FUNDAMENTAL
CONCEPTS IN
THE DESIGN OF
EXPERIMENTS

9780030435706

Charles R. Hicks

Assistant Dean
School of Humanities, Social Science and Education
Purdue University

HOLT, RINEHART AND WINSTON
NEW YORK   CHICAGO   SAN FRANCISCO   TORONTO   LONDON

FUNDAMENTAL CONCEPTS IN THE DESIGN OF EXPERIMENTS

February, 1965

Copyright © 1964 by Holt, Rinehart and Winston, Inc.

Library of Congress Catalog Card Number: 64-11344

23611-0114

Printed in the United States of America

PREFACE

It is the primary purpose of this book to present the fundamental concepts in the design of experiments using simple numerical problems, many from actual research work. These problems are selected to emphasize the basic philosophy of design. Another purpose is to present a logical sequence of designs that fit into a consistent outline; for every type of experiment, the distinctions among the experiment, the design, and the analysis are emphasized. Since this theme of experiment-design-analysis is to be highlighted throughout the text, the first chapter presents and explains this theme. The second chapter reviews statistical inference, and the remaining chapters follow a general outline, with an experiment-design-analysis summary at the end of each chapter.

The book is written for anyone engaged in experimental work who has a good background in statistical inference. It will be most profitable reading to those with a background in statistical methods including analysis of variance.

Some of the latest techniques have not been included. The reason for this is again the purpose of presenting the *fundamental* concepts in design to provide a background for reading journals in the field and understanding some of the more recent techniques. Although it is not assumed that every reader of this book is familiar with the calculus, some theory is presented where calculus is used. The reader should be able to grasp the underlying ideas of each chapter even if he must omit these sections.

This book evolved from a course in Design of Experiments given at Purdue University over the past four or five years. The author is indebted to Professors Gayle McElrath of the University of Minnesota and Clyde Kramer of Virginia Polytechnic Institute whose lectures, along with the author's, form the basis of this book. Credit is also due Mr. James Dick and Mr. Roland Rockwell, who took notes of the author's lectures.

I shall be forever indebted to the Univerity of Florida for granting me a visiting professorship during the academic year 1962–1963 with time to work on this book, and to Mrs. Alvarez of their Industrial Engineering Department for typing the manuscript.

Lafayette, Indiana   *Charles R. Hicks*
November, 1963

CONTENTS

Chapter 1　　THE EXPERIMENT, THE DESIGN, AND THE ANALYSIS 1
1.1 Introduction 1
1.2 The Experiment 1
1.3 The Design 2
1.4 The Analysis 3
1.5 Summary in Outline 4
Example 4

Chapter 2　　REVIEW OF STATISTICAL INFERENCE 9
2.1 Introduction 9
2.2 Estimation 10
2.3 Tests of Hypotheses 12
2.4 Power of a Test 14
2.5 How Large a Sample? 16
Problems 19

Chapter 3　　SINGLE-FACTOR EXPERIMENTS WITH NO
RESTRICTIONS ON RANDOMIZATION 21
3.1 Introduction 21
3.2 Analysis of Variance Rationale 23
3.3 After ANOVA — Tests on Means 28
3.4 Confidence Limits on Means 33
3.5 Components of Variance 33
3.6 General Regression Significance Test 35

3.7 Summary   *41*
Problems   *41*

Chapter 4   SINGLE-FACTOR EXPERIMENTS — RANDOMIZED
                 BLOCK DESIGN   *44*
                 4.1 Introduction   *44*
                 4.2 Randomized Complete Block Design   *46*
                 4.3 ANOVA Rationale   *48*
                 4.4 Interpretations   *49*
                 4.5 General Regression Significance Test Approach   *52*
                 4.6 Missing Values   *54*
                 4.7 Randomized Incomplete Blocks — Restriction on
                     Experimentation   *57*
                 4.8 Summary   *64*
                 Problems   *64*

Chapter 5   SINGLE-FACTOR EXPERIMENTS — LATIN AND
                 OTHER SQUARES   *66*
                 5.1 Introduction   *66*
                 5.2 Latin Squares   *66*
                 5.3 Graeco-Latin Squares   *68*
                 5.4 Youden Squares   *69*
                 5.5 Summary   *72*
                 Problems   *72*

Chapter 6   FACTORIAL EXPERIMENTS   *75*
                 6.1 Introduction   *75*
                 6.2 ANOVA Rationale   *85*
                 6.3 Remarks   *91*
                 6.4 Summary   *92*
                 Problems   *92*

Chapter 7 2^n FACTORIAL EXPERIMENTS   *95*
                 7.1 Introduction   *95*
                 7.2 2^2 Factorial   *95*
                 7.3 2^3 Factorial   *103*
                 7.4 2^n — Remarks   *106*
                 7.5 Summary   *108*
                 Problems   *109*

Chapter 8   QUALITATIVE AND QUANTITATIVE FACTORS   *110*
                 8.1 Introduction   *110*
                 8.2 Single Factor — Quantitative Levels   *112*
                 8.3 Two Factors — One Qualitative, One Quantitative   *115*

8.4 Two Factors — Both Quantitative   120
8.5 Summary   129
Problems   129

Chapter 9 3^n FACTORIAL EXPERIMENTS
9.1 Introduction   130
9.2 3^2 Factorial   130
9.3 3^3 Factorial   136
9.4 Summary   145
Problems   145

Chapter 10   FIXED, RANDOM AND MIXED MODELS   *148*
10.1 Introduction   148
10.2 Single-Factor Models   149
10.3 Two-Factor Models   151
10.4 EMS Rules   153
10.5 EMS Derivations   156
10.6 Remarks   162
Problems   163

Chapter 11   NESTED AND NESTED-FACTORIAL EXPERIMENTS   *165*
11.1 Introduction   165
11.2 Nested Experiments   166
11.3 ANOVA Rationale   169
11.4 Nested-Factorial Experiments   171
11.5 Summary   174
Problems   175

Chapter 12   EXPERIMENTS OF TWO OR MORE FACTORS —
RESTRICTIONS ON RANDOMIZATION   *179*
12.1 Introduction   179
12.2 Factorial Experiment in a Randomized
    Block Design   179
12.3 Factorial Experiment in a Latin Square Design   185
12.4 Remarks   186
12.5 Summary   187
Problems   188

Chapter 13   FACTORIAL EXPERIMENT — SPLIT-PLOT DESIGN   *190*
13.1 Introduction   190
13.2 A Pseudo F Test   197
13.3 Summary   199
Problems   199

Chapter 14   FACTORIAL EXPERIMENT — CONFOUNDING IN BLOCKS   201
                 14.1 Introduction   201
                 14.2 Confounding Systems   203
                 14.3 Block Confounding with Replication   206
                 14.4 Block Confounding — No Replication   209
                 14.5 Summary   218
                 Problems   219

Chapter 15   FRACTIONAL REPLICATION   221
                 15.1 Introduction   221
                 15.2 Aliases   222
                 15.3 Fractional Replications   223
                 15.4 Summary   231
                 Problems   231

Chapter 16   MISCELLANEOUS TOPICS   233
                 16.1 Introduction   233
                 16.2 Response Surface Experimentation   233
                 16.3 Evolutionary Operations (EVOP)   245

Chapter 17   SUMMARY   253

                 GLOSSARY OF TERMS   259
                 REFERENCES   263
                 STATISTICAL TABLES   265
                 Table A. Areas Under the Normal Curve   266
                 Table B. Student's Distribution   268
                 Table C. Table of Chi Square   269
                 Table D. F Distribution   270
                 Table E. Duncan's Multiple Ranges   276
                 Table F. Coefficients of Orthogonal Polynomials   278
                 ANSWERS TO ODD-NUMBERED PROBLEMS   279
                 INDEX   291

CHAPTER	The Experiment, The Design,
1	and The Analysis

1.1 Introduction

It is the objective of designed experiments to obtain more information for less cost than can be obtained by traditional experimentation. Often the experimenter is so anxious to collect data, stuff it into a neat little formula such as a "*t* test for the difference in means" and draw some conclusions that he pays no attention to how the data were collected. Much more valid conclusions could probably be made if more careful thought were given to the proper designing of an experiment before collecting and analyzing the data.

Throughout this book care will be taken to emphasize the three important phases of a project: the *experiment*, the *design*, and the *analysis*.

1.2 The Experiment

The experiment includes a statement of the problem to be solved. This sounds rather obvious, but in practice it often takes quite awhile to get general agreement as to the statement of a problem. It is important to bring out all points of view to establish just what the experiment is intended to do. A careful statement of the problem goes a long way toward its solution.

Choice must also be made as to the dependent variable or variables to be studied. Are these measurable? How accurately can they be measured on the instruments available? If they are not measurable, what type of response can be expected? If the results are simply *yes* or *no*, *go* or *no-go*, what type of distribution of such results is reasonable?

It is also necessary to define the independent variables or factors which may affect the dependent or response variable. Are these factors to be held constant, to assume certain specified levels, or to be averaged out by a process of randomization? Are levels of the factors to be set at certain fixed values, such as temperature at 70° F, 90° F, and 110° F, or are such levels to be set at random among all possible levels? Are the factors to be varied quantitative (such as temperature) or qualitative (operators)? All of the above considerations go into the definition of the experiment.

1.3   The Design

Of primary importance, since the remainder of this book will be devoted to it, is the design phase of a project. Many times an experiment is agreed upon, data are collected, and conclusions are drawn with little or no consideration given to *how* the data were collected. First, how many observations are to be taken? Considerations of how large a difference is to be detected, how much variation is present, and what size risks are to be tolerated are all important in deciding on the size of the sample to be taken for a given experiment. Without this information, the best alternative is to take as large a sample as possible. In practice this sample size is often quite arbitrary. However, as more and more tables become available, it should be possible to determine the sample size in a much more objective fashion (see Sec. 2.5).

Also of prime importance is the order in which the experiment is to be run, which should be random order. Once a decision has been made to control certain variables at specified levels, there are always a number of other variables which cannot be controlled. Randomization of the order of experimentation will tend to average out the effect of these uncontrolled variables.

For example, if an experimenter wishes to compare the average current flow through two types of computers and five of each type are to be tested, in what order are all ten to be tested? If the five of type I are tested, followed by the five of type II, and any general 'drift' in line voltage occurs during the testing, it may appear that the current flow is greater on the first five (Type I) than on the second five (Type II), yet the real cause is the "drift" in line voltage. A random order for testing allows any time trends to average out. It is desirable to have the average current flow in the type I and type II computers equal, if the computer types do not differ in this respect. Randomization will help accomplish this. Randomization will also permit the experimenter to proceed as if the errors of measurement are independent, a common assumption in most statistical analyses.

What is meant by random order? Is the whole experiment to be completely randomized, with each observation made only after consulting a table of random numbers, or tossing dice, or flipping a coin? Or, possibly, once a temperature bath is prepared, is the randomization made only within this particular temperature and another randomization made at another temperature? In other words, what is the randomization procedure and how are the units arranged for testing? Once this step has been agreed upon it is recommended that the experimenter keep a watchful eye on the experiment to see that it is actually conducted in the order prescribed.

Having agreed upon the experiment and the randomization procedure, a mathematical model can now be set up which should describe the experiment. This model will show the response variable as a function of all factors which are to be studied and any restrictions imposed on the experiment due to the method of randomization.

1.4 The Analysis

The final step, analysis, includes the procedure for data collection, data reduction, and the computation of certain test statistics to be used in making decisions about various aspects of an experiment. Analysis involves the computation of test statistics such as "t," "F," "χ^2," and their corresponding decision rules for testing hypotheses about the mathematical model. Once the test statistics have been computed, decisions must be made. These decisions should be made in terms which are meaningful to the experimenter. They should not be couched in statistical jargon such as "the third order $A \times B \times E$ interaction is significant at the 1 percent level," but instead should be expressed in graphical or tabular form, in order that they be clearly understood by the experimenter and by those persons who are to be "sold" by the experiment. The actual statistical tests should probably be included only in the appendix of a report on the experiment. These results should also be used as "feedback" to design a better experiment, once certain hypotheses seem tenable.

1.5   Summary in Outline

I. The Experiment
   A. Statement of problem
   B. Choice of response or dependent variable
   C. Selection of factors to be varied
   D. Choice of levels of these factors
      1. Quantitative or Qualitative
      2. Fixed or Random
   E. How factor levels are to be combined

II. The Design
   A. Number of observations to be taken
   B. Order of experimentation
   C. Method of randomization to be used
   D. Mathematical model to describe the experiment

III. The analysis
   A. Data collection and processing
   B. Computation of test statistics
   C. Interpretation of results for the experimenter

EXAMPLE 1.1. The following example [12]* is presented to show the three phases of the design of an experiment. It is not assumed that the reader is familiar with the design principles or analysis techniques in this problem. The remainder of the book is devoted to a discussion of many such principles and techniques, including those used in this problem.

An experiment was to be designed to study the effect of several factors on the power requirements for cutting metal with ceramic tools. The metal was cut on a lathe and the "y" or vertical component of a dynamometer reading was recorded. As this y-component is proportional to the horsepower requirements in making the cut, it was taken as the measured variable. The y-component is measured in millimeters of deflection on a recording instrument. Some of the factors which might affect this deflection are tool types, angle of tool edge bevel, type of cut, depth of cut, feed rate, and spindle speed. After much discussion, it was agreed to hold depth of cut constant at 0.100 in., feed rate constant at 0.012 in. per min, and spindle speed constant at 1000 rpm. These levels were felt to represent typical operating conditions. The main objective of the study was to determine the effect of the other three factors (tool type,

---

*Numbers in brackets [   ] refer to the References at the end of the book.

angle of edge bevel, and type of cut) on the power requirements. As only two ceramic tool types were available, this factor was considered at two levels. The angle of tool edge bevel was also set at two levels: 15 deg and 30 deg, representing the extremes for normal operation. The type of cut was either continuous or interrupted — again, two levels.

There are therefore two fixed levels for each of three factors, or eight experimental conditions (2^3) which may be set and which may affect the power requirements or y-deflection on the dynamometer. This is called a 2^3 factorial experiment, since both levels of each of the three factors are to be combined with both levels of all other factors. The levels of two factors (type of tool and type of cut) are qualitative, whereas the angle of edge bevel (15 deg and 30 deg) is a quantitative factor.

The question of design for this experiment involves the number of tests to be made under each of the eight experimental conditions. After some preliminary discussion of expected variability under the same set of conditions and the costs of wrong decisions, it was decided to take four observations under each of the eight conditions, making a total of 32 runs. The order in which these 32 units are to be put in a lathe and cut was to be completely randomized.

In order to completely randomize the 32 readings, the experimenter decided on the order of experimentation from the results of three coin tossings. A penny was used to represent the tool type (T): heads for one type, tails for the other. A nickel represented the angle of bevel (B): heads 30 deg, tails 15 deg, and a dime represented the type of cut (C): heads interrupted, tails continuous.

Thus if the first set of tosses came up THT, it would mean that the first tool to be used in the lathe would be of tool type 1, bevel 2, and subjected to the continuous type of cut. In Fig. 1.1 a data layout is given, showing each of the 32 experimental conditions. The numbers 1, 2, 3, 4, and 5 indicate the first five conditions to be run on the lathe, assuming the coins came up THT, TTH, HHT, HHT, HTH.

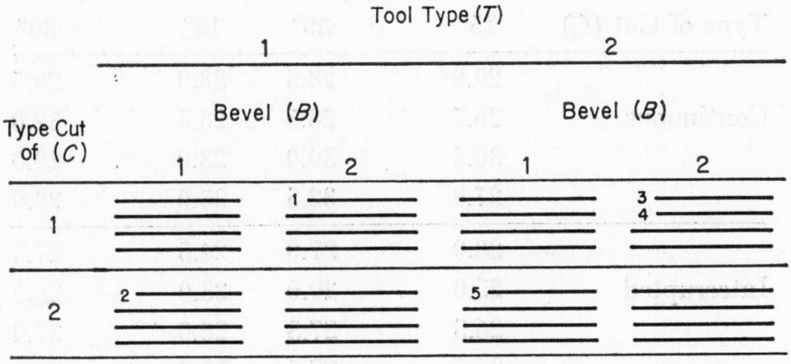

FIG. 1.1 Data layout of power consumption for ceramic tools.

In this layout it should be noted that the same set of conditions may be repeated (e.g., run three and four) before all eight conditions are run once. The only restriction on complete randomization here is that once four repeated measures have occurred in the same cell, no more will be run using those same conditions.

The coin flipping continues until the order of all 32 runs has been decided upon. This is a 2^3 factorial experiment with four observations per cell, run in a completely randomized manner. Complete randomization insures the averaging out of any effects which might be correlated with the time of the experiment. If the lathe-spindle speed should vary and all of the Type-1 tools were run through first and the Type-2 tools followed, it might be that this extraneous effect of lathe spindle speed would appear as a difference between tool types if the speed were faster at first and slower near the end of the experiment.

The mathematical model for this experiment and design would be
$$X_{ijkm} = \mu + T_i + B_j + TB_{ij} + C_k + TC_{ik} + BC_{jk} + TBC_{ijk} + \epsilon_{m(ijk)}$$
where X_{ijkm} represents the measured variable, μ, a common effect in all observations (the true mean of the population from which all the data came), and T_i represents the tool type effect where $i = 1, 2$. B_j stands for the angle of bevel where $j = 1, 2$. C_k is for the type of cut where $k = 1, 2$. $\epsilon_{m(ijk)}$ represents the random error in the experiment where $m = 1, 2, 3, 4$. The other terms stand for interactions between the main factors T, B, and C.

The analysis of this experiment consists of collecting 32 items of data in the spaces indicated in Fig. 1.1 in a completely randomized manner. The results in millimeter deflection are given in Table 1.1.

TABLE 1.1 — Data for Power Requirement Example

	Tool Type (T)			
	1		2	
	Bevel (B)		Bevel (B)	
Type of Cut (C)	15°	30°	15°	30°
	29.0	28.5	28.0	29.5
Continuous	26.5	28.5	28.5	32.0
	30.5	30.0	28.0	29.0
	27.0	32.5	25.0	28.0
	28.0	27.0	24.5	27.5
Interrupted	25.0	29.0	25.0	28.0
	26.5	27.5	28.0	27.0
	26.5	27.5	26.0	26.0

This experiment and the mathematical model suggest a three-way analysis of variance (ANOVA) which yields the results in Table 1.2.

TABLE 1.2 — ANOVA for Power Requirement Example

Source of Variation	df	Sum of Squares	Mean Square	EMS
Tool Types (T)	1	2.82	2.82	$\sigma_e^2 + 16\sigma_T^2$
Bevel (B)	1	20.32	20.32*	$\sigma_e^2 + 16\sigma_B^2$
$T \times B$ Interaction	1	0.20	0.20	$\sigma_e^2 + 8\sigma_{TB}^2$
Type of Cut (C)	1	31.01	31.01*	$\sigma_e^2 + 16\sigma_C^2$
$T \times C$ Interaction	1	0.01	0.01	$\sigma_e^2 + 8\sigma_{TC}^2$
$B \times C$ Interaction	1	0.94	0.94	$\sigma_e^2 + 8\sigma_{BC}^2$
$T \times B \times C$ Interaction	1	0.19	0.19	$\sigma_e^2 + 4\sigma_{TBC}^2$
$\epsilon_{m(ijk)}$ — Error	24	53.44	2.23	σ_e^2
TOTALS	31	108.93		

In testing the hypotheses that there is no type of tool effect, no bevel effect, no type of cut effect, and no interactions, the EMS column indicates that all observed mean squares are to be tested against the error mean square of 2.23 with 24 df (degrees of freedom). The proper test statistic is the F statistic (Appendix Table D) with 1 and 24 df. At the 5 percent significance level ($\alpha = 0.05$), the critical region of F is $F \geq 4.26$. Comparing each mean square with the error mean square indicates that only two hypotheses can be rejected: bevel has no effect on deflection and type of cut has no effect on deflection. None of the other hypotheses can be rejected, and it is concluded that only the angle of bevel and type of cut affect power consumption as measured by the y-deflection on the dynamometer. Tool type appears to have little effect on the y-deflection, and all interactions are negligible. Calculations on the original data of Table 1.2 show the following average y-deflections:

TABLE 1.3 — Average y-deflections

Tool Type	1	2
Average y-deflection	28.1	27.5
Bevel	15°	30°
Average y-deflection	27.0	28.6
Type of Cut	1	2
Average y-deflection	28.8	26.8

These averages seem to bear out the conclusions that bevel affects y-deflection, with a 30-deg bevel requiring more power than the 15-deg bevel (note the difference in average y-deflection of 1.6 mm), and that type of cut affects y-deflection, with a continuous cut averaging 2.0 mm more deflection than an interrupted cut. The difference of 0.6 mm in average deflection due to tool type is not significant at the 5 percent level. Graphing all four B, C combinations in Fig. 1.2 shows the meaning of no significant interaction.

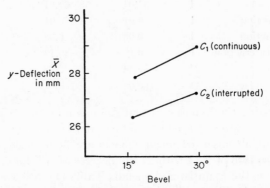

FIG. 1.2   *B,T Interaction for Power Requirement Example*

A brief examination of this graph indicates that the y-deflection is increased by an increase in degree of bevel. The fact that the line for the continuous cut (C_1) is above the line for the interrupted cut (C_2) shows that the continuous cut requires more power. The fact that the lines are nearly parallel is characteristic of no interaction between two factors. Or, it can easily be seen that an increase in the degree of bevel produced about the same average increase in y-deflection regardless of which type of cut was made. This is another way to interpret the presence of no interaction.

The experiment here was a three-factor experiment with two levels for each factor. The design was a completely randomized design and the analysis was a three-way ANOVA with four observations per cell. From the results of this experiment the experimenter not only found that two factors (angle of bevel and type of cut) affect the power requirements, but he has also determined that within the range of the experiment it makes little difference which ceramic tool type is used and that there are no significant interactions between the three factors.

This example is just one of many that might have been used to illustrate the three phases of the experiment: experiment, design, and analysis.

2 | Review of Statistical Inference

2.1 Introduction

The purpose of this chapter is to review basic concepts of statistical inference and also to introduce some of the definitions and notations which will be used throughout the book.

Present-day *statistics* may be defined as decision-making in the light of uncertainty. Uncertainty does not imply ignorance, merely that an exact determination of the outcome of an experiment is not possible. A range of possible outcomes can often be determined on the basis of past experience or from observed sample data. Assuming the range or pattern of variability to be expected, a decision can be made as to whether or not observed data could reasonably have been taken from a population which has this assumed pattern. Since random variation is present in all measurements, the real variation in an experiment must be detected in the presence of this random variation or measurement error. Thus, statistics may also be defined as decision making in the light of random variation.

Statistical inference refers to the process of inferring something about a population from a sample drawn from that population. The population is generally characterized by one or more *parameters*. A general population parameter will be designated as θ; whereas, other Greek letters will be used for specific parameters, such as the population mean (μ), the population variance (σ^2), and the population standard deviation (σ). Quantities computed from the sample values drawn from the population are called *sample statistics*; or simply, statistics. Examples include the sample mean

$$\bar{X} = \sum_{i=1}^{n} X_i/n$$

(where n is the number of observations in the sample), and the sample variance

$$s^2 = \sum_{i=1}^{n} (X_i - \bar{X})^2/n - 1$$

Italic letters will be used to designate sample statistics. The symbol u will be used to designate a general statistic corresponding to the population parameter, θ.

Most of statistical theory is based on the assumption that samples drawn are *random samples;* i.e., that each member of the population has an equal chance of being included in the sample and that the pattern of variation in the population is not changed by this deletion of the n members for the sample.

The notion of statistical inference may be divided into two parts: (1) estimation and (2) tests of hypotheses.

2.2   Estimation

The objective of statistical estimation is to make an estimate of a population parameter based on a sample statistic drawn from this population. Two types of estimates are usually needed: point estimates and interval estimates.

A *point estimate* is a single statistic used to estimate a parameter. For example, the sample mean ($\bar{X}$) is a point estimate of the population mean (μ). Point estimates are usually expected to have certain desirable characteristics. They should be unbiased, consistent, and have minimum variance.

An *unbiased statistic* is one whose expected or average value taken over an infinite number of similar samples equals the population parameter being estimated. Symbolically, $E(u) = \theta$, where $E(\ )$ means the expected value of the statistic in ( ).* The sample mean is an unbiased statistic, since it can be proved that

$$E(\bar{X}) = \mu$$

---

*$E(X) = \sum_i x_i p(x_i)$ when $p(x_i)$ is a discrete probability function.
  $= \int x f(x)\, dx$ when $f(x)$ is a probability density function (continuous).

Likewise, the sample variance as defined above is unbiased, since

$$E(s^2) = \sigma^2$$

Note that the sum of squares $\sum_{i=1}^{n} (X_i - \bar{X})^2$ must be divided by $n - 1$ and not by n if s^2 is to be unbiased. The sample standard deviation

$$s = \sqrt{\sum_{i=1}^{n} (X_i - \bar{X})^2/n - 1}$$

is not unbiased, since it can be shown that

$$E(s) \neq \sigma$$

This somewhat subtle point is proved in Burr [4] pp. 174–176.

A *consistent statistic* is one whose value comes closer and closer to the parameter as the sample size is increased. Symbolically

$$\lim_{n \to \infty} \Pr(|u_n - \theta| < \epsilon) \to 1$$

which expresses the notion that, as n increases, the probability approaches certainty (or one) that the statistic u_n, which depends on n, will be within a distance ϵ, however small, of the true parameter θ.

Minimum Variance applies where two or more statistics are being compared. If u_1 and u_2 are two estimates of the same parameter θ, the estimate having the smaller standard deviation is called the *minimum variance* estimate. This is shown diagrammatically in Fig. 2.1.

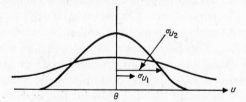

FIG. 2.1   *Minimum Variance Estimates*

In Fig. 2.1, $\sigma_{u_1} < \sigma_{u_2}$, and u_1 is then said to be the *minimum variance estimate*, as variance is the square of the standard deviation.

An *interval estimate* consists of the interval between two values of a sample statistic which is asserted to include the parameter in question. The band of values between these two limits is called a *confidence* interval for the parameter, since its width may be determined from the degree of confidence that is assumed when we say that the parameter lies in this band. Confidence limits (the end points of the confidence interval) are determined from the observed sample statistic, the sample size, and the degree of confidence desired. A 95-percent confidence interval on μ is given by

$$\bar{X} \pm 1.96 \frac{\sigma}{\sqrt{n}}$$

where 1.96 is taken from normal distribution values (see Appendix Table A), n is the sample size, and σ is the population standard deviation. If 100 sample means based on n observations each are computed, and 100 confidence intervals are set up using the above formula, we expect that about 95 of the 100 intervals will include μ. If only one interval is set up based on one sample of n, as is usually the case, we can state that we have 95 percent confidence that this interval includes μ. If σ is unknown, the "Student" t distribution (Appendix Table B) is used, and confidence intervals are given by

$$\bar{X} \pm t_{1-(\alpha/2)} \frac{s}{\sqrt{n}}$$

where s is the sample standard deviation and t has $n-1$ df.   100 $(1 - \alpha)$ percent gives the degree of confidence desired.

2.3   Tests of Hypotheses

A *statistical hypothesis* is an assumption about the population being sampled. It usually consists of assigning a value to one or more parameters of the population. For example, it may be hypothesized that the average number of miles per gallon obtained with a certain carburetor is 19.5. This is expressed as H_0: $\mu = 19.5$ mpg. The basis for the assignment of this value to μ usually rests on past experience with similar carburetors. Another example would be to hypothesize that the variance in weight of filled vials for the week is 40 (gram)² or H_0: $\sigma^2 = 40$ gm². When such hypotheses are to be tested, the other parameters of the population are either assumed or estimated from data taken on a random sample from this population.

A *test of a hypothesis* is simply a rule by which a hypothesis is either accepted or rejected. Such a rule is usually based on sample statistics, called *test statistics* when they are used to test hypotheses. For example, the rule might be to reject H_0: $\mu = 19.5$ mpg if a sample of 25 carburetors averaged 18.0 mpg $(\bar{X})$ or less when tested. The *critical region* of a test statistic consists of all values of the test statistic where the decision is made to reject H_0. In the example above, the critical region for the test statistic $\bar{X}$ is where $\bar{X} \leq 18.0$ mpg.

Since hypothesis testing is based on observed sample statistics computed on n observations, the decision is always subject to possible errors. If the hypothesis is really true and it is rejected by the sample, a *Type I error* is committed. The probability of a Type I error is designated as α. If the hypothesis is accepted when it is not true, i.e., some alternative hypothesis is true, a *Type II error* has been made and its probability is designated as β. These α and β error probabilities are often referred to as the risks of making incorrect decisions, and one of the objectives in hypothesis testing is to design a test whose α and β risks are both small. In most such test procedures α is set at some predetermined level, and the decision rule is then formulated in such a way as to minimize the other risk, β. In quality control work, α is the producer's risk and β the consumer's risk.

In order to review hypothesis testing, a series of steps can be taken which will apply to most types of hypotheses and test statistics. To help clarify these steps and to illustrate the procedure, a simple example will be given in parallel with the steps.

Steps in Hypothesis Testing	*Examples*
1. Set up the hypothesis and its alternative.	1. H_0: $\mu = 19.5$ mpg H_1: $\mu < 19.5$ mpg
2. Set the significance level of the test, α. (Size of the Type I error.)	2. $\alpha = 0.05$
3. Choose a test statistic to test H_0.	3. Test statistic: $\bar{X}$ or Standardized $\bar{X}$: $Z = \dfrac{\bar{X} - \mu}{\sigma/\sqrt{n}}$ [assume $\sigma = 2$]
4. Determine the sampling distribution of this test statistic when H_0 is true.	4. $\bar{X}$ is normally distributed with mean (μ) and standard deviation ($\sigma/\sqrt{n}$). Or Z is $N(0,1)$.
5. Set up a critical region on this test statistic where H_0 will be rejected in $(100)\alpha$ percent of the samples when H_0 is true.	5.

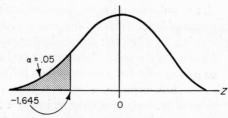

Critical region: $Z \leq -1.645$

6. Choose a random sample of n observations, compute the test statistic, and make a decision on H_0.

6. If $n = 25$ and $\bar{X} = 18.9$ mpg
$$Z = \frac{18.9 - 19.5}{2/\sqrt{25}} = -1.5$$
As $-1.5 > -1.645$, do not reject H_0.

In the example above a one-sided or one-tailed test was used. This is dictated by the alternative hypothesis, since we only wish to reject H_0 when low values of $\bar{X}$ are observed. The size of the significance level, α, is often set in an arbitrary fashion such as 0.05 or 0.01. It should reflect the seriousness of rejecting many carburetors when they are really satisfactory, or when the actual mean of the lot (population) is 19.5 mpg or better. In using the normal variate Z, σ is assumed known; a different test statistic would be used if σ is unknown, namely, "Student's" t. The critical region may also be expressed in terms of $\bar{X}$ using the critical Z value of -1.645

$$-1.645 = \frac{\bar{X}_c - 19.5}{2/\sqrt{25}}$$

or $\bar{X}_c = 18.8$, and the decision rule can be expressed as: Reject H_0 if $\bar{X} \leq 18.8$. Here $\bar{X} = 18.9$ and the hypothesis is not rejected.

The procedure outlined above may be used to test many different hypotheses. The nature of the problem will indicate what test statistic is to be used, and proper tables can be found to set up the required critical region. Well-known are such tests as those on a single mean, two means with various assumptions about the corresponding variances, one variance, and two variances. A good discussion of various tests may be found in Dixon and Massey [6] pp. 88–138.

2.4   Power of a Test

In the example given above no mention was made of the Type II error of size β. In order to compute the probability, β, of a Type II error, the hypothesis must be assumed untrue and some specific alternative assumed true. Then a value can be determined for the probability of accepting H_0 when the specified alternative H_1 is really true. Thus, β is a function of the specific alternative and several values of β will be obtained as μ is specified at various points below 19.5.

For example, when $\mu = 19.0$, the distribution of sample means around 19.0 would appear as in Fig 2.2.
Here the critical value of $\bar{X}, \bar{X}_c$ is still 18.8 as determined above, since the

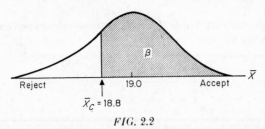

FIG. 2.2

hypothesis under test is $\mu = 19.5$ with an $\alpha = 0.05$. The probability of accepting H_0: $\mu = 19.5$ is indicated by the shaded region above 18.8, when actually $\mu = 19.0$. This probability is β and can be computed using normal distribution areas.

$$Z = \frac{18.8 - 19.0}{2/\sqrt{25}} = \frac{-0.2}{0.4} = -0.5$$

$\beta = 0.6915$ or 0.69 (from Appendix Table A)

If μ is assumed to be at 18.5, the results are

$$Z = \frac{18.8 - 18.5}{2/\sqrt{25}} = 0.75$$

$\beta = 0.2266$ or 0.23 (Appendix Table A)

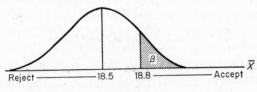

FIG. 2.3

Thus it is observed that β varies with the true value of μ, becoming smaller when μ is farther to the left of 19.5 mpg. Since β does vary with μ, a curve can be plotted of μ versus β.

This is called an *Operating Characteristic Curve*, used in testing

$$H_0: \mu = 19.5$$

with $\alpha = 0.05$, $\sigma = 2$, $n = 25$, versus

$$H_1: \mu < 19.5$$

Sometimes the complement of β is plotted, namely, the probability of rejecting H_0 for various values of μ. This plot of $1 - \beta$ versus μ is called the *power curve* for this test.

A table such as Table 2.1 makes these curves easy to plot using Appendix Table A.

TABLE 2.1 — Data for O.C. Curve

If $\mu =$	$Z = \dfrac{18.8 - \mu}{2/\sqrt{25}}$	β	$1 - \beta$
18.0	+2.00	0.02	0.98
18.3	+1.25	0.11	0.89
18.5	+0.75	0.23	0.77
19.0	−0.50	0.69	0.31
19.2	−1.00	0.84	0.16
19.5	−1.75	0.96	0.04*

*(approximately $= \alpha$)

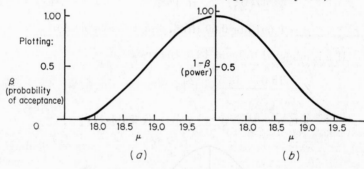

FIG. 2.4 O.C. and Power Curves

It should be noted that when μ is quite a distance from the hypothesized value of 19.5, the test does a fairly good job of detecting this shift; that is, if $\mu = 18.5$, the probability of rejecting 19.5 is 0.77, which is fairly high. On the other hand, if μ has shifted only slightly from 19.5, say 19.2, the probability of detection is only 0.16. The power of a test may be increased by increasing the sample size or increasing the risk α.

2.5 How Large a Sample?

The question of how large a sample to take from a population for making a test is one often asked of a statistician. This question can be answered provided the experimenter can answer each of the following questions.

1. How large a shift (from 19.5 to 19.0) in a parameter do you wish to detect?

2. How much variability is present in the population? [Based on past experience, $\sigma = 2$ mpg.]
3. What size risks are you willing to take? [$\alpha = 0.05$ and $\beta = 0.10$.]

If numerical values can be at least estimated in answering the above questions, the sample size may be determined. Set up two sampling distributions, one of the $\bar{X}$'s when H_0 is true, $\mu = 19.5$; and the other when the alternative to be detected is true, $\mu = 19.0$.

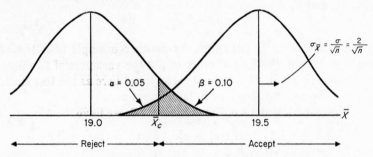

FIG. 2.5   *Determining Sample Size*

Indicate by $\bar{X}_c$ a value between the two μ's which will become a critical point, rejecting H_0 for observed values of $\bar{X}$ below it and accepting H_0 for $\bar{X}$ values above it. Indicate the α and β risks on the diagram. Set up two simultaneous equations, standardizing $\bar{X}_c$ first with respect to a μ of 19.5 (the α equation) and second with respect to a μ of 19.0 (the β equation). Solve these equations for n and $\bar{X}_c$.

$$\alpha \text{ equation: } \frac{\bar{X}_c - 19.5}{2/\sqrt{n}} = -1.645 \text{ (based on } \alpha = 0.05)$$

$$\beta \text{ equation: } \frac{\bar{X}_c - 19.0}{2/\sqrt{n}} = +1.282 \text{ (based on } \beta = 0.10)$$

Subtracting the second equation from the first and multiplying both sides of each equation by $\dfrac{2}{\sqrt{n}}$ gives

$$-0.5 = -2.927\left(\frac{2}{\sqrt{n}}\right)$$

$$\sqrt{n} = \frac{5.854}{0.5} = 11.71$$

$$n = (11.71)^2 = 136.9 \text{ or } 137$$

Keeping $\alpha = 0.05$ gives

$$\bar{X}_c = 19.5 - 1.645\left(\frac{2}{\sqrt{137}}\right) = 19.22 \text{ mpg}$$

The decision rule is then: Choose a random sample of 137 carburetors, and if the mean mpg of these is less than 19.22 mpg, reject H_0; otherwise, accept H_0.

Excellent tables are available for determining n for several tests of hypotheses, such as those in Davies [5] pp. 606–615 or Owen [13] pp. 19, 23, 36, 41, and ff.

EXAMPLE 2.1 (VARIANCE) As another example of a test of a hypothesis, consider testing whether or not the variances of two normal populations are equal. This example is included here as the test statistic involved has many applications in later chapters.

Following the steps outlined in Sec. 2.3, we have

1. H_0: $\sigma_1^2 = \sigma_2^2$ H_1: $\sigma_1^2 > \sigma_2^2$
2. $\alpha = 0.05$
3. Test Statistic

$$F = \frac{s_1^2}{s_2^2}$$

(often called the variance ratio, where s_1^2 is based on $n_1 - 1$ degrees of freedom and s_2^2 is based on $n_2 - 1$ degrees of freedom)

4. If the two samples are independently chosen from normal populations and H_0 is true, the F statistic follows a skewed distribution, formed as the ratio of two independent Chi-Square distributions. A table giving a few percentiles of this F distribution appears as Appendix Table D. This table is entered with $n_1 - 1$ df for the numerator and $n_2 - 1$ df for the denominator.

5. The critical region is set at $F \geq F_{0.95}$ in this example ($\alpha = 0.05$) with the degrees of freedom dependent on the size of the two samples.

6. If the first sample results are

$$n_1 = 8 \qquad s_1^2 = 156$$

and the second are

$$n_2 = 10 \qquad s_2^2 = 100$$

then

$$F = \frac{156}{100} = 1.56$$

and the critical region is $F \geq 3.29$ for 7 and 9 df. Hence, the hypothesis is not rejected.

PROBLEMS

2-1. For the following data on tensile strength in psi (pounds per square inch), determine the mean and variance of this sample:

Tensile Strength

in psi	Frequency
18,461	2
18,466	12
18,471	15
18,476	10
18,481	8
18,486	3
Total	50

2-2. Using the results of Prob. 2-1, test the hypothesis that the mean tensile strength of the population sampled is 18,470 psi [assume that $\sigma^2 = 40$, $\alpha = 0.05$].

2-3. Plot the O.C. curve for Prob. 2-2.

2-4. Determine how large a sample would be needed to detect a 10 psi increase in the mean tensile strength of Prob. 2-2 if $\alpha = 0.05$, $\beta = 0.02$, and $\sigma^2 = 40$.

2-5. Repeat Prob. 2-4 for the detection of a 10 psi shift in the mean in either direction.

2-6. For a sample mean of 124 grams based on 16 observations from a population whose variance is 25 gram^2, set up 90 percent confidence limits on the mean of the population.

The following problems may require test statistics not reviewed in this chapter but assumed to be known to the reader. The tables at the end of this book should be adequate for their solution.

2-7. For a sample variance of 62 based on 12 observations, test the hypothesis that the population variance is 40. Use a one-sided test and a 1 percent significance level.

2-8. For Prob. 2-7, set up 95 percent confidence limits (two-sided) on σ^2.

2-9. Two samples are taken, one from each of two machines. For this process

$$n_1 = 8, \bar{X}_1 = 42.2 \text{ grams}, s_1^2 = 10 \text{ gram}^2$$
$$n_2 = 15, \bar{X}_2 = 44.5 \text{ grams}, s_2^2 = 18 \text{ gram}^2$$

Test these results for a significant difference in variances.

2-10.   Test the results in Prob. 2-9 for a significant difference in means.

2-11.   Reflection light box readings before and after dichromating the interior of a metal cone were

Test No.	1	2	3	4	5	6	7	8
Before	6.5	6.0	7.0	6.8	6.5	6.8	6.2	6.5
After	4.4	4.2	5.0	5.0	4.8	4.6	5.2	4.9

Test for a significant difference in mean light box readings.

2-12.   To test the hypothesis that the fraction defective, p, of a process is 0.20, a sample of 100 pieces was drawn at random.

(a) Use an $\alpha = 0.05$, and set up a critical region for the number of observed defectives to test this hypothesis against a two-sided alternative.

(b) If the process now shifts to a 0.10 fraction defective, find the probability of an error of the second kind for this alternative.

(c) Without repeating the work, would you expect the β error to be the same if the process shifted to 0.30? Explain.

CHAPTER 3

Single-Factor Experiments with No Restrictions on Randomization

3.1 Introduction

In this and several subsequent chapters single-factor experiments will be considered. In this chapter no restrictions will be placed on the randomization so that the design will be completely randomized. Many of the techniques of analysis for a completely randomized single-factor experiment can be applied with little alteration to more complex experiments.

For example, the single factor could be steel manufacturers, where the main interest of an analyst centers on the effect of several different manufacturers on the hardness of steel purchased from them. It could be temperature in an instance where the experimenter is concerned about the effect of temperature on penicillin yield. Whenever only one factor is varied, whether the levels be quantitative or qualitative, fixed or random, the experiment is referred to as a *single-factor experiment*, and the symbol T_j will be used to indicate the effect of the j-th level of the factor. T_j suggests that the general factor may be thought of as a "treatment" effect.

If the order of experimentation applied to the several levels of the factor is completely random, so that any material to which the treatments might be applied is considered approximately homogeneous, the design is called a *completely randomized design*. The number of observations for each level of the treatment or factor will be determined from cost considerations and the power of the test. The model then becomes

$$X_{ij} = \mu + T_j + \epsilon_{ij}$$

where X_{ij} represents the i-th observation $(i = 1, 2, \cdots n_j)$ on the j-th treatment $(j = 1, 2, \cdots k$ levels). For example, X_{23} represents the second observation using level 3 of the factor. μ is a common effect for the whole experiment, T_j represents the effect of the j-th treatment, and ϵ_{ij} represents the random error present in the i-th observation on the j-th treatment.

The error term, ϵ_{ij}, is usually considered a normally and independently distributed random effect whose mean value is zero and whose variance is the same for all treatments or levels. This is expressed as: ϵ_{ij}'s are NID $(0, \sigma_e^2)$ where σ_e^2 is the common variance within all treatments. μ is always a fixed parameter, and $T_1, T_2, \cdots T_j, \cdots T_k$ are considered to be fixed parameters if the levels of treatments are fixed. It is also assumed that

$$\sum_{j=1}^{k} T_j = 0$$

If the k levels of treatments are chosen at random, the T_j's are assumed NID $(0, \sigma_T^2)$. Whether the levels are fixed or random depends upon how these levels are chosen in a given experiment.

The analysis of a single-factor, completely randomized experiment usually consists of a one-way analysis of variance test where the hypothesis, H_0: $T_j = 0$ for all j, is tested. If this hypothesis is true, then no treatment effects exist and each observation, X_{ij}, is made up of its population mean, μ, and a random error, ϵ_{ij}. After an analysis of variance (ANOVA), many other tests may be made, and some of these will be shown on the example which follows.

EXAMPLE 3.1. Interest is centered on the effect on tube conductivity of four different types of coating of TV tubes. As only four types of coating are used, the experiment is a single-factor experiment at four fixed levels, and these are also qualitative levels since no numerical value can be assigned to the four coatings. It is agreed that five observations per coating should be adequate and that the order for testing the 20 tubes can be completely randomized. A table of random numbers indicated the proper order for testing. A mathematical model might be

$$X_{ij} = \mu + T_j + \epsilon_{ij}$$

where $i = 1, 2, \cdots 5$, and $j = 1, 2, \cdots 4$.

There are four treatments (coatings) and five observations per coating. The data are shown in Table 3.1.

TABLE 3.1 — TV Tube-Coating Data

	Coating		
I	II	III	IV
56	64	45	42
55	61	46	39
62	50	45	45
59	55	39	43
60	56	43	41

An analysis of variance performed on these data gave the results in Table 3.2.

TABLE 3.2 — TV Tube-Coating Analysis

Source of Variation	df	Sum of Squares	Mean Square	EMS
Between Coatings (T_j)	3	1135.0	378.3	$\sigma_e^2 + 5\sigma_T^2$
Within Coatings or Error (ϵ_{ij})	16	203.2	12.7	σ_e^2
TOTALS	19	1338.2		

To test H_0: $T_j = 0$ for all $j = 1, 2, 3$, and 4, the test statistic is

$$F_{3,16} = \frac{378.3}{12.7} = 29.8$$

which is a highly significant value (see Appendix Table D). This indicates rejection of the hypothesis and a claim that there is a considerable difference in average conductivity between the four coatings. This result is no surprise when the data of Table 3.1 are examined.

3.2   Analysis of Variance Rationale

To review the basis for the F test in a one-way analysis of variance, k populations, each representing one level of treatment, can be considered with observations as shown in Table 3.3.

TABLE 3.3 — Population Layout for One-Way ANOVA

Treatment:	1	2 ········	j ········	k
	X_{11}	X_{12}	X_{1j}	X_{1k}
	X_{21}	X_{22}	X_{2j}	X_{2k}
	X_{31}	X_{32}	—	—
	—	—	—	—
	X_{i1}	X_{i2}	X_{ij}	X_{ik}
Population Means:	$\mu_{.1}$	$\mu_{.2}$ ········ $\mu_{.j}$	········	$\mu_{.k}$

Here the use of "dot notation" indicates a summing over all observations in the population. Since each observation could be returned to the population and measured, there could be an infinite number of observations taken on each population, so the average or $E(X_{i1}) = \mu_{.1}$, etc. μ will represent the average X_{ij} over all populations, or $E(X_{ij}) = \mu$. In the model T_j, the treatment effect can also be indicated by $\mu_{.j} - \mu$, and then the model is either

$$X_{ij} = \mu + T_j + \epsilon_{ij}$$

or

$$X_{ij} \equiv \mu + (\mu_{.j} - \mu) + (X_{ij} - \mu_{.j})$$

This last expression is seen to be an identity true for all values of X_{ij}. Expressed another way

$$X_{ij} - \mu \equiv (\mu_{.j} - \mu) + (X_{ij} - \mu_{.j}) \tag{3.1}$$

Since these means are unknown, random samples are drawn from each population and estimates can be made of the treatment means and the grand mean. If n_j observations are taken for each treatment where the numbers need not be equal, a sample layout would be as shown in Table 3.4.

TABLE 3.4 — Sample Layout for One-Way ANOVA

Treatment	1	2	.....	j	.....	k	
	X_{11}	X_{12}	$\cdots$	X_{1j}	$\cdots$	X_{1k}	
	X_{21}	X_{22}	$\cdots$	X_{2j}	$\cdots$	X_{2k}	
	.	.		.		.	
	.	.		.		.	
	.	.		.		.	
	X_{i1}	X_{i2}	$\cdots$	X_{ij}		X_{ik}	
	.	.		.		.	
	.	.		.		.	
	.			.		.	
	$X_{n_1 1}$	.		$X_{n_j j}$		.	
		.					
		$X_{n_2 2}$				$X_{n_k k}$	
Totals:	$T_{.1}$	$T_{.2}$	$\cdots$	$T_{.j}$	$\cdots$	$T_{.k}$	$T_{..}$
Number:	n_1	n_2	$\cdots$	n_j	$\cdots$	n_k	N
Means:	$\bar{X}_{.1}$	$\bar{X}_{.2}$	$\cdots$	$\bar{X}_{.j}$	$\cdots$	$\bar{X}_{.k}$	$\bar{X}_{..}$

Here $T_{.j}$ represents the total of the observations taken under treatment j, n_j the number of observations taken for treatment j, and $\bar{X}_{.j}$ is the observed mean for treatment j. $T_{..}$ represents the grand total of all observations taken where

$$T_{..} = \sum_{i=1}^{k} \sum_{i=1}^{n_j} X_{ij} = \sum_{j=1}^{k} T_{.j}$$

and

$$N = \sum_{j=1}^{k} n_j$$

and $\bar{X}_{..}$ is the mean of all N observations.

Note too that

$$\bar{X}_{..} = \sum_{j=1}^{k} n_j \bar{X}_{.j}/N$$

If these sample statistics are substituted for their corresponding population parameters in Eq. (3.1), we get a sample equation (also an identity) of the form

$$X_{ij} - \bar{X}_{..} \equiv (\bar{X}_{.j} - \bar{X}_{..}) + (X_{ij} - \bar{X}_{.j}) \tag{3.2}$$

This equation states that the deviation of any observation from the grand mean can be broken into two parts: the deviation of the observation from its own treatment mean plus the deviation of the treatment mean from the grand mean.

If both sides of Eq. (3.2) are squared and then added over both i and j, we have

$$\sum_{j=1}^{k} \sum_{i=1}^{n_j} (X_{ij} - \bar{X}_{..})^2 = \sum_{j=1}^{k} \sum_{i=1}^{n_j} (\bar{X}_{.j} - \bar{X}_{..})^2 + \sum_{j=1}^{k} \sum_{i=1}^{n_j} (X_{ij} - \bar{X}_{.j})^2$$

$$+ \sum_{j=1}^{k} \sum_{i=1}^{n_j} (\bar{X}_{.j} - \bar{X}_{..})(X_{ij} - \bar{X}_{.j}) \tag{3.3}$$

Examining the last expression on the right, we find that

$$\sum_{j=1}^{k} \sum_{i=1}^{n_j} (\bar{X}_{.j} - \bar{X}_{..})(X_{ij} - \bar{X}_{.j}) = \sum_{j=1}^{k} (\bar{X}_{.j} - \bar{X}_{..}) \left[\sum_{i=1}^{n_j} (X_{ij} - \bar{X}_{.j}) \right]$$

The term in brackets [ ] is seen to equal zero, as the sum of the deviations about the mean within a given treatment equals zero. Hence

$$\sum_{j=1}^{k} \sum_{i=1}^{n_j} (X_{ij} - \bar{X}_{..})^2 = \sum_{j=1}^{k} \sum_{i=1}^{n_j} (\bar{X}_{.j} - \bar{X}_{..})^2 + \sum_{j=1}^{k} \sum_{i=1}^{n_j} (X_{ij} - \bar{X}_{.j})^2 \tag{3.4}$$

This may be referred to as "the fundamental equation of analysis of variance," and it expresses the idea that the total sum of squares of deviations from the grand mean is equal to the sum of squares of deviations between treatment means and the grand mean plus the sum of squares of deviations within treatments. In Chapter 2 an unbiased estimate of population variance was determined by dividing the sum of squares $\sum_{i=1}^{n} (X_i - \bar{X})^2$ by the corresponding number of degrees of freedom, $n - 1$. If the hypothesis being tested in analysis of variance is true, namely, that $T_j = 0$ for all j, or that there is no treatment effect, then $\mu_{.1} = \mu_{.2} = \cdot = \mu_{.j} \cdots = \mu_{.k}$ and all there is in the model is the population mean, μ, and random error, ϵ_{ij}. Then, any one of the three terms in Eq. (3.4) may be used to give an unbiased estimate of this common population variance. For example, dividing the left-hand term by its degrees of freedom, $N - 1$, will yield an unbiased estimate of population variance, σ^2. Within the j-th treatment, $\Sigma_i(X_{ij} - \bar{X}_{.j})^2$ divided by $n_j - 1$ degrees of freedom would yield an unbiased estimate of the variance within the j-th treatment. If the variances within the k treatments are really all alike, their estimates may be pooled to give $\Sigma_{j=1}^{k} \Sigma_{i=1}^{n_j}$ $(X_{ij} - \bar{X}_{.j})^2$ with degrees of freedom

$$\sum_{j}^{k} (n_j - 1) = N - k$$

which will give another estimate of the population variance. Still another estimate can be made by first estimating the variance, $\sigma_{\bar{X}}^2$, between means drawn from a common population with $\sigma_X^2 = n_j\sigma_{\bar{X}.j}^2$. An unbiased estimate for $\sigma_{\bar{X}}^2$ is given by $\Sigma_{j=1}^{k} (\bar{X}_{.j} - \bar{X}_{..})^2/k - 1$ so that an unbiased estimate of

$$\sigma_X^2 = \sum_{j=1}^{k} n_j(\bar{X}_{.j} - \bar{X}_{..})^2/k - 1$$

which is found by summing the first term on the right hand side of (Eq. 3.4) over i and dividing by $k - 1$ df. Thus there are three unbiased estimates of σ^2 possible from the data in a one-way ANOVA if the hypothesis is true. Now all three are not independent since the sum of squares is additive in Eq. (3.4). However, it can be shown that if each of the terms (sums of squares) on the right of Eq. (3.4) is divided by its proper degrees of freedom, it will yield two independent, chi-square distributed, unbiased estimates of σ^2 when H_0 is true. If two such independent, unbiased estimates of the same variance are compared, their ratio can be shown to be distributed as F with $k - 1$, $N - k$ degrees of freedom. If, then, H_0 is true, the test of the hypothesis can be made using a critical region of the F distribution with the observed F at $k - 1$ and $N - k$ degrees of freedom given by

$$F_{k-1,N-k} = \frac{\displaystyle\sum_{j=1}^{k} n_j(\bar{X}_{.j} - \bar{X}_{..})^2/k - 1}{\displaystyle\sum_{j=1}^{k} \sum_{i=1}^{n_j} (X_{ij} - \bar{X}_{.j})^2/N - k} \tag{3.5}$$

The critical region is usually taken as the upper tail of the F distribution, rejecting H_0 if $F \geq F_{1-\alpha}$ where α is the area above $F_{1-\alpha}$. In this F ratio, the sum of squares between treatments is always put into the numerator, and then a significant F will indicate that the differences between means has something in it besides the estimate of variance. It probably indicates that there is a real difference in treatment means ($\mu_{.1}$, $\mu_{.2}$, etc.) and that H_o should be rejected. These unbiased estimates of population variance, sums of squares divided by df, are also referred to as *Mean Squares*.

The actual computing of sums of squares indicated in Eq. (3.5) above is much easier if they are first expanded and rewritten in terms of treatment totals. These computing formulae are given in Table 3.5.

TABLE 3.5 — *ANOVA Table for One-Way ANOVA*

Source of Variation	df	Sum of Squares (SS)	Mean Square (MS
Between Treatments (T_j)	$k-1$	$$\sum_{j=1}^{k} n_j(\bar{X}_{.j} - \bar{X}_{..})^2$$ $$= \sum_{j=1}^{k} \frac{T_{.j}^2}{n_j} - \frac{T_{..}^2}{N}$$	$SS_{\text{treatments}}/k-1$
Within Treatments or Error (ϵ_{ij})	$N-k$	$$\sum_{j=1}^{k}\sum_{i=1}^{n_j} (X_{ij} - \bar{X}_{.j})^2$$ $$= \sum_{j=1}^{k}\sum_{i=1}^{n_j} X_{ij}^2 - \sum_{j=1}^{k} \frac{T_{.j}^2}{n_j}$$	$SS_{\text{error}}/N-k$
Totals	$N-1$	$$\sum_{j=1}^{k}\sum_{i=1}^{n_j} (X_{ij} - \bar{X}_{..})^2$$ $$= \sum_{j=1}^{k}\sum_{i=1}^{n_j} X_{ij}^2 - \frac{T_{..}^2}{N}$$	

Applying the above formulae to the problem data in Table 3.1, the data may first be coded by subtracting 50 from all readings (coding will leave the F statistic unchanged in value). Table 3.6 shows the coded data and useful statistics computed from these data

TABLE 3.6—*Coded TV Coating Data*

Treatment:	1	2	3	4	
	6	14	-5	-8	
	5	11	-4	-11	
	12	0	-5	-5	
	9	5	-11	-7	
	10	6	-7	-9	
$T_{.j}$:	42	36	-32	-40	$T_{..} = 6$
n_j:	5	5	5	5	$N = 20$
$\sum_{i=1}^{n_j} X_{ij}^2$:	386	378	236	340	$\sum_{j=1}^{k}\sum_{i=1}^{n_j} X_{ij}^2 = 1340$

The sums of squares can be computed quite easily from this table. The total sum of squares states, "square each observation, add over all observations, and subtract the correction term." This latter is the grand total squared and divided by the total number of observations

$$SS_{total} = \sum_{j=1}^{k} \sum_{i=1}^{n_j} X_{ij}^2 - \frac{T_{..}^2}{N} = 1340 - \frac{(6)^2}{20} = 1338.2$$

The sum of squares between treatments is found by totaling n_j observations for each treatment, squaring this total, dividing by the number of observations, adding for all treatments, and then subtracting the correction term

$$SS_{treatment} = \sum_{j=1}^{k} \frac{T_{.j}^2}{n_j} - \frac{T_{..}^2}{N} = \frac{(42)^2}{5} + \frac{(36)^2}{5} + \frac{(-32)^2}{5} + \frac{(-40)^2}{5}$$
$$- \frac{(6)^2}{20} = 1135.0$$

The sum of squares for error is then determined by subtraction

$$SS_{error} = SS_{total} - SS_{treatment} = 1338.2 - 1135.0 = 203.2$$

These results are then displayed as in Table 3.2, and the F test is run on the $H_0 \colon T_j = 0$ as shown before. The "expected mean square" or "EMS" column is discussed in more detail later (see Chapter 10). It represents the average value of the mean square under the model being used. No assumption is made that H_0 is true in computing this EMS. In this problem the value 12.7 is an unbiased estimate of σ_e^2; whereas 378.3 is an unbiased estimate of $\sigma_e^2 + 5\sigma_T^2$ where σ_T^2 is the true variance between treatments. Now, if H_0 is true, all treatment effects are the same, σ_T^2 would be zero, and both mean squares would be estimates of σ_e^2. Obviously, the considerable difference between means is beyond what could be considered as chance variation (σ_e^2); hence σ_T^2 is quite real.

No distinction is made at this point between whether σ_T^2 represents the variance among an infinite number of treatment population means (of which the ones observed are but a random sample), or whether σ_T^2 represents variation between k fixed treatment means. In the latter case

$$\sigma_T^2 = \sum_{j=1}^{k} T_{.j}^2 / k - 1$$

as discussed in more detail in Chapter 10.

3.3   After ANOVA — Tests on Means

Having concluded, as in the problem above, that there is a significant difference in treatment means, questions naturally arise, "Which means differ?" "Does the mean of the first coating differ from the mean of the second?" "Does the average of 1 and 2 differ from the average of 3 and 4?" The answers to questions about means, after ANOVA, may be handled in two ways, depending upon when — before the experiment is performed or after the data are collected — a selection is made of those contrasts among means that are to be of interest.

Tests on Means Set Prior to Experimentation — Orthogonal Contrasts

If the above decision is made prior to the running of an experiment, such comparisons can usually be set without disturbing the risk, α, of the original ANOVA. This means that the contrasts must be chosen with care, and the number of such contrasts should not exceed the number of degrees of freedom between the treatment means. The method usually used here is called the *method of orthogonal contrasts*, and such contrasts must first be defined.

A *contrast*, C_m, is defined on the observed totals of the treatments as follows

$$C_m = \sum_{j=1}^{k} c_{jm} T_{.j}$$

is a contrast if

$$\sum_{j=1}^{k} c_{jm} = 0$$

for equal n_j's in the columns.

Two contrasts, C_m and C_q, are said to be *orthogonal contrasts*, provided

$$\sum_{j=1}^{k} c_{jm} c_{jq} = 0$$

for equal n's.

The sums of squares for a contrast are given by

$$SS_{C_m} = \frac{(C_m)^2}{n \sum_{j=1}^{k} c_{jm}^2}$$

To apply this procedure to the problem above, three orthogonal contrasts may be set up since there are three df between treatments. One such set of three might be

$$\left\{\begin{array}{l} C_1 = T_{.1} \qquad\qquad\quad - T_{.4} \\ C_2 = \qquad\quad T_{.2} - T_{.3} \\ C_3 = T_{.1} - T_{.2} - T_{.3} + T_{.4} \end{array}\right\} \qquad (3.6)$$

C_1 is a contrast to compare the mean of the first treatment with the fourth, C_2 compares the second treatment with the third, and C_3 compares the average of treatment one and four with the average of two and three. The coefficients of the $T_{.j}$'s for the three contrasts are given in Table 3.7.

TABLE 3.7 — Orthogonal Coefficients

	$T_{.1}$	$T_{.2}$	$T_{.3}$	$T_{.4}$
C_1	+1	0	0	−1
C_2	0	+1	−1	0
C_3	+1	−1	−1	+1

It can be seen from Table 3.7 that the sum of coefficients, c_{jm}'s, adds up to zero for each contrast, and that the sum of products of coefficients of each pair of contrasts is also zero.

For the example given in Sec. 3.2, using the coded data in Table 3.6, the contrasts are

$$C_1 = +1(42) + 0(36) + 0(-32) - 1(-40) = 82$$

$$C_2 = 0(42) + 1(36) - 1(-32) + 0(-40) = 68$$

$$C_3 = +1(42) - 1(36) - 1(-32) + 1(-40) = -2$$

The corresponding sums of squares are

$$\text{SS}_{C_1} = \frac{(82)^2}{5(2)} = \frac{6724}{10} = 672.4$$

$$\text{SS}_{C_2} = \frac{(68)^2}{5(2)} = \frac{4624}{10} = 462.4$$

$$\text{SS}_{C_3} = \frac{(-2)^2}{5(4)} = \frac{4}{20} = \frac{0.2}{1135.0}$$

Each sum of squares for a contrast has 1 df, and the total sum of squares for the treatments is 1135.0 as in Table 3.2. Each of these sums of squares may be tested against the error mean square with 1 and 16 df as follows

$$H_1: T_1 = T_4 \qquad F_{1,16} = \frac{672.4/1}{12.7} = 52.9$$

$$H_2: T_2 = T_3 \qquad F_{1,16} = \frac{462.4/1}{12.7} = 36.4$$

$$H_3: T_1 + T_4 = T_2 + T_3 \qquad F_{1,16} = \frac{0.2/1}{12.7} = 0.016$$

Comparing these with $F_{1,16}$ at the 5 percent significance level, which is 4.49 (Appendix Table D), the first two hypotheses are rejected and the third one is not. We can therefore conclude that there is a significant difference in the mean conductivity between the first and fourth coating and between the second and third coating. However, there is no significant difference between the average of coatings one and four and two and three. These results can be assessed only if the decision is made beforehand as to the contrasts to be performed.

As this method of orthogonal contrasts is used quite often in experimental design work, the definitions and formulae are given below for the case of unequal numbers of observations per treatment

C_m is a *contrast* if

$$\sum_{j=1}^{k} n_j c_{jm} = 0$$

and C_m and C_q are *orthogonal contrasts* if

$$\sum_{j=1}^{k} n_j c_{jm} c_{jq} = 0$$

The *sum of squares for such contrasts* is given by

$$\mathrm{SS}_{C_j} = \frac{(C_m)^2}{\sum\limits_{j=1}^{k} n_j\, c_{jm}^2}$$

Tests on Means After Experimentation — Multiple Range Test

If the decision on what comparisons to make is withheld until after the data are examined, comparisons may still be made, but the α level is altered because such decisions are not taken at random but are based on observed results. Several methods have been introduced to handle such situations [11], but only the Duncan Multiple Range test [7] will be given here.

After the data have been compiled the following steps are taken.

1. Arrange the k means in order from low to high.

2. Enter the ANOVA table and take the error mean square with its degrees of freedom.

3. Obtain the standard error of the mean for each treatment

$$s_{\bar{x}.j} = \sqrt{\frac{\text{Error mean square*}}{\text{No. of observations in } \bar{X}_{.j}}}$$

---

*Where this error mean square is the one used as the denominator in the F test on means, $\bar{X}_{.j}$'s.

4. Enter Duncan's table (Appendix Table E) of significant ranges at the α level desired, using n_2 = degrees of freedom for error mean square and $p = 2, 3, \ldots k$, and list these $k - 1$ ranges.

5. Multiply these ranges by $s_{\bar{x}.j}$ to form a group of $k - 1$ least significant ranges.

6. Test the observed ranges between means, beginning with largest versus smallest, which is compared with the least significant range for $p = k$; then test largest versus second smallest with the least significant range for $p = k - 1$; etc. Continue this for second largest versus smallest, etc. until all $k(k - 1)/2$ possible pairs have been tested. The sole exception to the rule above is that no difference between two means can be declared significant if the two means concerned are both contained in a subset with a nonsignificant range.

To see how this works, consider the coded data of the problem in Tables 3.1, 3.2, and 3.6. Here the means are

$$\bar{X}_{.j}: \text{Treatment} \quad \frac{1 \qquad 2 \qquad 3 \qquad 4}{8.4 \quad 7.2 \quad -6.4 \quad -8.0}$$

Following the steps given above:

    1. $k = 4$ means are -8.0 -6.4 7.2   8.4
       for treatments   4   3   2   1

    2. From Table 3.2, Error MS $= 12.7$ with 16 df

    3. Standard error of a mean is

$$s_{\bar{x}.j} = \sqrt{\frac{12.7}{5}} = 1.59$$

    4. From Appendix Table E at the 5 percent level, the significant ranges are, for $n_2 = 16$:

$$p = \quad 2 \qquad 3 \qquad 4$$
$$\text{Ranges} = 3.00 \quad 3.15 \quad 3.23$$

    5. Multiplying by the standard error of 1.59, the least significant ranges (LSR) are

$$p = \quad 2 \qquad 3 \qquad 4$$
$$\text{LSR} = 4.77 \quad 5.01 \quad 5.13$$

    6.

Largest versus smallest:	1 versus 4 $= 16.4 > 5.13$
Largest versus next smallest:	1 versus 3 $= 14.8 > 5.01$
Largest versus next largest:	1 versus 2 $=\ \ 1.2 < 4.77$
Second largest versus smallest:	2 versus 4 $= 15.2 > 5.01$
Second largest versus next largest:	2 versus 3 $= 13.6 > 4.77$
Third largest versus smallest:	3 versus 4 $=\ \ 1.6 < 4.77$

Here there is a significant difference between treatments 1 and 4, 1 and 3, 2 and 4, and 2 and 3, but not between 1 and 2 or 3 and 4. This may be shown by underlining means which are not significant and could therefore have come from a common population. These appear on a one dimensional scale as shown in Fig. 3.1.

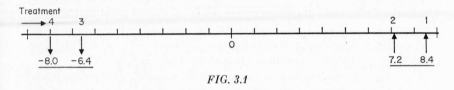

FIG. 3.1

Here any two means *not* underscored by the same line are significantly different, and any two means underscored by the same line are *not* significantly different.

3.4   Confidence Limits on Means

After an analysis of variance, it is often desirable to set confidence limits on a treatment mean. The $100(1 - \alpha)$ percent confidence limits on $\mu_{.j}$ are given by

$$\bar{X}_{.j} \pm t_{1-(\alpha/2)} \cdot \sqrt{\frac{\text{Mean square used to test treatment mean square}}{n_j}} \qquad (3.6)$$

where the mean square used to test treatment mean square is the error mean square in a one-way ANOVA but may be a different mean square in more complex analyses. The degrees of freedom used with the Student t statistic are the degrees of freedom which correspond to the mean square used for testing the treatment mean.

In Example 3.1, 95-percent confidence limits on the mean conductivity for the first coating, $\mu_{.1}$, would be $\bar{X}_{.1} \pm t_{0.975} \sqrt{12.7/5}$ with 16 df on t. On coded data, $8.4 \pm 2.12 \sqrt{12.7/5}$ (t from Appendix Table B), or, 8.4 ± 3.37, or, from 5.03 to 11.77. Decoding by adding 50 gives 55.03 to 61.77 for 95-percent confidence limits on $\mu_{.1}$.

3.5   Components of Variance

In Example 3.1 the levels of the factor were considered as fixed, since only four coatings were available and a decision was desired on the effect of these four coatings only. If, however, the levels of the factor were random (such as operators, days, or samples where the levels in the experiment might have been chosen at random from a large number of possible levels) the model is then called a *random model*, and inferences are to be extended to all levels of the population (of which the observed four levels are random samples). In a random model, the experimenter is not usually interested in testing hypotheses, setting confidence limits or making contrasts in means; rather, he is interested in estimating components of variance. How much of the variance in the experiment might be considered as due to true differences in treatment means, and how much might be due to random error about these means?

In order to see how a component of variance or random model may be analyzed, assume that the four levels of the factor in Example 3.1 represent four operators. Assume further that these operators have been chosen at random from a large population of operators. (Actually an infinite population is assumed.) The question is whether or not the operators can affect the conductivity of the tube by the way they administer the coating. If they do indeed affect this conductivity, how much of the variance in conductivity is due to operators and how much is random error?

In order to determine the components of variance, the observed mean squares are set equal to their expected mean squares and these equations are solved for the best estimates of the components of variance. For the example, data from Table 3.2 are assumed to be for operators rather than coatings, with results as before.

TABLE 3.8 — *ANOVA Table for Components of Variance Example*

Source of Variation	df	SS	MS	EMS
Between Operators (O_j)	3	1135.0	378.3	$\sigma_e^2 + 5\sigma_0^2$
Error (ϵ_{ij})	16	203.2	12.7	σ_e^2
Total	19		Model: $X_{ij} = \mu + O_j + \epsilon_{ij}$	

If we set the MS column equal to the EMS column, the symbol s^2 will replace σ^2, since the resulting mean square is only an estimate of the expected mean square.

$$378.3 = s_e^2 + 5s_0^2$$
$$12.7 = s_e^2$$
$$s_0^2 = \frac{378.3 - 12.7}{5} = 73.1$$

Hence, the total variance can be estimated as

$$s_T^2 = s_0^2 + s_e^2 = 73.1 + 12.7 = 85.8$$

with about $73.1/85.8 = 85$ percent of this total variance attributable to differences between operator means and the remaining $12.7/85.8 = 15$ percent due to error.

It is interesting to note that if the standard deviation of the whole experiment is estimated

$$s_T = \sqrt{85.8} = 9.26$$

and this is multiplied by 4, or $4(9.26) = 37.0$, we might expect this $\pm 2s_T$ to cover the range of observed readings. An examination of Table 3.1 shows a maximum reading of 64 and a minimum of 39 or a range of 25 for this rather small sample of 20 readings. So the variance breakdown by operators and errors is at least a reasonable one.

3.6 General Regression Significance Test

A method will be presented in this section that can be used on any ANOVA problem but is much more general than the method of Sec. 3.2. The results of this General Regression Significance Test will be the same as given above when applied to the example, but the method is important as it can easily be extended to more complicated problems. This method will be given in three parts: (1) the steps in a general regression significance test, (2) these steps applied to the example of this chapter, (3) some of the theory behind this method.

Steps in General Regression Significance Test

In the model, $X_{ij} = \mu + T_j + \epsilon_{ij}$, let m be the least-squares best estimate of μ, t_j a similar estimate of T_j, and e_{ij} of ϵ_{ij}. Proceed with the following steps:

1. Obtain totals for each term in the model which is a distinct classification.

2. Obtain the grand total of the experiment.

3. Obtain normal equations, one equation for each total in steps 1 and 2 above. These equations are in terms of the estimates of the parameters.

4. Solve these equations for m and the t_j's.

5. Obtain regression sum of squares due to all estimates.

6. Rewrite the model, omitting the parameters assumed to be zero when the hypothesis under test is true.

7. Determine normal equations for this reduced model.

8. Solve these equations and determine the regression sum of squares due to the estimates left. Call these estimates primed from original, e.g., m'.

9. Obtain between-treatments sum of squares:

$$SS_{\text{between treatments}} = SS_{\text{regression}}\ (m,t) - SS_{\text{regression}}\ (m')$$

10. Obtain

$$SS_{\text{error}} = \sum_{j=1}^{k} \sum_{i=1}^{n_j} X_{ij}^2 - SS_{\text{regression}}\ (m,t)$$

11. Make F test where

$$F = \frac{SS_{\text{treatment}}/\text{df}}{SS_{\text{error}}/\text{df}}$$

to test hypothesis that treatment effects are zero.

EXAMPLE 3.2. (Based on Coded Data in Table 3.6)

Following the above steps with the data below, we have

1. Distinct Classification — 4 treatments $T_{.j}$: 42 36 -32 -40
2. $T_{..} = 6$
3. Normal equations:

$$\left\{\begin{array}{l} 6 = 20m + 5t_1 + 5t_2 + 5t_3 + 5t_4 \\ 42 = 5m + 5t_1 \\ 36 = 5m + 5t_2 \\ -32 = 5m + 5t_3 \\ -40 = 5m + 5t_4 \end{array}\right\}$$

Note that the coefficients of m and the t_j's are the number of times that estimate appears in the total on the left-hand side of the equation.

4. Since

$$\sum_{j=1}^{k} t_j = 0$$

the first equation becomes

$$6 = 20m \text{ and } m = \frac{6}{20} = 0.3$$

The others give

$$t_1 = \frac{42 - 5m}{5} = 8.1$$

$$t_2 = \frac{36 - 5m}{5} = 6.9$$

$$t_3 = \frac{-32 - 5m}{5} = -6.7$$

$$t_4 = \frac{-40 - 5m}{5} = -8.3$$

$$\sum_{j=1}^{4} t_j = 0$$

5. Regression sum of squares is found by multiplying each term on the left of the equations (the totals) by the corresponding estimates obtained in Step 4.

$$SS_{regression} \ (m,t_j\text{'s}) = 6(0.3) + 42(8.1) + 36(6.9) + (-32)(-6.7)$$
$$+ (-40)(-8.3)$$

$$= 1.8 + 340.2 + 248.4 + 214.4 + 332.0$$

$$= 1136.8$$

6. $\quad X_{ij} = \mu + \epsilon_{ij}$

7. $\quad\quad 6 = 20m'$

8. $m' = \dfrac{6}{20} = 0.3$ (as before)

$$SS_{regression} \ (m') = 6(.3) = 1.8$$

9. $SS_{between \ treatments} = SS_{regression} \ (m,t) - SS_{regression} \ (m')$

$$= 1136.8 - 1.8 = 1135.0$$

10. $SS_{error} = \sum\limits_{j} \sum\limits_{i} X_{ij}^2 - SS_{regression} \ (m,t)$

$$= 1340 - 1136.8 = 203.2$$

11. $F = \dfrac{SS_{treatment}/df}{SS_{error}/df} = \dfrac{1135.0/3}{203.2/16} = \dfrac{378.3}{12.7}$

$F = 29.8$ (as before)

Rationale for General Regression Significance Test

Consider the model

$$X_{ij} = \mu + T_j + \epsilon_{ij}$$

To find the least squares best estimates of the parameters μ, T_1, T_2, $\cdots T_k$, form the sum of squares of the errors

$$\sum_{j} \sum_{i} \epsilon_{ij}^2 = \sum_{j} \sum_{i} (X_{ij} - \mu - T_j)^2 \qquad (3.7)$$

The object is to find estimates of $\mu = m$, $T_j = t_j$ which will minimize the sum of squares of these errors. To minimize, differentiate partially with respect to μ, take $j = 1, 2 \cdots k$ and differentiate partially with respect to $T_1, T_2 \cdots T_k$:

for $\qquad \dfrac{\partial}{\partial \mu}\left(\sum_i \sum_j \epsilon_{ij}^2\right) = 2 \sum_i \sum_j (X_{ij} - \mu - T_j)(-1) = 0$

for $T_1 \qquad \dfrac{\partial}{\partial T_1}\left(\sum_i \epsilon_{i1}^2\right) = 2 \sum_i (X_{i1} - \mu - T_1)(-1) = 0$

for $T_2 \qquad \dfrac{\partial}{\partial T_2}\left(\sum_i \epsilon_{i2}^2\right) = 2 \sum_i (X_{i2} - \mu - T_2)(-1) = 0$

.

.

.

for $T_k \qquad \dfrac{\partial}{\partial T_k}\left(\sum_i \epsilon_{ik}^2\right) = 2 \sum_i (X_{ik} - \mu - T_k)(-1) = 0$

From these equations the least-squares normal equations are written

$$\sum_{i=1}^{n}\sum_{j=1}^{k} X_{ij} = \sum_i \sum_j \mu + \sum_i \sum_j T_j$$

$$\sum_i X_{i1} = \sum_i \mu + \sum_i T_1$$

$$\sum_i X_{i2} = \sum_i \mu + \sum_i T_2$$

$$\cdot \qquad \cdot \qquad \cdot$$
$$\cdot \qquad \cdot \qquad \cdot$$
$$\cdot \qquad \cdot \qquad \cdot$$

$$\sum_i X_{ik} = \sum_i \mu + \sum_i T_k$$

When they are added as indicated these become

$$\left.\begin{aligned}
T_{..} &= Nm + n\sum_{j=1}^{k} t_j \\[4pt]
T_{.1} &= nm + nt_1 \\[4pt]
T_{.2} &= nm \qquad\quad + nt_2 \\[2pt]
&\quad\;\; \cdot \\
&\quad\;\; \cdot \\
&\quad\;\; \cdot \\
T_{.k} &= nm \qquad\quad\;\; + nt_k
\end{aligned}\right\} \qquad\qquad (3.8)$$

where μ and T have been replaced by m and t_j as they are estimates of the parameters. These equations are the normal equations of Step 3. Solving these for m and the t_j's gives

$$\text{Since } \sum_{j=1}^{k} t_j = 0$$

$$m = \frac{T_{..}}{N} = \bar{X}_{..}$$

$$t_1 = \frac{T_{.1} - nm}{n} = \frac{T_{.1}}{n} - \frac{T_{..}}{N} = \bar{X}_{.1} - \bar{X}_{..}$$

$$t_2 = \frac{T_{.2} - nm}{n} = \frac{T_{.2}}{n} - \frac{T_{..}}{N} = \bar{X}_{.2} - \bar{X}_{..}$$

$$\cdot \qquad \cdot \qquad \cdot$$
$$\cdot \qquad \cdot \qquad \cdot$$
$$\cdot \qquad \cdot \qquad \cdot$$

$$t_k = \frac{T_{.k} - nm}{n} = \frac{T_{.k}}{n} - \frac{T_{..}}{N} = \bar{X}_{.k} - \bar{X}_{..}$$

To obtain the regression sum of squares due to this regression of X_{ij} on m and the t_j's, consider the error sum of squares, Eq. (3.7), and substitute the best estimates

$$\sum_i \sum_j e_{ij}^2 = \sum_i \sum_j (X_{ij} - m - t_j)^2$$

$$\text{SS}_{\text{error}} = \sum_i \sum_j (X_{ij} - [m + t_j])^2$$

$$= \sum_i \sum_j X_{ij}^2 - 2 \sum_i \sum_j X_{ij}(m + t_j) + \sum_i \sum_j (m + t_j)^2$$

$$= \sum_i \sum_j X_{ij}^2 - 2m \sum_i \sum_j X_{ij} - 2 \sum_i \sum_j X_{ij}t_j + m^2 N$$

$$\quad + 2m \sum_i \sum_j t_j + \sum_i \sum_j t_j^2$$

$$= \sum_i \sum_j X_{ij}^2 - 2m \sum_i \sum_j X_{ij} - 2 \sum_i \sum_j X_{ij}t_j$$

$$\quad + m\left[Nm + n \sum_j t_j \right] + \sum_j t_j[nm + nt_j]$$

where the fifth term $(2m\Sigma_i \Sigma_j t_j)$ is divided in half in the two bracketed expressions. From the least squares Eq. (3.8) above, these terms in [ ] may be replaced by $T_{..}$ and $T_{.j}$ respectively, and the resulting SS_{error} is

$$SS_{error} = \sum_i \sum_j X_{ij}^2 - 2mT_{..} - 2\sum_i \sum_j X_{ij}t_j + mT_{..} + \sum_j T_{.j}t_j$$

or

$$SS_{error} = \sum_i \sum_j X_{ij}^2 - mT_{..} - \sum_j T_{.j}t_j$$

The regression sum of squares is equal to the total sum of squares less the error sum of squares

$$\therefore SS_{regression}\ (m,t) = \sum_i \sum_j X_{ij}^2 - SS_{error}$$

$$= mT_{..} + \sum_j T_{.j}t_j$$

Note that this is each estimate $m,t_1, \cdots t_k$, multiplied by the corresponding terms on the left of Eq. (3.8) and added.

In general, then

$$SS_{regression}\ (m,t) = mT_{..} + \sum_j T_{.j}t_j$$

$$SS_{regression}\ (m,t) = (\bar{X}_{..})(T_{..}) + T_{.1}(\bar{X}_{.1} - \bar{X}_{..}) + T_{.2}(\bar{X}_{.2} - \bar{X}_{..})$$

$$+ \cdots + T_{.k}(\bar{X}_{.k} - \bar{X}_{..})$$

If H_0 is assumed true, so that $T_j = 0$ for all j, the model becomes

$$X_{ij} = \mu + \epsilon'_{ij}$$

Again, applying least squares to this error

$$\sum_i \sum_j \epsilon'^2_{ij} = (X_{ij} - \mu)^2$$

and the estimate of $\mu = m' = \bar{X}_{..}$

$$SS_{regression}\ (m'\ only) = m'T_{..} = (\bar{X}_{..})(T_{..})$$

then $SS_{treatments} = SS_{regression}\ (m,t) - SS_{regression}\ (m')$

$$= (\bar{X}_{..})(T_{..}) + \sum_j T_{.j}(\bar{X}_{.j} - \bar{X}_{..}) - (\bar{X}_{..})(T_{..})$$

$$SS_{treatments} = \sum_j T_{.j}(\bar{X}_{.j} - \bar{X}_{..}) = \sum_j T_{.j}\left(\frac{T_{.j}}{n} - \frac{T_{..}}{N}\right)$$

$$= \sum_j \frac{T_{.j}^2}{n} - \frac{T_{..}}{N}\sum_j T_{.j}$$

$$= \sum_j \frac{T_{.j}^2}{n} - \frac{T_{..}^2}{N} \qquad as \qquad \sum_j^k T_{.j} = T_{..}$$

and $\mathrm{SS}_{\mathrm{error}} = \sum_i \sum_j X_{ij}^2 - \mathrm{SS}_{\mathrm{regression}}\ (m,t)$

$$= \sum_i \sum_j X_{ij}^2 - (\bar{X}_{..})(T_{..}) - \sum_j T_{.j}(\bar{X}_{.j} - \bar{X}_{..})$$

$$= \sum_i \sum_j X_{ij}^2 - \frac{T_{..}^2}{N} - \sum_j \frac{T_{.j}^2}{n} + \frac{T_{..}^2}{N}$$

$$= \sum_i \sum_j X_{ij}^2 - \sum_j \frac{T_{.j}^2}{n}$$

and the F test becomes

$$F = \frac{\mathrm{SS}_{\mathrm{treatments}}/\mathrm{df}}{\mathrm{SS}_{\mathrm{error}}/\mathrm{df}} = \frac{\left.\sum_j \dfrac{T_{.j}^2}{n} - \dfrac{T_{..}^2}{N}\right/ k - 1}{\left.\sum_i \sum_j X_{ij}^2 - \sum_j \dfrac{T_{.j}^2}{n}\right/ N - k}$$

which is identical with the expression for F from Table 3.5 if the n_j's are all equal.

3.7 Summary

In this chapter consideration has been given to

Experiment	*Design*	*Analysis*
Single Factor	Completely Randomized	One-way ANOVA

In applying the ANOVA techniques, certain assumptions should be kept in mind:

1. The process is in control; i.e., it is repeatable.
2. The population distribution being sampled is normal.
3. The variance of the errors within all k levels of the factor are homogeneous.

Many texts [2], [5], discuss these assumptions and what may be done if they are not met in practice.

PROBLEMS

3-1. Assuming a completely randomized design, do a one-way analysis of variance on the following data in order to familiarize yourself with the technique:

	Factor A				
Levels:	1	2	3	4	5
Measurements:	8	4	1	4	10
	6	−2	2	6	8
	7	0	0	5	7
	5	−2	−1	5	4
	8	3	−3	4	9

3-2.   The cathode warm-up time in seconds was determined for three (3) different tube types using eight (8) observations on each type of tube. The order of experimentation was completely randomized. The results were

Tube Type:	A		B		C	
Warm-up	19	20	20	40	16	19
Time	23	20	20	24	15	17
In	26	18	32	22	18	19
Seconds:	18	35	27	18	26	18

Do an analysis of variance on these data and test the hypothesis that the three (3) tube types require the same average warm-up time.

3-3.   For Prob. 3-2, set up orthogonal contrasts between the tube types and test your contrasts for significance.

3-4.   Set up 95 percent confidence limits for the average warm-up time for Tube Type C in Prob. 3-2.

3-5.   Use Duncan's Multiple Range method to test for differences between tube types.

3-6.   The following data are on the pressure in a torsion spring for several settings of the angle between the legs of the spring in a free position:

Angle of Legs of Spring

67	71	75	79	83
83	84	86	89	90
85	85	87	90	92
	85	87	90	
	86	87	91	
	86	88		
	87	88		
		88		
		88		
		88		
		89		
		90		

Assuming a completely randomized design, complete a one-way analysis of variance for this experiment and state your conclusion concerning the effect of angle on the pressure in the spring.

3-7. Set up orthogonal contrasts for the angles in Prob. 3-6.

3-8. Do Prob. 3-1 using the general regression significance test.

3-9. Show that the expanded forms for the sums of squares in Table 3.5 are correct.

3-10. Assume that the levels of Factor A in Prob. 3-1 were chosen at random, and determine the proportion of variance attributable to differences in level means and the proportion due to error.

CHAPTER	*Single-Factor Experiments —*
4	*Randomized Block Design*

4.1 Introduction

Consider the problem of determining whether or not different brands of tires exhibit different amounts of tread loss after 20,000 miles of driving. A fleet manager wishes to consider four brands which are available and make some decision about which brand might show the least amount of tread wear after 20,000 miles. The brands to be considered are A, B, C, and D, and although driving conditions might be simulated in the laboratory, he wants to try these four brands under actual driving conditions. The variable to be measured is the difference in maximum tread thickness on a tire between the time it is mounted on the wheel of a car and after it has completed 20,000 miles on this car. The measured variable, X_{ij}, is this difference in thickness in millimeters, and the only factor of interest is brands — say T_j where $j = 1, 2, 3$, and 4.

Since the tires must be tried on cars and since some measure of error is necessary, more than one tire of each brand must be used and a set of four of each brand would seem quite practical. This means 16 tires, four each of four different brands, and a reasonable experiment would involve at least four cars. Designating the cars as I, II, III, and IV, one might put Brand A's four tires on Car I, Brand B's on Car II, etc. with a design as shown in Table 4.1.

One look at this design shows its fallibility, since averages for brands are also averages for cars. If the cars travel over different terrains,

44

TABLE 4.1 — Design 1 for Tire Brand Test

	Car:	I	II	III	IV
		A	B	C	D
	Brand	A	B	C	D
Distribution:		A	B	C	D
		A	B	C	D

using different drivers, any apparent brand differences are also car differences. This design is called completely confounded, since we cannot distinguish between brands and cars in the analysis.

A second attempt at design might be to try a completely randomized design, as given in Chapter 3. Assigning the 16 tires to the four cars in a completely random manner might give results as in Table 4.2.

TABLE 4.2 — Design 2 for Tire Brand Test

Car:	I	II	III	IV
Brand	C(12)	A(14)	D(10)	A(13)
Distribution	A(17)	A(13)	C(11)	D(9)
and Loss	D(13)	B(14)	B(14)	B(8)
in Thickness:	D(11)	C(12)	B(13)	C(9)

In Table 4.2 the loss in thickness is given for each of the 16 tires. The purpose of complete randomization here is to average out any car differences which might affect the results. The model would be

$$X_{ij} = \mu + T_j + \epsilon_{ij} \quad \text{with} \quad j = 1,2,3,4 \quad i = 1,2,3,4$$

An analysis of variance on these data gives the results in Table 4.3.

TABLE 4.3 — ANOVA for design 2

Source	df	SS	MS
Brands	3	30.6	10.2
Error	12	50.3	4.2
TOTALS	15	80.9	

The F test shows $F_{3,12} = 2.43$, and the 5 percent critical region for F is $F_{3,12} \geq 3.49$ (Appendix Table D), so there is no reason to reject the hypothesis of equal average tread loss among the four brands.

4.2   Randomized Complete Block Design

A more careful examination of design 2 in Table 4.2 will reveal some glaring disadvantages of the completely randomized design in this problem. One thing to be noted is that Brand A is never used on Car III nor Brand B on Car I. Also any variation within Brand A may reflect variation between Cars I, II, and IV. Thus, the random error may not be merely experimental error but may include variation between cars. Since the chief objective of experimental design is to reduce the experimental error, a better design might be one in which car variation is removed from error variation. Although the completely randomized design averaged out the car effects, it did not eliminate the variance among cars. A design which requires that each brand be used once on each car is a *randomized complete block design*, given in Table 4.4.

TABLE 4.4 — Design 3 — Randomized Block Design for Tire Brand Test

Car:	I	II	III	IV
Brand	$B(14)$	$D(11)$	$A(13)$	$C(9)$
Distribution	$C(12)$	$C(12)$	$B(13)$	$D(9)$
and Loss	$A(17)$	$B(14)$	$D(11)$	$B(8)$
in Thickness:	$D(13)$	$A(14)$	$C(10)$	$A(13)$

In this design the order in which the four brands are placed on a car is random and each car gets one tire of each brand. In this way better comparisons can be made between brands since they are all driven over approximately the same terrain, etc. This provides a more homogeneous environment in which to test the four brands. In general, these groupings for homogeneity are called *blocks* and randomization is now restricted within blocks. This design also allows the car (block) variation to be independently assessed and removed from the error term. The model for this design is

$$X_{ij} = \mu + B_i + T_j + \epsilon_{ij} \tag{4.1}$$

where B_i now represents the block effect (car effect) in the example above.

The analysis of this model is a two-way analysis of variance, since the block effect may now also be isolated. A slight rearrangement of the data in Table 4.4 and a coding by subtracting 13 from all readings gives Table 4.5.

The total sum of squares is computed as in Chapter 3:

$$\text{SS}_{\text{total}} = \sum_{j=1}^{4} \sum_{i=1}^{4} X_{ij}^2 - \frac{T_{..}^2}{N}$$

$$= 95 - \frac{(-15)^2}{16} = 80.9$$

TABLE 4.5 — Randomized Block Coded Data for Tire Brand Test

Car	A	B	C	D	$T_{i.}$
			Brand		
I	4	1	-1	0	4
II	1	1	-1	-2	-1
III	0	0	-3	-2	-5
IV	0	-5	-4	-4	-13
$T_{.j}$	5	-3	-9	-8	$-15 = T_{..}$
$\sum_{i=1}^{4} X_{ij}^2$	17	27	27	24	$95 = \sum_{i}^{4}\sum_{j}^{4} X_{ij}^2$

The brand (treatment) sum of squares is computed as usual

$$SS_{brand} = \sum_j \frac{T_{.j}^2}{n} - \frac{T_{..}^2}{N}$$

$$= \frac{(5)^2 + (-3)^2 + (-9)^2 + (-8)^2}{4} - \frac{(-15)^2}{16} = 30.6$$

Since the car (block) effect is similar to the brand effect but totaled across the rows of Table 4.5, the car sum of squares is computed exactly like the brand sum of squares, using row totals, $T_{i.}$'s, instead of column totals. Calling the number of treatments (brands) in general k, then

$$SS_{car} = \sum_{i=1}^{n} \frac{T_{i.}^2}{k} - \frac{T_{..}^2}{N}$$

$$= \frac{(4)^2 + (-1)^2 + (-5)^2 + (-13)^2}{4} - \frac{(-15)^2}{16} = 38.6$$

The error sum of squares is now the remainder after subtracting both brand and car sum of squares from the total sum of squares

$$SS_{error} = SS_{total} - SS_{brand} - SS_{car}$$

$$= 80.9 - 30.6 - 38.6 = 11.7$$

Table 4.6 is an ANOVA table of these data.

TABLE 4.6 — ANOVA for Randomized Block Design of Tire Brand Test

Source	df	SS	MS	EMS
Brands	3	30.6	10.2	$\sigma_e^2 + 4\sigma_T^2$
Cars	3	38.6	12.9	$\sigma_e^2 + 4\sigma_B^2$
Error	9	11.7	1.3	σ_e^2
TOTALS	15	80.9		

To test the hypothesis, H_0: $\mu_{.1} = \mu_{.2} = \mu_{.3} = \mu_{.4}$, the ratio is

$$F_{3,9} = \frac{10.2}{1.3} = 7.8$$

which is significantly larger than the corresponding critical F even at the 1 percent level (Appendix Table D). The hypothesis of equal brand means is thus rejected. It is to be noted that this hypothesis could not be rejected using a completely randomized design. The randomized block design which allows for removal of the block (car) effect definitely reduced the error variance estimate from 4.2 to 1.3.

It is also possible, if desired, to test the hypothesis that the average tread loss of all four cars is the same. H_1: $\mu_{1.} = \mu_{2.} = \mu_{3.} = \mu_{4.}$ and $F_{3,9} = 12.9/1.3 = 9.9$, which is also significant at the 1 percent level (Appendix Table D). Here this hypothesis is rejected and a car-to-car variation is detected.

Even though an effect due to cars (blocks) has been isolated, the main objective is still to test brand differences. Thus it is still a single-factor experiment, the blocks representing only a restriction on complete randomization due to the environment in which the experiment was conducted. Other examples include testing differences in materials which are fed into several different machines, testing differences in fertilizers which must be spread on several different plots of ground, testing the effect of different teaching methods on several pupils. In these examples the blocks are machines, plots, and pupils, respectively, and the levels of the factors of interest can be randomized within each block.

4.3   ANOVA Rationale

For this randomized complete block design, the model is

$$X_{ij} = \mu + B_i + T_j + \epsilon_{ij} \tag{4.2}$$

or

$$X_{ij} = \mu + (\mu_{i.} - \mu) + (\mu_{.j} - \mu) + (X_{ij} - \mu_{i.} - \mu_{.j} + \mu) \tag{4.3}$$

where $\mu_{i.}$ represents the true mean of block i. The last term can be obtained by subtracting the treatment and block deviations from the overall deviation, as follows

$$(X_{ij} - \mu) - (\mu_{i.} - \mu) - (\mu_{.j} - \mu) \equiv X_{ij} - \mu_{i.} - \mu_{.j} + \mu$$

Best estimates of the parameters in Eq. (4.3) give the sample model (after moving $\bar{X}_{..}$ to the left of the equation)

$$X_{ij} - \bar{X}_{..} = (\bar{X}_{i.} - \bar{X}_{..}) + (\bar{X}_{.j} - \bar{X}_{..}) + (X_{ij} - \bar{X}_{i.} - \bar{X}_{.j} + \bar{X}_{..})$$

Squaring both sides and adding with $i = 1, 2, \cdots n$, $j = 1, 2, \cdots k$

$$\sum_{i=1}^{n}\sum_{j=1}^{k} (X_{ij} - \bar{X}_{..})^2 = \sum_{i}^{n}\sum_{j}^{k} (\bar{X}_{i.} - \bar{X}_{..})^2 + \sum_{i}^{n}\sum_{j}^{k} (\bar{X}_{.j} - \bar{X}_{..})^2$$

$$+ \sum_{i}^{n}\sum_{j}^{k} (X_{ij} - \bar{X}_{i.} - \bar{X}_{.j} + \bar{X}_{..})^2 + 3 \text{ cross-products} \qquad (4.4)$$

A little algebraic work on the sums of the cross products will show that they all reduce to zero and the remaining equation becomes the fundamental equation of a two-way analysis of variance. The equation states that

$$\text{SS}_{\text{total}} = \text{SS}_{\text{block}} + \text{SS}_{\text{treatment}} + \text{SS}_{\text{error}}$$

one sum of squares for each variable term in the model [Eq. (4.2)]. Each sum of squares has associated with it its degrees of freedom, and dividing any sum of squares by its degrees of freedom will yield an unbiased estimate of population variance, σ_e^2, if the hypotheses under test are true.

The breakdown of degrees of freedom here is

$$
\begin{array}{cccc}
\text{Total} & \text{Blocks} & \text{Treatments} & \text{Error} \\
(nk - 1) = (n - 1) + & (k - 1) & + (n - 1)(k - 1)
\end{array}
$$

The error degrees are derived from the remainder

$$(nk - 1) - (n - 1) - (k - 1) = nk - n - k + 1 = (n - 1)(k - 1)$$

It can be shown that each sum of squares on the right of Eq. (4.4) when divided by its degrees of freedom provides mean squares which are independently Chi-Square distributed, so that the ratio of any two of them is distributed as F.

The sums of squares formulae given in Eq. (4.4) are usually expanded and rewritten to give formulae which are easier to apply. These are shown in Table 4.7.

The sum of squares formulae given in Table 4.7 are the ones applied to the data of Table 4.5 where $nk = N$.

4.4   Interpretations

Since the above example shows significant differences in brand effects, it might be desirable to make further investigation of the brand means. Orthogonal contrasts could be made on these if set prior to experimentation, or tests like Duncan's Multiple Range Test could be made

TABLE 4.7 — ANOVA for Randomized Block Analysis

Source	df	SS	MS
Between Blocks (B_i)	$n - 1$	$\displaystyle\sum_i^n \frac{T_{i\cdot}^2}{k} - \frac{T_{\cdot\cdot}^2}{nk}$	$SS_{\text{blocks}}/n - 1$
Between Treatments (T_j)	$k - 1$	$\displaystyle\sum_j^k \frac{T_{\cdot j}^2}{n} - \frac{T_{\cdot\cdot}^2}{nk}$	$SS_{\text{treatments}}/k - 1$
Error (ϵ_{ij})	$(n-1)(k-1)$	$\displaystyle\sum_i^n \sum_j^k X_{ij}^2 - \sum_{i=1}^n \frac{T_{i\cdot}^2}{k}$ $\displaystyle\qquad - \sum_{j=1}^k \frac{T_{\cdot j}^2}{n} + \frac{T_{\cdot\cdot}^2}{nk}$	$SS_{\text{error}}/(n-1)(k-1)$
TOTALS	$nk - 1$	$\displaystyle\sum_i^n \sum_j^k X_{ij}^2 - \frac{T_{\cdot\cdot}^2}{nk}$	

after experimentation. For the latter the means are arranged in order of magnitude as follows (coded):

Brands:	C	D	B	A
$T_{\cdot j}$	-9	-8	-3	5
$\bar{X}_{\cdot j}$	-2.25	-2.00	-0.75	1.25

The standard error of a treatment (brand) mean is

$$s_{\bar{X}\cdot j} = \sqrt{\frac{1.3}{4}} = 0.57$$

The tabled ranges are $Z_{p,9\text{df}}(.05)$

$$Z_{2,9}(.05) = 3.20$$

$$Z_{3,9}(.05) = 3.34$$

$$Z_{4,9}(.05) = 3.41$$

And the least significant ranges for this example are

$$R_2 = (3.20)(.57) = 1.82$$

$$R_3 = (3.34)(.57) = 1.90$$

$$R_4 = (3.41)(.57) = 1.94$$

Testing the brand averages

$$A - C =   1.25 - (-2.25) = 3.5 > 1.94^*$$

$$A - D =   1.25 - (-2.00) = 3.25 > 1.90^*$$

$$A - B =   1.25 - (-0.75) = 2.00 > 1.82^*$$

$$B - C = -0.75 - (-2.25) = 1.50 < 1.90$$

$$B - D = -0.75 - (-2.00) = 1.25 < 1.82$$

$$D - C = -2.00 - (-2.25) = 0.25 < 1.82$$

These results show A significantly greater than all other brands, but the other three do not differ significantly from each other. This is shown graphically in Fig. 4.1. Since a high average means a large loss in tread,

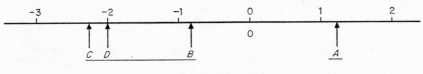

FIG. 4.1

these results indicate that Brand A is the poorest of the four tested, but there is little difference in the other three brands. Confidence limits might be set on Brand A

$$\bar{X}_{.1} \pm t_{1-(\alpha/2)} s_{\bar{x}.j}, \text{ with 9 df on } t.$$

$$1.25 \pm (2.26)(0.57)$$

$$1.25 \pm 1.29$$

or

$$-0.04 \text{ to } 2.54$$

Decoded: 12.96 to 15.54 mm

Similar tests might be run on car effects if there is any concern about these four specific cars. Often the cars are selected at random and it might be desirable to estimate the variance in car means. From Table 4.6:

$$s_e^2 = 1.3$$

$$s_e^2 + 4s_c^2 = 12.9$$

$$s_c^2 = \frac{12.9 - 1.3}{4} = \frac{11.6}{4} = 2.9$$

4.5   General Regression Significance Test Approach

A randomized block design may also be analyzed by the General Regression Significance Test approach given in Chapter 3. The only essential difference is that there are n more totals taken across the k treatments, making $(n + k + 1)$ least squares normal equations in $n + k + 1$ unknowns. For the randomized block model

$$X_{ij} = \mu + B_i + T_j + \epsilon_{ij}$$

The least-squares best estimates give a model

$$X_{ij} = m + b_i + t_j + e_{ij}$$

where $i = 1,2, \cdots n; j = 1,2, \cdots k$.

Applying this approach to the coded data of Table 4.5 on brands and cars, the following normal equations result

$$\left.\begin{aligned}
-15 &= 16m + 4b_1 + 4b_2 + 4b_3 + 4b_4 + 4t_1 + 4t_2 + 4t_3 + 4t_4 \\
4 &= 4m + 4b_1 \qquad\qquad\qquad\quad + t_1 + t_2 + t_3 + t_4 \\
-1 &= 4m \quad + 4b_2 \qquad\qquad\quad + t_1 + t_2 + t_3 + t_4 \\
-5 &= 4m \qquad\quad + 4b_3 \qquad\quad + t_1 + t_2 + t_3 + t_4 \\
-13 &= 4m \qquad\qquad\quad + 4b_4 + t_1 + t_2 + t_3 + t_4 \\
5 &= 4m + b_1 + b_2 + b_3 + b_4 + 4t_1 \\
-3 &= 4m + b_1 + b_2 + b_3 + b_4 \qquad + 4t_2 \\
-9 &= 4m + b_1 + b_2 + b_3 + b_4 \qquad\qquad + 4t_3 \\
-8 &= 4m + b_1 + b_2 + b_3 + b_4 \qquad\qquad\qquad + 4t_4
\end{aligned}\right\} \qquad (4.5)$$

Since

$$\sum_{i=1}^{4} b_i = \sum_{j=1}^{4} t_j = 0$$

these can be solved easily to give

$$m = -\frac{15}{16} = -0.94$$

$$b_1 = \frac{4 - 4\left(-\dfrac{15}{16}\right)}{4} = 1.94$$

$$b_2 = \frac{-1 - 4\left(-\dfrac{15}{16}\right)}{4} = +0.69$$

$$b_3 = \frac{-5 - 4\left(-\dfrac{15}{16}\right)}{4} = -0.31$$

$$b_4 = \frac{-13 - 4\left(-\dfrac{15}{16}\right)}{4} = -2.31$$

$\left.\vphantom{\begin{array}{c}1\\1\\1\\1\\1\\1\\1\\1\end{array}}\right\} \sum_i b_i = 0.01$ (or approximately 0)

$$t_1 = \frac{5 - 4\left(-\dfrac{15}{16}\right)}{4} = +2.19$$

$$t_2 = \frac{-3 - 4\left(-\dfrac{15}{16}\right)}{4} = 0.19$$

$$t_3 = \frac{-9 - 4\left(-\dfrac{15}{16}\right)}{4} = -1.31$$

$$t_4 = \frac{-8 - 4\left(-\dfrac{15}{16}\right)}{4} = -1.06$$

$\left.\vphantom{\begin{array}{c}1\\1\\1\\1\\1\\1\\1\\1\end{array}}\right\} \sum_j t_j = .01$ (or approximately 0)

The $SS_{\text{regression}}$ $(m, b_i, t_j) = (-15)(-0.94) + 4(1.94) - 1(0.69)$

$$-5(-0.31) - 13(-2.31) + 5(2.19) - 3(0.19)$$

$$-9(-1.31) - 8(-1.06) = 83.40$$

The $SS_{\text{error}} = \displaystyle\sum_i^4 \sum_j^4 X_{ij}^2 - SS_{\text{regression}} \ (m, b_i, t_j)$

$$= 95 - 83.40 = 11.60$$

which agrees within rounding error with the value in ANOVA Table 4.6.

To determine the treatment sum of squares, assume no treatment effect; therefore, the reduced model is

$$X_{ij} = m' + b'_i + e'_{ij}$$

The normal equations for this model turn out to be the same as the first five equations in Eq. (4.5), so that the estimates are

$$m' = m = -0.94$$

$$b'_1 = b_1 = 1.94$$

$$b'_2 = b_2 = 0.69$$

$$b'_3 = b_3 = -0.31$$

$$b'_4 = b_4 = -2.31$$

and

$$SS_{regression} \ (m, b_i) = (-15)(-0.94) + 4(1.94) - 1(0.69)$$
$$-5(-0.31) - 13(-2.31) = 52.75$$

Hence

$$SS_{treatments} = SS_{regression} \ (m, b_i, t_j) - SS_{regression} \ (m, b_i)$$

$$= 83.40 - 52.75 = 30.65$$

agreeing with 30.6 of Table 4.6. If block sums of squares are desired, assume block effect zero and use the reduced model

$$X_{ij} = m'' + t''_j + e''_{ij}$$

The normal equations are now equations 1, 6, 7, 8 and 9 in Eq. (4.5) with the same solutions as before, and

$$SS \ (m, t_j) = (-15)(-.94) + 5(2.19) - 3(0.19) - 9(-1.31)$$
$$-8(-1.06) = 44.75$$

Hence

$$SS_{blocks} = SS_{regression} \ (m, b_i, t_j) - SS_{regression} \ (m, t_j)$$

$$= 83.40 - 44.75 = 38.65$$

agreeing with 38.6 of Table 4.6.

4.6 Missing Values

Occasionally in a randomized block design an observation is lost. A vial may break, an animal may die, or a tire may disintegrate, so that there occurs one or more missing observations in the data. For a single-factor completely randomized design this presents no problem, since the analysis of variance can be run with unequal n_j's. But for a two-way analysis this means a loss of orthogonality, since for some blocks the $\Sigma_j t_j$ no longer equals zero, and for some treatments the $\Sigma_i b_i$ no longer equals zero. When blocks and treatments are orthogonal, the block totals are added over all treatments and vice-versa. If one or more observations are missing, the usual procedure is to replace the value with one which makes the sum of the squares of the errors a minimum.

In the tire brand test example, suppose that the Brand C tire on Car III blew out and was ruined before completing the 20,000 miles. The resulting data appear below where y is put in place of this missing value.

TABLE 4.8 — Missing Value Example

Car	Brand A	B	C	D	$T_i.$
I	4	1	-1	0	4
II	1	1	-1	-2	-1
III	0	0	y	-2	$y - 2$
IV	0	-5	-4	-4	-13
$T._j$	5	-3	$y - 6$	-8	$y - 12 = T_{..}$

Now the $SS_{error} = SS_{total} - SS_{treatment} - SS_{block}$

$$= \sum_i \sum_j X_{ij}^2 - \sum_j \frac{T_{.j}^2}{n} - \sum_i \frac{T_{i.}^2}{k} + \frac{T_{..}^2}{nk}$$

For this example

$$SS_{error} = 4^2 + 1^2 + \cdots + y^2 + \cdots + (-4)^2$$

$$- \frac{(5)^2 + (-3)^2 + (y-6)^2 + (-8)^2}{4}$$

$$- \frac{(4)^2 + (-1)^2 + (y-2)^2 + (-13)^2}{4} + \frac{(y-12)^2}{16}$$

In order to find the y-value which will minimize this expression, it is differentiated with respect to y and set equal to zero. As all constant terms have their derivates zero

$$\frac{d(SS_{error})}{dy} = 2y - \frac{2(y-6)}{4} - \frac{2(y-2)}{4} + \frac{2(y-12)}{16} = 0$$

Solving gives

$$16y - 4y + 24 - 4y + 8 + y - 12 = 0$$

$$9y = -20$$

$$y = -\frac{20}{9} = -2.2$$

If this value is now used in the y-position, the resulting ANOVA table is as shown in Table 4.9.

TABLE 4.9 — ANOVA for Tire Brands Test Example
Adjusted for a Missing Value

Source	df	SS	MS
Cars (B_i)	3	28.7	9.5
Brands (T_j)	3	38.3	12.7
Error (ϵ_{ij})	8	11.2	1.4
TOTALS	14	78.2	

The resulting ANOVA is not too different from before, but the degrees of freedom for the error term are reduced by one, since there are only 15 actual observations and y is determined from these 15 readings. This procedure can be used on any reasonable number of missing values by differentiating the error sum of squares partially with respect to each such missing value and setting it equal to zero, giving as many equations as unknown values to be solved for these missing values.

In general, for one missing value, y_{ij}, it can be shown that

$$y_{ij} = \frac{nT'_{i.} + kT'_{.j} - T'_{..}}{(n-1)(k-1)} \tag{4.6}$$

where the primed totals $(T'_{i.}, T'_{.j}$ and $T'_{..})$ are the totals indicated without the missing value, y. In our example

$$y_{ij} = y_{33} = \frac{4(-2) + 4(-6) - (-12)}{(3)(3)}$$

$$y_{33} = \frac{-20}{9} = -2.2 \text{ (as before)}$$

Another approach to the missing value problem is to set up the least squares normal equations without the missing value and solve them as usual. They will, of course, be more difficult to solve now as certain $\Sigma_j t_j$ and $\Sigma_i b_i$ are not zero. For this problem with one missing value, the results are the same.

4.7   Randomized Incomplete Blocks — Restriction on Experimentation

Method for Balanced Blocks

In some randomized block designs it may not be possible to apply all treatments in every block. If there were, for example, six brands of tires to test in the preceding example, only four could be tried on a given car (not using the spare), and such a block would be incomplete, having only four out of the six treatments in it.

Take the problem of determining the effect on current flow of four treatments applied to the coils of TV tube filaments. As each treatment application requires some time, it is not possible to run several observations of these treatments in one day. If days were taken as blocks, all four treatments must be run in random order on each of several days in order to have a randomized block design. After checking, it is found that even four treatments cannot be completed in a day; three are the most that can be run. The question then is: Which treatments are to be run on the first day, which on the second, and so forth, if information is desired on all four treatments?

The solution to this problem is to use a balanced incomplete block design. An *incomplete block design* is simply one in which there are more treatments than can be put in a single block. A *balanced incomplete block design* is an incomplete block design in which every pair of treatments occurs the same number of times in the experiment. Tables of such designs may be found in Fisher and Yates [8]. The number of blocks necessary for balancing will depend upon the number of treatments that can be run in a single block.

For the example mentioned there are four treatments and only three treatments can be run in a block. The balanced design for this problem requires four blocks (days) as shown in Table 4.10.

TABLE 4.10 — Balanced Incomplete Block Design
for TV Filament Example

Blocks (Days)	Treatments				$T_{i.}$
	A	B	C	D	
1	2	—	20	7	29
2	—	32	14	3	49
3	4	13	31	—	48
4	0	23	—	11	34
$T_{.j}$	6	68	65	21	$160 = T_{..}$

In this design only Treatments A, C, and D are run on the first day; B, C, and D on the second day, and so forth. Note that each pair of treatments, such as AB, occurs together twice in the experiment. A and B occur together on days three and four; C and D occur together on days one and two; etc. As in randomized complete block designs, the order in which the three treatments are run on a given day is completely randomized.

The analysis of such a design is easier if some new notation is introduced. Let

b = number of blocks in the experiment $(b = 4)$

t = number of treatments in the experiment $(t = 4)$

k = number of treatments per block $(k = 3)$

r = number of replications of a given treatment throughout the experiment $(r = 3)$

N = total number of observations

$= bk = tr \ (N = 12)$

λ = number of times each pair of treatments appears together throughout the experiment

$= r(k - 1)/(t - 1) \ (\lambda = 2)$

Table 4.10 has the current readings after they have been coded by subtracting 513 milliamperes and the block and treatment totals. The analysis for a balanced incomplete block design proceeds as follows:

1. Calculate the total sum of squares as usual.

$$SS_{total} = \sum_i \sum_j X_{ij}^2 - \frac{T_{..}^2}{N}$$

$$= 3478 - \frac{(160)^2}{12} = 1344.67$$

2. Calculate the block sum of squares, ignoring treatments.

$$SS_{block} = \sum_{i=1}^{b} \frac{T_{i.}^2}{k} - \frac{T_{..}^2}{N}$$

$$= \frac{(29)^2 + (49)^2 + (48)^2 + (34)^2}{3} - \frac{(160)^2}{12} = 100.67$$

3. Calculate treatment effects, adjusting for blocks.

$$SS_{treatments} = \frac{\sum_{j=1}^{t} Q_j^2}{k\lambda t} \tag{4.7}$$

where

$$Q_j = kT_{.j} - \sum_i n_{ij}T_{i.} \tag{4.8}$$

where $n_{ij} = 1$ if treatment j appears in block i, and $n_{ij} = 0$ if treatment j does *not* appear in block i. Note that $\Sigma_i n_{ij}T_{i.}$ is merely the sum of all block totals which contain treatment j.

For the data given

$$Q_1 = 3(6) - [29 + 48 + 34] = 18 - 111 = -93$$

$$Q_2 = 3(68) - 131 = \quad 73$$

$$Q_3 = 3(65) - 126 = \quad 69$$

$$Q_4 = 3(21) - 112 = \underline{-49}$$
$$0$$

. . .

Note that

$$\sum_{j=1}^{t} Q_j = 0$$

which is always true.

Then $SS_{treatments} = \dfrac{(-93)^2 + (73)^2 + (69)^2 + (-49)^2}{3(2)4} = 880.83$

4. Calculate the error sum of squares by subtraction

$$SS_{error} = SS_{total} - SS_{blocks} - SS_{treatments}$$

$$= 1344.67 - 100.67 - 880.83 = 363.17$$

Table 4.11 summarizes in an ANOVA table.

TABLE 4.11 — ANOVA for Incomplete Block Example

Source	df	SS	MS
Blocks (days)	3	100.67	—
Treatments (adjusted)	3	880.83	293.61
Error	5	363.17	72.63
TOTALS	11	1344.67	

An F test gives $F_{3,5} = 293.61/72.63 = 4.04$, which is not significant at the 5 percent level (Appendix table D).

In Table 4.11 the error degrees of freedom are determined by subtraction rather than as the product of the block and treatment degrees of freedom. However, this error degrees of freedom is seen to be the product of treatment and block degrees of freedom (9) if 4 is subtracted for the four missing values in the design.

In some incomplete block designs it may be desirable to test for a block effect. The mean square for blocks was not computed in Table 4.11 since it had not been adjusted for treatments. In the case of a *symmetrical balanced incomplete randomized block design*, where $b = t$, the block sum of squares may be adjusted in the same manner as the treatment sums of squares

$$Q'_i = rT_{i.} \ - \sum_j n_{ij}T_{.j}$$
$$Q'_1 = 3(29) - \ 92 = -5$$
$$Q'_2 = 3(49) - 154 = -7$$
$$Q'_3 = 3(48) - 139 = +5$$
$$Q'_4 = 3(34) - \ 95 = +7$$
$$\sum_i Q'_i = \ 0$$

$$\text{SS}_{\text{blocks}} = \sum_{i=1}^{b} (Q'_i)^2/r\lambda b = \frac{(-5)^2 + (-7)^2 + (5)^2 + (7)^2}{3(2)4} = 6.17$$

and

$$\text{SS}_{\text{treatments (unadj)}} = \frac{6^2 + 68^2 + 65^2 + 21^2}{3} - \frac{(160)^2}{12} = 975.34$$

The results of this adjustment and the one in treatments may now be summarized for this symmetrical case as shown in Table 4.12.

TABLE 4.12 — ANOVA Table for Incomplete Block Example for Both Treatments and Blocks

Source	df	SS	MS
Blocks (adjusted)	3	6.17	2.06
Blocks	(3)	(100.67)	—
Treatments (adjusted)	3	880.83	293.61
Treatments	(3)	(975.34)	—
Errors	5	363.17	72.63
TOTALS	11	1344.67	

The terms in parentheses are inserted only to show how the error term was computed for one adjusted effect and one unadjusted effect

$$\text{SS}_{\text{error}} = \text{SS}_{\text{total}} - \text{SS}_{\text{treatments(adj)}} - \text{SS}_{\text{blocks}}$$
$$= 1344.67 - 880.83 - 100.67 = 363.17$$

Or

$$SS_{error} = SS_{total} - SS_{treatments} - SS_{blocks(adj)}$$
$$= 1344.67 - 975.34 - 6.17 = 363.17$$

It should be noted also that the final sum of squares values used in Table 4.12 to get the mean square values do not add up to the total sum of squares. This is characteristic of a nonorthogonal design. The F test for blocks was not run because its value is obviously extremely small, which indicates no day-to-day effect on current flow.

For nonsymmetrical or unbalanced designs, the general regression method may be a useful alternative. If contrasts are to be computed for an incomplete block design, it can be shown that the sum of squares for a contrast is given by

$$SS_{C_m} = \frac{(C_m)^2}{\left(\sum_{j=1}^{t} c_{jm}^2 \right) k\lambda t} \tag{4.9}$$

where contrasts (C_m) are made on the Q_j's rather than $T_{.j}$'s.

General Regression Approach to Randomized Incomplete Block Design

Applying the general regression significance test to the data in Table 4.10, the normal equations are

$$
\left.
\begin{aligned}
160 &= 12m + 3t_1 + 3t_2 + 3t_3 + 3t_4 + 3b_1 + 3b_2 + 3b_3 + 3b_4 \\
29 &= 3m + t_1 \quad\quad + t_3 + t_4 + 3b_1 \\
49 &= 3m \quad\quad + t_2 + t_3 + t_4 \quad\quad + 3b_2 \\
48 &= 3m + t_1 + t_2 + t_3 \quad\quad\quad\quad + 3b_3 \\
34 &= 3m + t_1 + t_2 \quad\quad + t_4 \quad\quad\quad\quad\quad\quad + 3b_4 \\
6 &= 3m + 3t_1 \quad\quad\quad\quad + b_1 \quad\quad + b_3 + b_4 \\
68 &= 3m \quad\quad + 3t_2 \quad\quad\quad\quad\quad\quad + b_2 + b_3 + b_4 \\
65 &= 3m \quad\quad\quad + 3t_3 \quad\quad + b_1 + b_2 + b_3 \\
21 &= 3m \quad\quad\quad\quad + 3t_4 + b_1 + b_2 \quad\quad + b_4
\end{aligned}
\right\} \tag{4.10}
$$

Since

$$\sum_i b_i = \sum_j t_j = 0$$

from the first equation in Eq. (4.10)

$$m = \frac{160}{12}$$

The method for solving for the t's is as follows: Multiply the sixth equation in Eq. (4.10) by 3 and add it to the third equation.

$$6\text{th} \times 3: \quad 18 = 9m + 9t_1 \qquad\qquad + 3b_1 \qquad + 3b_3 + 3b_4$$

$$3\text{rd:} \quad \underline{49 = 3m \qquad + t_2 + t_3 + t_4 \qquad\qquad + 3b_2}$$

$$\text{adding: } 67 = 12m + 9t_1 + t_2 + t_3 + t_4 + 3\sum_i^4 b_i$$

$$\text{or: } 67 = 12m + 8t_1 + \sum_{j=1}^4 t_j + 3\sum_{i=1}^4 b_i$$

$$\text{or: } \quad t_1 = \frac{67 - 12m}{8} \quad \text{since} \quad \sum t_j = \sum b_i = 0$$

$$= \frac{67 - 12\left(\dfrac{160}{12}\right)}{8} = \frac{67 - 160}{8} = \frac{-93}{8}$$

In this same manner, using the seventh and second equations gives

$$t_2 = \frac{233 - 160}{8} = \frac{73}{8}$$

Using the eighth and fifth equations gives

$$t_3 = \frac{229 - 160}{8} = \frac{69}{8}$$

Using the ninth and fourth equations gives

$$t_4 = \frac{111 - 160}{8} = \frac{-49}{8}$$

$$\sum_{j=1}^4 t_j = 0$$

Note that these t_j's are proportional to the Q_j's, as $t_j = Q_j/8$.

By a similar elimination of t's, the b's can be obtained. The second and seventh equations give

$$2\text{nd} \times 3: \quad 87 = 9m + 3t_1 \qquad + 3t_3 + 3t_4 + 9b_1$$

$$7\text{th:} \quad \underline{68 = 3m \qquad + 3t_2 \qquad\qquad\qquad + b_2 + b_3 + b_4}$$

$$\text{Adding: } 155 = 12m + 3\sum_j t_j + 8b_1 + \sum_i b_i$$

$$b_1 = \frac{155 - 12m}{8} = \frac{155 - 160}{8} = -\frac{5}{8}$$

Likewise: $b_2 = \dfrac{153 - 160}{8} = -\dfrac{7}{8}$

$b_3 = \dfrac{165 - 160}{8} = \dfrac{5}{8}$

$b_4 = \dfrac{167 - 160}{8} = \dfrac{7}{8}$

$$\sum_{i=1}^{4} b_i = 0$$

Again these b_i's are proportional to the Q_i''s.

$$\text{SS}_{\text{regression}}\,(m, b_i, t_j) = mT_{..} + \sum_i b_i T_{i.} + \sum_j t_j T_{.j}$$

$$\text{SS}_{\text{regression}}\,(m, b, t) = \left(\frac{160}{12}\right)(160) + \left(-\frac{5}{8}\right)(29) + \left(-\frac{7}{8}\right)(49)$$

$$+ \left(\frac{5}{8}\right)(48) + \left(\frac{7}{8}\right)(34) + \left(-\frac{93}{8}\right)(6) + \left(\frac{73}{8}\right)(68)$$

$$+ \left(\frac{69}{8}\right)(65) + \left(-\frac{49}{8}\right)(21) = 3114.83$$

$$\text{SS}_{\text{error}} = \sum_i \sum_j X_{ij}^2 - \text{SS}_{\text{regression}}\,(m, b, t)$$

$$= 3478 - 3114.83 = 363.17 \text{ (as before)}$$

To test H_0: $T_j = 0$ for all j, the reduced model is $X_{ij} = m' + b_i' + e_{ij}'$, and the normal equations are

$$160 = 12m' + 3b_1' + 3b_2' + 3b_3' + 3b_4'$$
$$29 = 3m' + 3b_1'$$
$$49 = 3m' + 3b_2'$$
$$48 = 3m' + 3b_3'$$
$$34 = 3m' + 3b_4'$$

Solving $m' = 160/12$ (as before) but

$$b_1' = \frac{29 - 3m}{3} = -\frac{11}{3}$$

$$b_2' = \frac{49 - 3m}{3} = \frac{9}{3}$$

$$b_3' = \frac{48 - 3m}{3} = \frac{8}{3}$$

$$b_4' = \frac{34 - 3m}{3} = -\frac{6}{3}$$

$$\sum b_i' = 0$$

Note that the b_i''s are different from the b_i's so that the

$$SS_{\text{regression}} \; (m, \; b_i') = \left(\frac{160}{12}\right)(160) + (29)\left(-\frac{11}{3}\right) + (49)\left(\frac{9}{3}\right)$$

$$+ \; 48\left(\frac{8}{3}\right) + 34\left(-\frac{6}{3}\right) = 2234.00$$

The $SS_{\text{treatments(adj)}} = SS_{\text{regression}} \; (m, \; b, \; t) - SS_{\text{regression}} \; (m, \; b')$

$$= 3114.83 - 2234.00 = 880.83 \text{ (as before)}$$

A similar procedure would give $SS_{\text{blocks(adj)}}$ if desired.

4.8 Summary

Experiment	*Design*	*Analysis*

I. Single Factor

1. Completely Randomized   1. One-way ANOVA
$$X_{ij} = \mu + T_j + \epsilon_{ij}$$
2. Randomized Block   2.
$$X_{ij} = \mu + T_j + B_i + \epsilon_{ij}$$
   a. Complete   *a.* Two-way ANOVA
   b. Incomplete-Balanced   *b.* Special formulae
   c. Incomplete-General   *c.* Regression method

PROBLEMS

4-1.   The effects of four (4) types of graphite coaters on light box readings are to be studied. As these readings might differ from day to day, observations are to be taken on each of the four (4) types every day for three (3) days. The order of testing of the four (4) types on any given day can be randomized. The results are

	Graphite Coater Type			
Day	M	A	K	L
1	4.0	4.8	5.0	4.6
2	4.8	5.0	5.2	4.6
3	4.0	4.8	5.6	5.0

Analyze these data as a randomized block design and state your conclusions.

4-2.   Set up orthogonal contrasts among coater types and analyze for Prob. 4-1.

4-3. Use Duncan's multiple range test to compare 4 coater types means for Prob. 4-1.

4-4. Solve Prob. 4-1 by the general regression method.

4-5. If the reading on type K for the second day was missing, what missing value should be inserted and what is the analysis now?

4-6. Data on screen color difference on a television tube measured in degrees K are to be compared for four operators. On a given day only three operators can be used in the experiment. A balanced incomplete block design gave results as follows:

Day	Operator			
	A	B	C	D
Monday	780	820	800	—
Tuesday	950	—	920	940
Wednesday	—	880	880	820
Thursday	840	780	—	820

Do a complete analysis of these data and discuss your findings with regard to differences between operators.

4-7. Run orthogonal contrasts on the operators in Prob. 4-6.

4-8. Determine the missing values in the table for Prob. 4-6.

4-9. Use these missing values to obtain the error sum of squares for Prob. 4-6.

4-10. Complete an analysis of variance of Prob. 4-6 using the error sum of squares as determined in Prob. 4-9. Compare your results with those in Prob. 4-6.

CHAPTER 5

Single-Factor Experiments— Latin and Other Squares

5.1 Introduction

The reader may have wondered about a possible position effect in the problem on testing tire brands in Chapter 4. Experience shows that rear tires get different wear than front tires and even different sides of the same car may show different amounts of tread wear. In the randomized block design of Chapter 4, the four brands were randomized onto the four wheels of each car with no regard for position. The effect of position on wear could be balanced out by rotating the tires every 5,000 miles, giving each brand 5,000 miles on each wheel. However, if this is not feasible, the positions can impose another restriction on the randomization in such a way that each brand is not only used once on each car but also only once in each of the four possible positions: left-front, left-rear, right-front, and right-rear.

5.2 Latin Squares

A design in which each treatment appears once and only once in each row (position) and once and only once in each column (cars) is called a *Latin Square Design*. Interest is still centered on one factor, treatments, but two restrictions are placed on the randomization. An example of one such 4 × 4 Latin Square is shown in Table 5.1.

Such a design is only possible when the number of levels of both

TABLE 5.1 — 4 × 4 Latin Square Design

	Car			
Position	I	II	III	IV
1	C	D	A	B
2	B	C	D	A
3	A	B	C	D
4	D	A	B	C

restrictions equals the number of treatment levels. In other words, it must be a square. It is not true that all randomization is lost in this design, as the particular Latin Square to be used on a given problem may be chosen at random from several possible Latin Squares of the required size. Tables of such squares are found in Fisher and Yates [8].

The analysis of the data in a Latin Square Design is a simple extension of previous analyses where the data are now added in a third direction — positions. If the data of Table 4.5 in Chapter 4 are imposed on the Latin Square of Table 5.1, the result could be that shown in Table 5.2, letters still representing tire brand.

TABLE 5.2 — *Latin Square Data on Tire Wear*

	Car				
Position	I	II	III	IV	$T_{..k}$
1	$C = -1$	$D = -2$	$A = 0$	$B = -5$	-8
2	$B = 1$	$C = -1$	$D = -2$	$A = 0$	-2
3	$A = 4$	$B = 1$	$C = -3$	$D = -4$	-2
4	$D = 0$	$A = 1$	$B = 0$	$C = -4$	-3
$T_{i..}$	4	-1	-5	-13	$T_{...} \equiv -15$

Totals by Treatments are

$$T_{.j.} = \frac{A \quad B \quad C \quad D}{5, \ -3, \ -9, \ -8}$$

where the model is now

$$X_{ijk} = \mu + B_i + T_j + \gamma_k + \epsilon_{ijk}$$

and γ_k represents the positions effect. Since the only new totals are for positions, a positions sum of squares can be computed as

$$SS_{positions} = \frac{(-8)^2 + (-2)^2 + (-2)^2 + (-3)^2}{4} - \frac{(-15)^2}{16} = 6.2$$

and

$$SS_{error} = SS_{total} - SS_{treatments} - SS_{cars} - SS_{positions}$$
$$= 80.9 - 30.6 - 38.6 - 6.2 = 5.5$$

Table 5.3 is the ANOVA table for these data.

TABLE 5.3 — Latin Square ANOVA

Source	df	SS	MS	EMS
Brands (T_j)	3	30.6	10.2	$\sigma_e^2 + 4\sigma_T^2$
Cars (B_i)	3	38.6	12.9	$\sigma_e^2 + 4\sigma_B^2$
Positions (γ_k)	3	6.2	2.1	$\sigma_e^2 + 4\sigma_\gamma^2$
Error (ϵ_{ijk})	6	5.5	0.9	σ_e^2
TOTALS	15	80.9		

Once again another restriction placed on the randomization has further reduced the experimental error, although the position effect is not significant at the 5 percent level. This further reduction of error variance is attained at the expense of degrees of freedom, since now the estimate of σ_e^2 is based on only 6 df instead of 9 df as in the randomized block design. This means less precision in estimating this error variance. But the added restrictions should be made if the environmental conditions suggest them. After discovering that positions had no significant effect, some investigators might "pool" the positions sum of squares with the error sum of squares and obtain a more precise estimate of σ_e^2; namely, 1.3, as given in Table 4.6 of Chapter 4. However, there is a danger in "pooling," as it means "accepting" a hypothesis of no position effect, and the investigator has no idea about the possible error involved in "accepting" an hypothesis. Naturally if the degrees of freedom on the error term are reduced much below that of Table 5.3 there will have to be some pooling to get a reasonable yardstick for assessing other effects.

5.3 Graeco-Latin Squares

In some experiments still another restriction may be imposed on the randomization and the design may be a Graeco-Latin Square such as Table 5.4 exhibits.

TABLE 5.4 — Graeco-Latin Square Design

Position	Car			
	I	II	III	IV
1	$A\alpha$	$B\beta$	$C\gamma$	$D\delta$
2	$B\gamma$	$A\delta$	$D\alpha$	$C\beta$
3	$C\delta$	$D\gamma$	$A\beta$	$B\alpha$
4	$D\beta$	$C\alpha$	$B\delta$	$A\gamma$

In this design the third restriction is at levels α, β, γ, δ, and not only do these each appear once and only once in each row and each column, but they appear once and only once with each level of treatment, A, B, C, or D. The model for this would be

$$X_{ijkm} = \mu + B_i + T_j + \gamma_k + W_m + \epsilon_{ijkm}$$

where W_m is the effect of the latest restriction with levels α, β, γ, δ. An outline of the analysis appears in Table 5.5.

TABLE 5.5 — Graeco-Latin Analysis Outline

Source	df
B_i	3
T_j	3
γ_k	3
W_m	3
ϵ_{ijkm}	3
TOTAL	15

Such a design may not be very practical, as only 3 df are left for the error variance.

5.4   Youden Squares

When the conditions for a Latin Square are met except for the fact that only three treatments are possible (e.g., in one block because only three positions are available) and where there are four blocks altogether, the design is an incomplete Latin Square. This design is called a *Youden Square*. One such Youden Square is illustrated in Table 5.6.

TABLE 5.6 — Youden Square Design

Blocks	Positions 1	2	3
I	A	B	C
II	D	A	B
III	B	C	D
IV	C	D	A

Note that the addition of a column (D, C, A, B) would make this a Latin Square if another position were available. A situation calling for a Youden

Square might occur if four materials are to be tested on four machines but there were only three heads on each machine whose orientation might affect the results.

The analysis of a Youden Square proceeds like the incomplete block analysis. Assuming hypothetical values for some measured variable X_{ijk} where

$$X_{ijk} = \mu + B_i + T_j + \gamma_k + \epsilon_{ijk}$$

and

$$i = 1, \cdots 4 \qquad j = 1, 2, \cdots 4 \qquad k = 1, 2, 3$$

we might have the data of Table 5.7.

TABLE 5.7 — Youden Square Data

	Position			
Block	1	2	3	$T_{i..}$
I	A 2	B 1	C 0	3
II	$D - 2$	A 2	B 2	2
III	$B - 1$	$C - 1$	$D - 3$	-5
IV	C 0	$D - 4$	A 2	-2
$T_{..k}$	-1	-2	$+1$	$-2 = T_{...}$

$$\left. \begin{array}{l} t = b = 4 \\ r = k = 3 \\ \lambda = 2 \end{array} \right\}$$

Treatment totals of A, B, C, D are

$$T_{.j.} = 6, 2, -1, -9$$

From this table

$$\mathrm{SS}_{\text{total}} = \sum_i \sum_j \sum_k X_{ijk}^2 - \frac{T_{...}^2}{N} = 48 - \frac{(-2)^2}{12} = 47.67$$

Position effect may first be ignored, since every position occurs once and only once in each block and once with each treatment, so that positions are orthogonal to blocks and treatments.

$$\mathrm{SS}_{\text{block (ignoring treatments)}} = \frac{(3)^2 + (2)^2 + (-5)^2 + (-2)^2}{3} - \frac{(-2)^2}{12}$$

$$= \frac{42}{3} - \frac{1}{3} = \frac{41}{3} = 13.67$$

For treatment sum of squares adjusted for blocks we get

$$Q_1 = 3(+6) - 3 = 15$$

$$Q_2 = 3(\ 2) - 0 = 6$$

$$Q_3 = 3(-1) - (-4) = 1$$

$$Q_4 = 3(-9) - (-5) = -22$$

$$\sum_i Q_i = 0$$

$$SS_{treatments} = \frac{(15)^2 + (6)^2 + (1)^2 + (-22)^2}{4.6} = 31.08$$

$$SS_{position} = \frac{(-1)^2 + (-2)^2 + (1)^2}{4} - \frac{(-2)^2}{12} = 1.17$$

$$SS_{error} = SS_{total} - SS_{block} - SS_{treatment \ (adj)} - SS_{position}$$

$$= 47.67 - 13.67 - 31.08 - 1.17$$

$$= 1.75$$

The analysis appears in Table 5.8.

TABLE 5.8 — Youden Square ANOVA

Source	df	SS	MS
Treatments T_j(adjusted)	3	31.08	10.36
Blocks B_i	3	13.67	—
Positions γ_k	2	1.17	0.58
Error ϵ_{ijk}	3	1.75	0.58
TOTALS	11	47.67	

The position effect here is not significant and it might be desirable to pool it with the error, getting

$$s_e^2 = \frac{1.17 + 1.75}{2 + 3} = \frac{2.92}{5} = 0.58$$

as an estimate of error variance, with 5 df. Then the treatment effect is highly significant. The block mean square not given as blocks must be adjusted by treatments if block effects are to be assessed. The procedure is the same as shown in Chapter 4 on incomplete block designs.

5.5 Summary

Experiment	*Design*	*Analysis*

I. Single Factor

1. Completely Randomized
$X_{ij} = \mu + T_j + \epsilon_{ij}$

    1. One-Way ANOVA

2. Randomized Block
$X_{ij} = \mu + T_j + B_i + \epsilon_{ij}$

    2.

    a. Complete

       a. Two-Way ANOVA

    b. Incomplete-Balanced

       b. Special ANOVA

    c. Incomplete-General

       c. Regression Method

3. Latin Square
$X_{ijk} = \mu + B_i + T_j + \gamma_k + \epsilon_{ijk}$

    3.

    a. Complete

       a. Three-Way ANOVA

    b. Incomplete-Youden Square

       b. Special ANOVA [like 2(b)]

4. Graeco-Latin Square
$X_{ijkm} = \mu + B_i + T_j + \gamma_k + W_m + \epsilon_{ijkm}$

    4. a. Four-Way ANOVA

It might be emphasized once again that, so far, interest has been centered on a single factor (treatments) for the discussion in Chapters 3, 4, and 5. The special designs simply represent restrictions on the randomization. In the next chapter, two or more factors will be considered.

PROBLEMS

5-1. In a research study at Purdue University on metal-removal rate, five electrode shapes were studied, shapes *A*, *B*, *C*, *D* and *E*. The removal was accomplished by an electric discharge between the electrode and the material being cut. For this experiment five holes were cut in five workpieces, and the order of electrodes was arranged so that only one electrode shape was used in the same position on each of the five workpieces. Thus, the design was a Latin Square design, with workpieces (strips) and positions on the strip as restrictions on the randomization. Several variables were studied, one of which was the Rc hardness of metal where each hole was to be cut. The results were as follows:

	Position				
Strips	1	2	3	4	5
I	$A(64)$	$B(61)$	$C(62)$	$D(62)$	$E(62)$
II	$B(62)$	$C(62)$	$D(63)$	$E(62)$	$A(63)$
III	$C(61)$	$D(62)$	$E(63)$	$A(63)$	$B(63)$
IV	$D(63)$	$E(64)$	$A(63)$	$B(63)$	$C(63)$
V	$E(62)$	$A(61)$	$B(63)$	$C(63)$	$D(62)$

Analyze these data and test for an electrode effect, position effect, and strip effect on Rc hardness.

5-2. The times in hours necessary to cut the holes in Prob. 5-1 were recorded as follows:

	Position				
Strips	1	2	3	4	5
I	$A(3.5)$	$B(2.1)$	$C(2.5)$	$D(3.5)$	$E(2.4)$
II	$E(2.6)$	$A(3.3)$	$B(2.1)$	$C(2.5)$	$D(2.7)$
III	$D(2.9)$	$E(2.6)$	$A(3.5)$	$B(2.7)$	$C(2.9)$
IV	$C(2.5)$	$D(2.9)$	$E(3.0)$	$A(3.3)$	$B(2.3)$
V	$B(2.1)$	$C(2.3)$	$D(3.7)$	$E(3.2)$	$A(3.5)$

Analyze these data for the effect of electrodes, strips, and positions on time.

5-3. Analyze the electrode effect further in Prob. 5-2 and make some statement as to which electrodes are best, if the shortest cutting time is the most desirable factor.

5-4. A composite measure of screen quality was made on screens using four lacquer concentrations, four standing times, four acryloid concentrations (A, B, C, D) and four acetone concentrations (α, β, Γ, Δ). A Graeco-Latin Square design was used with data recorded as follows:

	Lacquer Concentrations			
Standing Times	1/2	1	$1\frac{1}{2}$	2
30	$C\beta(16)$	$B\Gamma(12)$	$D\Delta(17)$	$A\alpha(11)$
20	$B\alpha(15)$	$C\Delta(14)$	$A\Gamma(15)$	$D\beta(14)$
10	$A\Delta(12)$	$D\alpha(6)$	$B\beta(14)$	$C\Gamma(13)$
5	$D\Gamma(9)$	$A\beta(9)$	$C\alpha(8)$	$B\Delta(9)$

Do a complete analysis of these data.

5-5. If, in Prob. 5-2, it were found that there is not room on the strips for a cut in the fifth position, consider the data for four positions only and analyze as a Youden Square.

5-6. Explain why a three-level Graeco-Latin Square is not a feasible design.

Factorial Experiments

6.1 Introduction

In the preceding three chapters, all of the experiments involved only one factor and its effect on a measured variable. Several different designs were considered, but all of these represented restrictions of the randomization where interest was still centered in the effect of a single factor.

Suppose there are now two factors of interest to the experimenter, for example, the effect of both temperature and altitude on the current flow in a small computer. One traditional method is to hold altitude constant and vary the temperature and then hold temperature constant and change the altitude, or, in general, hold all factors constant except one and take current flow readings for several levels of this one factor, then choose another factor to vary, holding all others constant, and so forth. In order to examine this type of experimentation, consider a very simple example in which temperature is to be set at 25°F and 55°F only and altitudes of 0-K and 3-K are to be used. If one factor is to be varied at a time, the altitude may be set for sea level or 0-K and the temperature varied from 25°F to 55°F. Suppose the current flow changed from 210 ma to 240 ma with this temperature increase. Now there is no way to assess whether or not this 30-ma increase is real or due to chance. Unless there is available some previous estimate of the error variability, the experiment must be repeated in order to obtain an estimate of the error or chance variability within the experiment. If the experiment is now repeated and the resultant readings are 205 ma and 230 ma as the temperature is varied from 25°F to 55°F, it seems obvious, without any formal statistical analysis, that there is a real increase in current flow, since for each repetition the increase is large compared to the variation in current flow within a given temperature. Graphically these results appear as in Fig. 6.1.

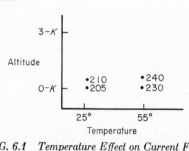

FIG. 6.1   Temperature Effect on Current Flow

Four experiments have now been run to determine the effect of temperature at 0-K altitude only. To check the effect of altitude, the temperature can be held at 25°F and the altitude varied to 3-K by adjustment of pressure in the laboratory. Using the results already obtained at 0-K (assuming they are representative), two observations of current flow are now taken at 3-K with the results shown in Fig. 6.2.

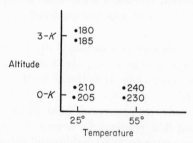

FIG. 6.2   Temperature and Altitude Effect on Current Flow

From these experiments the temperature increase is seen to increase the current flow an average of

$$\frac{30 \text{ ma} + 25 \text{ ma}}{2} = 27.5 \text{ ma}$$

and the increase in altitude decreases the current flow on the average of

$$\frac{30 \text{ ma} + 20 \text{ ma}}{2} = 25 \text{ ma}$$

This information is gained after 6 experiments have been performed and no information is available on what would happen at a temperature of 55°F and an altitude of 3-K.

An alternative experimental arrangement would be a factorial arrangement where each temperature level is combined with each altitude and only four experiments are run. Results of four such experiments might appear as in Fig. 6.3.

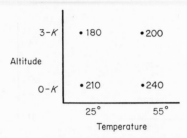

FIG. 6.3   Factorial Arrangement of Temperature and Altitude Effect on Current Flow

With this experiment, one estimate of temperature effect on current flow is 240 ma − 210 ma = 30 ma at 0-K, and another estimate is 200 − 180 ma = 20 ma at 3-K. Hence, two estimates can be made of temperature effect (average (30 + 20)/2 = 25 ma) using all four observations without necessarily repeating any observation at the same point. Using the same four observations, two estimates of altitude effect can be determined: 180 − 210 = −30 ma at 25°F, and 200 − 240 = −40 ma at 55°F, an average decrease of 35 ma for a 3-K increase in altitude. Here, with just four observations instead of six, valid comparisons have been made on both temperature and altitude and, in addition some information has been obtained as to what happens at 55°F and altitude 3-K.

From this simple example, some of the advantages of a factorial experiment can be seen:

1. More efficiency than one-factor-at-a-time experiments (here four sixths or two thirds the amount of experimentation).

2. All data are used in computing both effects. (Note that all four observations are used in determining the average effect of temperature and the average effect of altitude.)

3. Some information is gleaned on possible interaction between the two factors. (In the example, the increase in current flow of 20 ma at 3-K was of about the same order of magnitude as the 30-ma increase at 0-K. If these increases had differed considerably, interaction might be said to be present.)

These advantages are even more pronounced as the number of levels of the two factors is increased. A *factorial experiment* is one in which all levels of a given factor are combined with all levels of every other factor in the experiment. Thus, if four temperatures are considered at three altitudes, a 4×3 factorial experiment would be run requiring 12 different experimental conditions. In the example above, if the current flow were 160 ma for 55°F and 3-K, the results could be shown as in Fig. 6.4.

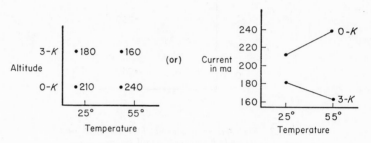

FIG. 6.4   Interaction in a Factorial Experiment

From the right-hand diagram of Fig. 6.4, note that as the temperature is increased from 25°F to 55°F at 0-K, the current flow increases by 30 ma, but at 3-K for the same temperature increase the current flow *decreased* by 20 ma. When a change in one factor produces a different change in the response variable at one level of another factor than at other levels of this factor, there is an *interaction* between the two factors. This is also observable in Fig. 6.4 (right diagram) as the two altitude lines are not parallel. If the data of Fig. 6.3 are plotted we get the relations pictured in Fig. 6.5.

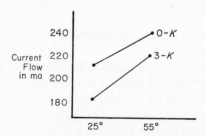

FIG. 6.5   No-Interaction Temperature Diagram in Temperature-Altitude Study

It is seen that the lines are much more nearly parallel and no interaction is said to be present. An increase in temperature at 0-K produces about that same increase in current flow (30 ma) as at 3-K

(20 ma). Now a word of warning is necessary: lines can be made to look nearly parallel or quite diverse depending on the scale chosen; therefore, it is necessary to run statistical tests in order to determine whether or not the interaction is statistically significant. It is only possible to test the significance of such interaction if more than one observation is taken for each experimental condition. The graphic procedure shown above is given merely to give some insight into what interaction is and how it might be displayed for explaining the factorial experiment. The following example will illustrate the computation of interaction.

EXAMPLE 6.1. An experiment is to be conducted to determine the effects of three different types of phosphor and two types of face-plate glass on the light output in a TV tube. Light output is the measured variable; it is measured in microamperes (μa). The value of cathode current required to give 30 ft-lamberts of light output is what is actually to be recorded. As only three phosphor types are available and two types of face-plate glass, the experiment would be a 3×2 factorial experiment. Both factors are at fixed levels, since these are the only types available, and both factors are also qualitative.

For the design of the experiment, it was agreed to take three observations under each of the six (3×2) experimental conditions, as previous data showed that results on cathode current were quite repeatable with respect to detectable differences between phosphor types and glass types. The experimenter agreed that it would be no problem to completely randomize the order for running the 18 experiments — three at each of six experimental conditions. In fact the six "cells" could be numbered 1, 2, $\cdots$ 6, and dice rolled to determine which experimental conditions would be run first, which second, etc., until all 18 were completed. To see this procedure in more detail, consider the sample layout in Table 6.1.

TABLE 6.1 — Data Layout for Phosphor, Glass-Type Experiment

Glass	Phosphor Type					
Type	*A*		*B*		*C*	
1	1	9	3	14	5	1
		12		15		6
		13		16		7
2	2	4	4	3	6	2
		8		5		10
		18		17		11

Dice are rolled and the results are as follows: 5, 6, 4, 2, 4, 5, 5, 2, 1, 6, 6, 1, 1, 3, X, X, 3, X, 3, X, 4, where a repeated value (X) is ignored after three such values have been obtained, and the last observation is not needed since it must be a two in order to have just three observations per cell. In Table 6.1 the order of experimentation dictated by the dice toss is given (condition 5 is first, condition 6 is second, and so on) by numbers, 1, 2, $\cdots$ 18. This illustrates only one possible method for complete randomization. A table of random numbers could be used, or simply, six numbers on chips could be drawn out at random (replacing each time) to decide which of the six conditions to run 1st, 2nd, 3rd, etc. This may seem like so much busywork, but it is very important to employ some objective method of randomization because lack of randomization may seriously influence the results of the experiment. If, for example, there were a change in the house voltage during the last third of the test and all of the Type C phosphor were run after this change occurred, it would be impossible to determine whether or not an increase in cathode current was due to Type C phosphor or to this change in voltage. By randomization, Table 6.1 shows that for the last third of the experiment the numbers 13, 14, 15, 16, 17, and 18 are quite well spread throughout the experiment. The above scheme shows one way to completely randomize a 3 $\times$ 2 factorial with three observations per cell, the only restriction being that three observations will be made under the same experimental conditions. It is a great advantage in the analysis if the number of observations per cell can be kept equal.

The experiment is now a 3 $\times$ 2 factorial experiment with 3 observations per cell executed as a completely randomized design. The mathematical model can be evolved from the completely randomized model of Chapter 3 as

$$X_{ij} = \mu + T_j + \epsilon_{ij} \tag{6.1}$$

In this experiment there are 3 $\times$ 2 = 6 experimental conditions, often called *treatment combinations*. Hence, there are five degrees of freedom between these six treatment combinations and 2 $\times$ 6 = 12 degrees of freedom within treatments. A one-way ANOVA layout appears in Table 6.2.

TABLE 6.2 — ANOVA Layout

Source	df	SS
Between Treatments	5	
Within Treatments	12	
TOTAL	17	

However, since the two factors are arranged in a factorial manner, or are *crossed*, as some say, 2 df may be assigned to phosphor type (columns of Table 6.1) and 1 df may be assigned to glass type (rows of Table 6.1). This leaves $5 - 2 - 1 = 2$ df between treatment combinations, or between cells not accounted for. These 2 df are associated with the interaction between phosphor and glass types. The model is then

$$X_{ijk} = \mu + P_i + G_j + PG_{ij} + \epsilon_{k(ij)} \qquad (6.2)$$

where

P_i represents the phosphor type $i = 1, 2, 3$
G_j represents the glass type $j = 1, 2$
PG_{ij} represents the interaction between P and G
$\epsilon_{k(ij)}$ represents the random error within the cell i, j where $k = 1, 2, 3$

The parentheses ( ) are used to indicate that the three observations are within each of the six cells. Sometimes these observations are said to be "nested" within the cell. This notation will be most advantageous in later chapters. An ANOVA layout now appears as in Table 6.3.

TABLE 6.3 — *Second ANOVA Layout*

Source	df	SS
Between treatments	5	
Phosphor types		2
Glass types		1
$P \times G$ interaction		2
Within treatments	12	
TOTAL	17	

From the models and the ANOVA layout, it should be noted that the two main effects (P and G) and their interaction ($P \times G$) come from a breakdown of the treatment effect and do not come from the random error. In Chapters 4 and 5, the block and position effects were taken from the random error in an attempt to reduce this error because of design limitations; in the factorial experiment the design is still completely randomized and that model fits the situation with no adjustment of the error term.

For the analysis of this experiment, data were collected according to the randomization scheme of Table 6.1. After coding each value by subtracting 260 μa and dividing each reading by 5, the coded results are as shown in Table 6.4.

TABLE 6.4 — Phosphor, Glass-Type Data (Coded)

Glass	Phosphor Type		
Type	A	B	C
1	4	8	2
	6	10	5
	5	7	6
2	−6	0	−8
	−5	−4	−7
	−4	−5	−6

To simplify the analysis, the six treatment combinations could be arranged as a single classification ANOVA as in Table 6.5.

TABLE 6.5 — Phosphor, Glass-Type Data in a One-Way Arrangement

Treatment:	$P_A G_1$	$P_A G_2$	$P_B G_1$	$P_B G_2$	$P_C G_1$	$P_C G_2$	
	4	−6	8	0	2	−8	
	6	−5	10	−4	5	−7	
	5	−4	7	−5	6	−6	
$T_{.j}$	15	−15	25	−9	13	−21	$T_{..} = 8$
$\sum_{i=1}^{3} X_{ij}^2$	77	77	213	41	65	149	$\sum_i \sum_j X_{ij}^2 = 622$

In Table 6.5, the subscripts on the P and G indicate the levels of these factors in each treatment combination. Using the methods given in Sec. 3.2, a one-way ANOVA gives the values shown in Table 6.6.

TABLE 6.6 — One-Way ANOVA on Phosphor, Glass Data

Source	df	SS
Between treatments	5	585.11
Within treatments	12	33.33
TOTALS	17	618.44

As the 5 df between treatments can be broken down into phosphor type, glass type and interaction degrees of freedom, so can the sums of squares. Returning to Table 6.4, the phosphor type totals (columns) are given by

$$T_{.j}: \quad 0 \quad 16 \quad -8 \qquad T_{..} = 8$$

and the sum of squares for this main effect is

$$SS_P = \frac{0^2 + (16)^2 + (-8)^2}{6} - \frac{(8)^2}{18}$$
$$= 53.33 - 3.56 = 49.77$$

and the glass type totals (rows) are given by

$$T_{i.} \quad 53 \quad -45 \qquad T_{..} = 8$$

and the sum of squares for this main effect is

$$SS_G = \frac{(53)^2 + (-45)^2}{9} - \frac{(8)^2}{18}$$
$$= 537.11 - 3.56 = 533.55$$

using the methods of Sec. 4.2 of a two-way ANOVA. Totalling these two sums of squares, $49.77 + 533.55 = 583.32$, leaves $585.11 - 583.32 = 1.79$ for the $P \times G$ interaction sum of squares. Summarizing this in an ANOVA table, we get Table 6.7.

TABLE 6.7 — *ANOVA for Phosphor, Glass-Type Problem:*
3 × 2 with 3 Observations Per Cell

Source	df	SS	MS
Phosphor type	2	49.77	24.88
Glass type	1	533.55	533.55
$P \times G$ interaction	2	1.79	0.89
Error or within cells	12	33.33	2.78
TOTALS	17	618.44	

In interpreting the above results, three different hypotheses may be tested:

H_1: $P_i = 0$ for all i (no phosphor-type effect)

$$F_{2,12} = \frac{24.88}{2.78} = 8.95$$

which is significant at the 1 percent level (see Appendix Table D).

H_2: $G_j = 0$ for all j (no glass-type effect)

$$F_{1,12} = \frac{533.55}{2.78} = 191.92$$

which is *highly* significant.

H_3: $PG_{ij} = 0$ for all i and j (no $P \times G$ interaction effect)

$$F_{2,12} = \frac{0.89}{2.78}$$

which is less than one and hence not significant.

Since both factors are fixed, all tests are made by using the error mean square in the denominator of the F test. (Variations of this procedure are discussed in Chapter 10.) The results of these three tests show that glass type has a very decided effect on cathode current and hence on light output, and that phosphor type also affects light output but there is no significant interaction. This latter may be interpreted to mean that as light output changes for the three phosphor types, these changes are about the same for each glass type. Graphically (using coded cell totals from Table 6.4) we get Fig. 6.6.

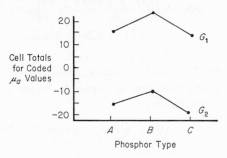

FIG. 6.6   Phosphor, Glass-Type Plot

The large gap between the two glass-type curves illustrates the sizeable glass-type effect. The trend in each curve over the three phosphor types indicates a phosphor-type effect, and the fact that the two curves are nearly parallel demonstrates the presence of little or no interaction.

Since only two glass types were used, it is obvious that the second glass type (G_2) is the better as the current flow is considerably less, which means that the light output of these tubes is higher than for glass type 1. To compare the three phosphor types, a Duncan test may be used on the coded phosphor type averages. These are

Phosphor Type:	A	B	C
$\bar{X}_{.j}$:	0	2.67	-1.33

Using the method given in Sec. 3.3, we have

	C	A	B
Means:	-1.33	0	2.67

$MS_{error} = 2.78$ (with 12 df)

Standard error of $\bar{X}_{.j} = \sqrt{\dfrac{2.78}{6}} = 0.68$

Tabled ranges are Z_p, 12 df (.05) (Appendix Table E)

$$Z_{2,12}(.05) = 3.08 \qquad R_{2,12} = (3.08)(.68) = 2.09$$

and

$$Z_{3,12}(.05) = 3.23 \qquad R_{3,12} = (3.23)(.68) = 2.20$$

Testing phosphor type differences gives

$$B - C = 2.67 - (-1.33) = 4.00 > 2.20^*$$

$$B - A = 2.67 - \quad 0 \quad = 2.67 > 2.09^*$$

$$A - C = \quad 0 \quad - (-1.33) = 1.33 < 2.09$$

so at the 5 percent level of significance B differs from both A and C, whereas there is no significant difference between A and C. It is therefore concluded that phosphor type B is inferior since it requires a significantly higher cathode current and hence lower light output than A or C.

Combining these results on the two factors (since there is no significant interaction), we find that the best combination of glass type and phosphor type to give maximum light output (minimum cathode current) would be Glass Type 2 and either Phosphor Type A or C, whichever is more economical to use.

It should be pointed out that in calculating interaction it is not necessary to rewrite Table 6.4 as in Table 6.5, but only to note that the interaction sum of squares is found by subtracting the sum of squares for each main effect from the cell sum of squares. These cells are formed by all levels of these two main effects.

It might also be noted that in the model for this problem, it is assumed that the errors ($\epsilon_{k(ij)}$'s) are NID $(0, \sigma_e^2)$. This means that the variances within each of the six cells in this problem are assumed to have come from normal populations with equal variances. Since the ranges of the coded data in the six cells are 2, 2, 3, 5, 4, and 2, this seems like a safe assumption.

6.2   ANOVA Rationale

For a two-factor factorial experiment with n observations per cell run as a completely randomized design, a general model would be

$$X_{ijk} = \mu + A_i + B_j + AB_{ij} + \epsilon_{k(ij)} \qquad (6.3)$$

where A and B represent the two factors; $i = 1, 2, \cdots a$ levels of factor

$A, j = 1, 2, \cdots b$ levels of factor B, and $k = 1, 2, \cdots n$ observations per cell. In terms of population means this becomes

$$X_{ijk} - \mu_{...} \equiv (\mu_{i..} - \mu_{...}) + (\mu_{.j.} - \mu_{...}) + (\mu_{ij.} - \mu_{i..} - \mu_{.j.} + \mu_{...}) \\ + (X_{ijk} - \mu_{ij.}) \qquad (6.4)$$

where $\mu_{ij.}$ represents the true mean of the i,j cell or treatment combination. Justification for the interaction term in the model comes from subtracting A and B main effects from the cell effect as follows

$$(\mu_{ij.} - \mu_{...}) - (\mu_{i..} - \mu_{...}) - (\mu_{.j.} - \mu_{...}) = \mu_{ij.} - \mu_{i..} - \mu_{.j.} + \mu_{...}$$

If each mean is now replaced by its sample estimate, the resulting sample model is

$$X_{ijk} - \bar{X}_{...} = (\bar{X}_{i..} - \bar{X}_{...}) + (\bar{X}_{.j.} - \bar{X}_{...}) \\ + (\bar{X}_{ij.} - \bar{X}_{i..} - \bar{X}_{.j.} + \bar{X}_{...}) + (X_{ijk} - \bar{X}_{ij.})$$

If this expression is now squared and summed over i, j, and k, all cross products vanish, and the results give

$$\sum_i^a \sum_j^b \sum_k^n (X_{ijk} - \bar{X}_{...})^2 = \sum_i^a \sum_j^b \sum_k^n (\bar{X}_{i..} - \bar{X}_{...})^2$$

$$+ \sum_i^a \sum_j^b \sum_k^n (\bar{X}_{.j.} - \bar{X}_{...})^2 + \sum_i^a \sum_j^b \sum_k^n (\bar{X}_{ij.} - \bar{X}_{i..} - \bar{X}_{.j.} + \bar{X}_{...})^2$$

$$+ \sum_i^a \sum_j^b \sum_k^n (X_{ijk} - \bar{X}_{ij.})^2$$

which again expresses the idea that the total sum of squares can be broken down into the sum of squares between means of factor A, plus the sum of squares between means of factor B, plus the sum of squares of $A \times B$ interaction, plus the error sum of squares (or within cell sum of squares). Each sum of squares is seen to be independent of the others; hence, if any such sum of squares is divided by its associated degrees of freedom the results are independently Chi-Square distributed, and F tests may be run.

The degrees-of-freedom breakdown would be

$$(abn - 1) \equiv (a - 1) + (b - 1) + (a - 1)(b - 1) + ab(n - 1)$$

the interaction one being cell df = $(ab - 1)$ minus the main effects df, $(a - 1)$ and $(b - 1)$ or $(ab - 1) - (a - 1) - (b - 1) = ab - a - b + 1 = (a - 1)(b - 1)$, and within each cell the degrees of freedom are $n - 1$ and there are ab such cells giving $ab(n - 1)$ df for error. An

ANOVA table (Table 6.8) can now be set up expanding and simplifying the sum of squares expressions using totals.

TABLE 6.8 — *General ANOVA for Two-Factor Factorial with n Replications per Cell*

Source	df	SS	MS
Factor A_i	$a - 1$	$\sum_i^a \dfrac{T_{i..}^2}{nb} - \dfrac{T_{...}^2}{nab}$	Each SS divided by its df
Factor B_j	$b - 1$	$\sum_j^b \dfrac{T_{.j.}^2}{na} - \dfrac{T_{...}^2}{nab}$	
$A \times B$ Interaction	$(a-1)(b-1)$	$\sum_i^a \sum_j^b \dfrac{T_{ij.}^2}{n} - \sum_i^a \dfrac{T_{i..}^2}{nb}$ $- \sum_j^b \dfrac{T_{.j.}^2}{na} + \dfrac{T_{...}^2}{nab}$	
Error $\epsilon_{k(ij)}$	$ab(n-1)$	$\sum_i^a \sum_j^b \sum_k^n X_{ijk}^2 - \sum_i^a \sum_j^b \dfrac{T_{ij.}^2}{n}$	
TOTALS	$abn - 1$	$\sum_i^a \sum_j^b \sum_k^n X_{ijk}^2 - \dfrac{T_{...}^2}{nab}$	

The formulae for sum of squares in Table 6.8 provide good computational formulae for a two-way ANOVA with replication. The error sum of squares might be rewritten as

$$\text{SS}_{\text{error}} = \sum_i^a \sum_j^b \left[\sum_k^n X_{ijk}^2 - \frac{T_{ij.}^2}{n} \right]$$

which points up the fact that the sum of squares within each of the $a \times b$ cells is being pooled or added for all such cells. This depends on the assumption that the variance within all cells came from populations with equal variance. The interaction sum of squares can also be rewritten as

$$\left(\sum_i^a \sum_j^b \frac{T_{ij.}^2}{n} - \frac{T_{...}^2}{nab} \right) - \left(\sum_i^a \frac{T_{i..}^2}{nb} - \frac{T_{...}^2}{nab} \right) - \left(\sum_j^b \frac{T_{.j.}^2}{na} - \frac{T_{...}^2}{nab} \right)$$

which shows again that interaction is calculated by subtracting the main effects sum of squares from the cell sum of squares.

EXAMPLE 6.2. To extend the factorial idea a bit further, consider a problem with three factors. Such a problem was presented in Chapter 1 on the effect of tool type, angle of bevel, and type of cut on power consumption for ceramic-tool-cutting. Reference to this problem will point out the phases of experiment, design and analysis as followed in Example 6.1.

It is a $2 \times 2 \times 2$ factorial experiment with 4 observations per cell run in a completely randomized manner. The mathematical model is

$$X_{ijk} = \mu + T_i + B_j + TB_{ij} + C_k + TC_{ik} + BC_{jk} + TBC_{ijk} + \epsilon_{m(ijk)}$$

where TBC_{ijk} represents a three-way interaction.

The data for this example are given in Table 1.1 and the ANOVA table in Table 1.2. That this analysis is a simple extension of the methods used on Example 6-1 will be shown with the coded data from Table 1.1 (see Table 6.9).

TABLE 6.9 — Coded Ceramic Tool Data of Table 1.2, Code: 2(X–28.0)

Type of Cut	Tool Type				
	1		2		
	Bevel Angle		Bevel Angle		
	15°	30°	15°	30°	
Continuous	2	1	0	3	
	−3	1	1	8	
	5 (42)	4 (99)	0 (37)	2 (77)	25
	−2 / 2	9 / 15	−6 / −5	0 / 13	
Interrupted	0	−2	−7	−1	
	−6	2	−6	0	
	−3 (54)	−1 (10)	0 (101)	−2 (21)	−38
	−3 / −12	−1 / −2	−4 / −17	−4 / −7	
	−10	13	−22	+6	−13

Table 6.9 shows the total for each small cell and the sum of the squares of the cell observations. These results will be useful in doing the ANOVA. By this time, we should be able to set up the steps in the analysis without recourse to formulas in dot notation, etc.

First the total sum of squares: Add the squares of all readings (the circled numbers) and subtract a correction term. The grand total = −13 squared, divided by the number of observations (32).

$$SS_{total} = 441 - \frac{(-13)^2}{32} = 435.72$$

Tool type sum of squares: add for each tool type. The totals are $+3$ and -16; square these and divide by the number of observations per type (16), add these results for both types, and subtract the correction term, thus

$$SS_{\text{tool type}} = \frac{3^2 + (-16)^2}{16} - \frac{(-13)^2}{32} = 11.28$$

Bevel angle sum of squares: same procedure on the totals for each bevel angle, -32 and 19.

$$SS_{\text{bevel angle}} = \frac{(-32)^2 + (19)^2}{16} - \frac{(-13)^2}{32} = 81.28$$

Type of cut sum of squares: same procedure, with cut totals of 25 and -38.

$$SS_{\text{type of cut}} = \frac{(25)^2 + (-38)^2}{16} - \frac{(-13)^2}{32} = 124.03$$

For the $T \times B$ interaction, ignore type of cut and use cell totals for the $T \times B$ cells. These are -10, 13, -22, $+6$.

$$SS_{T \times B \text{ interaction}} = \frac{(-10)^2 + (13)^2 + (-22)^2 + (6)^2}{8} - \frac{(-13)^2}{32}$$
$$- 11.28 - 81.28 = 0.78$$

For $T \times C$ interaction, ignore bevel angle and the cell totals become 17, -14, 8, -24.

$$SS_{T \times C \text{ interaction}} = \frac{(17)^2 + (-14)^2 + (8)^2 + (-24)^2}{8} - \frac{(-13)^2}{32}$$
$$- 11.28 - 124.03 = 0.03$$

For $B \times C$ interaction, ignore tool type and the cell totals become -3, 28, -29, -9.

$$SS_{B \times C \text{ interaction}} = \frac{(-3)^2 + (28)^2 + (-29)^2 + (-9)^2}{8} - \frac{(-13)^2}{32}$$
$$- 81.28 - 124.03 = 3.78$$

For the three-way interaction $T \times B \times C$, consider the totals of the smallest cells, 2, 15, -5, 13, -12, -2, -17 and -7; from this cell sum of squares subtract *not only* the main effects sum of squares *but also* the 3, 2-way interaction sum of squares. Thus

$SS_{T \times B \times C}$ interaction

$$= \frac{(2)^2 + (15)^2 + (-5)^2 + (13)^2 + (-12)^2 + (-2)^2 + (-17)^2 + (-7)^2}{4}$$

$$- \frac{(-13)^2}{32} - 11.28 - 81.28 - 124.03 - 0.78 - 0.03 - 3.78 = 0.79$$

By subtraction

$$SS_{\text{error}} = 213.75$$

These results are displayed in Table 6.10.

TABLE 6.10 — ANOVA Table for Ceramic-Tool Problem

Source	df	SS	MS
Tool type (T_i)	1	11.28	11.28
Bevel angle (B_j)	1	81.28	81.28
$T \times B$ interaction (TB_{ij})	1	0.78	0.78
Type of cut (C_k)	1	124.03	124.03
$T \times C$ interaction (TC_{ik})	1	0.03	0.03
$B \times C$ interaction (BC_{jk})	1	3.78	3.78
$T \times B \times C$ interaction (TBC_{ijk})	1	0.79	0.79
Error $(\epsilon_{m(ijk)})$	24	213.75	8.91
TOTALS	31	435.72	

If the results displayed in Table 6.10 are compared with those in Table 1.2, they appear to differ considerably. Actually they give the same F-test results, but, in Table 6.10, the data were coded involving multiplication by 2; the data of Table 1.2 are uncoded. Multiplication by 2 will multiply the variance or mean square by 4, so, if all mean square values in Table 6.10 are divided by 4, the results are the same as in Table 1.2. For example, on tool types $11.28/4 = 2.82$, and error $213.75/4 = 53.44$. It is worth noting that any decoding is unnecessary for determining the F ratios. However, if one wishes confidence limits on the original data or components of variance on the original data, it may be necessary to decode the results.

The interpretation of the results of this example are given in Chapter 1. The purpose of presenting it again in this chapter is to show that factorial experiments with three or more factors can easily be analyzed by simple extension of the methods of this chapter.

6.3 Remarks

Since the examples in this chapter have contained several replications within a cell, it would be well to examine a situation involving only one observation per cell. In this case, $k = 1$, and the model is written as

$$X_{ij} = \mu + A_i + B_j + AB_{ij} + \epsilon_{ij}$$

A glance at the last two terms indicates that we cannot distinguish between the interaction and the error — they are hopelessly confounded. Then, the only reasonable situation for running one observation per cell is one in which past experience generally assures us that there is no interaction. In such a case, the model is written as

$$X_{ij} = \mu + A_i + B_j + \epsilon_{ij}$$

It may also be noted that this model looks very much like the model for a randomized block design for a single factor experiment (Chapter 4). In Chapter 4 that model was written as

$$X_{ij} = \mu + T_j + B_i + \epsilon_{ij}$$

Even though the models do look alike and an analysis would be run in the same way, this latter is a single-factor experiment — treatments are the factor — and B_i represents a restriction on the randomization. In the factorial model, there are two factors of interest, A_i and B_j, and the design is completely randomized. It is, however, assumed in the randomized-block situation that there is no interaction between treatments and blocks. This is often a more reasonable assumption for blocks and treatments since blocks are often chosen at random; for a two-factor experiment an interaction between A and B may very well be present, and some external information must be available in order to assume that no such interaction exists. If the experimenter is not sure about interaction, he must take more than one observation per cell and test the hypotheses of no interaction.

As the number of factors increase, however, the presence of higher-order interactions is much more unlikely, so it is fairly safe to assume no four-way, five-way, etc., interactions. Even if these were present, they would be difficult to explain in practical terms.

6.4   Summary

Experiment	*Design*	*Analysis*

I. Single Factor

1. Completely Randomized
   $X_{ij} = \mu + T_j + \epsilon_{ij}$

   1. One-way ANOVA

2. Randomized Block
   $X_{ij} = \mu + T_j + B_i + \epsilon_{ij}$

   2.

   a. Complete   *a.* Two-way ANOVA

   b. Incomplete (Balanced)   *b.* Special ANOVA

   c. Incomplete (General)   *c.* Regression Method

3. Latin Square
   $X_{ijk} = \mu + B_i + T_j + \gamma_k + \epsilon_{ijk}$

   3.

   a. Complete   *a.* Three-way ANOVA

   b. Incomplete (Youden Square)   *b.* Special ANOVA [like 2(*b*)]

4. Graeco-Latin Square
   $X_{ijkm} = \mu + B_i + T_j + \gamma_k + W_m + \epsilon_{ijkm}$

   4. Four-way ANOVA

II. Two or more Factors
   A. Factorial (crossed)

1. Completely Randomized
   $X_{ijk} = \mu + A_i + B_j + AB_{ij} + \epsilon_{k(ij)}$ etc.
   for more factors.

   1.

   a. General case   *a.* ANOVA with Interactions

PROBLEMS

6-1.   To determine the effect of exhaust index (in seconds) and pump heater voltage (in volts) on the pressure inside a vacuum tube (in microns of mercury), three exhaust indexes and two voltages are chosen at fixed values. For each combination of exhaust index and voltage, two tests are made. The order of experimentation is completely randomized. The results are as follows:

Pump Heater Voltage	Exhaust Index (Seconds)		
	60	90	150
127	0.048	0.028	0.007
	0.058	0.033	0.015
220	0.062	0.014	0.006
	0.054	0.010	0.009

Do an analysis of variance on these data and test the effect of exhaust index, heater voltage, and interaction on the pressure.

6-2.   Plot the results of Prob. 6-1 to show that your conclusions are reasonable.

6-3.   For any significant effects in Prob. 6-1, test further between the levels of the significant factors.

6-4.   For Prob. 6-1, what combination of exhaust index and heater voltage would you recommend if a minimum pressure is desired? Explain your choice.

6-5.   Adhesive force on gummed material was determined under three fixed humidity and three fixed temperature conditions. Four readings were made under each set of conditions. The experiment was completely randomized and the results set out in an ANOVA table as follows:

Source	df	SS	MS
Humidity		9.07	
Temperature		8.66	
$H \times T$ Interaction		6.07	
Error			
TOTAL		52.30	

Complete this table.

6-6.   For the data in Prob. 6-5, test all indicated hypotheses and state your conclusions.

6-7.   Set up a mathematical model for the experiment in Prob. 6-5 and indicate the hypotheses to be tested in terms of your model.

6-8.   The object of an experiment is to determine thrust forces in drilling at different speeds, feeds, and in different materials. Five speeds are used, three feeds, and two materials with two samples tested under each set of conditions. The order of the experiment is completely randomized and the levels of all factors are fixed. The following data are recorded on thrust forces after subtracting 200 from all readings:

Materials	Feeds	Speeds 100	220	475	715	870
B_{10}	0.004	122	108	108	66	80
		110	85	60	50	60
	0.008	332	276	248	248	276
		330	310	295	275	310
	0.014	640	612	543	612	696
		500	500	450	610	610
V_{10}	0.004	192	136	122	108	136
		170	130	85	75	75
	0.008	386	333	318	472	499
		365	330	330	350	390
	0.014	810	779	810	893	1820
		725	670	750	890	890

Do a complete analysis of this experiment and state your conclusions.

6-9.   Plot any results in Prob. 6-8 which are significant.

6-10.   Set up tests on means where suitable and draw conclusions.

2ⁿ Factorial Experiments

7.1 Introduction

In the last chapter, factorial experiments were considered and a general method for their analysis was given. There are a few special cases which are of considerable interest in future designs. One of these is the case of n factors where each factor is at just two levels. These levels might be two extremes of temperature, two extremes of pressure, two time values, two machines, etc. Although this may seem like a rather trivial case since only two levels are involved, it is, nevertheless, very useful for at least two reasons: to introduce notation and concepts useful when more involved designs are discussed and to illustrate what main effects and interactions really are in this simple case. It is also true that in practice many experiments are run at just two levels of each factor. The ceramic-tool-cutting example of Chapters 1 and 6 is a $2 \times 2 \times 2$, or 2^3 factorial, with four observations per cell. Throughout this chapter, the two levels will be considered as fixed levels. This is quite reasonable because the two levels are chosen at points near the extremes, rather than at random.

7.2 2² Factorial

The simplest case to consider is one in which two factors are of interest and each factor is set at just two levels. This is a $2 \times 2 = 2^2$ factorial and the design will be considered as completely randomized.

Example 6.1 is of this type. The factors are temperature and altitude, and each is set at two levels: temperature at 25 °F and 55 °F and altitude at 0-K and 3-K. This gives four treatment combinations, displayed in Fig. 6.3, where the response variable is the current flow in milliamperes. In order to generalize a bit, consider temperature as Factor A and altitude as Factor B. The model for this completely randomized design would be

$$X_{ij} = \mu + A_i + B_j + AB_{ij} + \epsilon_{ij} \qquad (7.1)$$

where $i = 1,2$ and $j = 1,2$ in this case. Unless there is some replication, of course, no assessment of interaction can be made independent of error. From the data of Fig. 6.3, when both temperature (A) and altitude (B) are at their low levels, the response is 210 ma. This may be designated by subscripts on AB as follows: $A_0B_0 = 210$ ma. Following this notation, A_1B_0 means A at its high level and B at its low level, or temperature 55 °F and altitude 0-K. The response is $A_1B_0 = 240$ ma. Likewise $A_0B_1 = 180$ ma and $A_1B_1 = 200$ ma. Since a 2^n experiment is encountered so often in the literature, most authors have adopted another notation for these treatment combinations. For this new notation, just the subscripts on AB are used as exponents on the small letters ab. If both factors are at their low levels, $a^0b^0 = (1)$, and (1) represents the response of both factors at their low level. $a^0b^1 = b$ represents B at its high level and A at its low level, $a^1b^0 = a$ represents the high level of A and low level of B, and $a^1b^1 = ab$ represents the response when both factors are at their high levels. This notation can easily be extended to more factors, provided only two levels of each factor are involved.

For the example of Fig. 6.3, the treatment combinations can be represented by the vertices of a square as in Fig. 7.1.

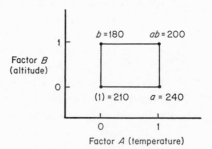

FIG. 7.1 2^2 Factorial Experiment

In Fig. 7.1, the low and high levels of Factors A and B are represented by 0 and 1, respectively, on the A and B axes. The intersection of these levels in the plane of the figure shows the four treatment combinations. For example: $00 = (1)$ represents both factors at their low levels, $10 = a$ represents A high, B low, etc., $01 = b$, $11 = ab$. These expressions are only symbolic and are to be considered as merely a mnemonic device to simplify the design and its analysis. The normal order for writing these treatment combinations is: (1), a, b, ab. Note that (1) is written first, then the high level of each factor with the low level of the other (a, b), and the fourth term is the algebraic product of the second and third (ab). When a third factor is introduced, it is placed at the end of this sequence and then multiplied by all of its predecessors. For example, if Factor C is also present at two levels, the treatment combinations are

$$(1), a, b, ab, c, ac, bc, abc$$

which can be represented as the vertices of a cube.

Returning to Fig. 7.1, we find that the *effect of a factor* is defined as the change of response produced by a change in the level of that factor. At the low level of B, the effect of A is then $240 - 210$ or $a - (1)$; whereas the effect of A at the high level of B is $200 - 180$ or $ab - b$. The average effect of A is then

$$A = \tfrac{1}{2}[a - (1) + ab - b]$$

or

$$A = \tfrac{1}{2}[-(1) + a - b + ab]$$

Note that the coefficients on this A effect are all $+1$ when A is at its high level in the treatment combinations $(+a, +ab)$ and the coefficients are all -1 when A is at its low level as in (1) and b. Note also that

$$2A = -(1) + a - b + ab$$

is a contrast as defined in Sec. 3.3 (the sum of its coefficients are $-1 + 1 - 1 + 1 = 0$). This concept will be useful, as the sum of squares due to this contrast or effect can easily be determined.

The average effect of B, based on low level of A $[180 - 210 = b - (1)]$ and high level of A $(200 - 240 = ab - a)$, is

$$B = \tfrac{1}{2}[b - (1) + ab - a]$$

or

$$B = \tfrac{1}{2}[-(1) - a + b + ab]$$

and again it is seen that the same four responses are used, but $+1$ coefficients are on the treatment combinations for the high level of B and -1 coefficients for the low level of B. Also $2B$ is a contrast.

To determine the effect of the interaction between A and B, note that, at the high level of B the A effect is $ab - b$, and at the low level of B the A effect is $a - (1)$. If these two effects differ, there is an interaction between A and B. Thus the interaction is the average *difference* between these two differences

$$AB = \tfrac{1}{2}\{(ab - b) - [a - (1)]\}$$

$$= \tfrac{1}{2}[ab - b - a + (1)]$$

or

$$= \tfrac{1}{2}[(1) - a - b + ab]$$

Here again the same four treatment combinations are used with a different combination of coefficients. Note that $2AB$ is also a contrast, and all contrasts $2A$, $2B$, $2AB$ are orthogonal to each other. Summarizing in normal order gives

$$2A = -(1) + a - b + ab$$

$$2B = -(1) - a + b + ab$$

$$2AB = +(1) - a - b + ab$$

Note that the interaction effect takes the responses on one diagonal of the square with $+1$ coefficients and the responses on the other diagonal with -1 coefficients. Note also that the coefficients for the interaction effect can be found by multiplying the corresponding coefficients of the two main effects. As the only coefficients used are $+1$'s and -1's, the proper coefficients on the treatment combinations for each main effect and interaction can be determined from Table 7.1.

TABLE 7.1 — *Coefficients for Effects in a 2^2 Factorial Experiment*

Treatment Combination	Effects		
	A	B	AB
(1)	−	−	+
a	+	−	−
b	−	+	−
ab	+	+	+

From Table 7.1 the orthogonality of the effects is easily seen, as well as the generation of the interaction coefficients from the main effect coefficients.

Another approach to the interaction between A and B would be to consider that at the high level of A the effect of B is $ab - a$, and at the low level of A the effect of B is $b - (1)$, so that the average difference is

$$AB = \tfrac{1}{2}[(ab - a) - (b - (1))]$$
$$= \tfrac{1}{2}[ab - a - b + (1)]$$
$$= \tfrac{1}{2}[+(1) - a - b + ab]$$

which is the same expression as given before.

For the response data of Fig. 7.1, the effects are

$$A = \tfrac{1}{2}(-210 + 240 - 180 + 200) = 25 \text{ ma}$$
$$B = \tfrac{1}{2}(-210 - 240 + 180 + 200) = -35 \text{ ma}$$
$$AB = \tfrac{1}{2}(+210 - 240 - 180 + 200) = -5 \text{ ma}$$

Since $2A$, $2B$ and $2AB$ are contrasts, the sum of squares due to a contrast is

$$SS_{C_m} = \frac{(\text{contrast})^2}{n \sum c_{im}^2}$$

where n is the number of observations in each total (here $n = 1$). Also $\sum c_{im}^2 = 1 + 1 + 1 + 1 = 4$ (or 2^2). From this definition

$$SS_A = \frac{[2(25)]^2}{4} = 625$$

$$SS_B = \frac{[2(-35)]^2}{4} = 1225$$

$$SS_{AB} = \frac{[2(-5)]^2}{4} = 25$$

$$SS_{\text{total}} = 1875$$

Since each effect and the interaction has but 1 df and there is no measure of error as only one observation was taken in each cell, this ANOVA is quite trivial, but it does show another approach to analysis based on effects. The simple ANOVA table would be that shown by Table 7.2.

TABLE 7.2 — ANOVA for a 2² Factorial with No Replication

Source	df	SS	MS
A_i	1	625	625
B_j	1	1225	1225
(Error or AB_{ij})	1	25	25
TOTALS	3	1875	

If the general methods of Chapter 6 are used on the data in Fig. 7.1 (coded by subtracting 200), the results are those in Table 7.3.

TABLE 7.3 — *Coded Data of Fig. 7.1*

Factor B	Factor A		
	0	1	
0	$+10$	$+40$	$+50$
1	-20	0	-20
	-10	$+40$	$+30$

$$SS_{total} = (10)^2 + (-20)^2 + (40)^2 + (0)^2 - \frac{(30)^2}{4} = 1875$$

$$SS_A = \frac{(-10)^2 + (40)^2}{2} - \frac{(30)^2}{4} = 850 - 225 = 625$$

$$SS_B = \frac{(50)^2 + (-20)^2}{2} - \frac{(30)^2}{4} = 1450 - 225 = 1225$$

$$SS_{AB} \text{ (by subtraction)} = 1875 - 625 - 1225 = 25$$

which are the same Sums of Squares as given in Table 7.2. Even though no separate measure of error is available, a glance at the Mean Squares of Table 7.2 shows that both main effects are large compared to the interaction effect.

The results of this section can easily be extended to cases where there are r replications in the cells, by using cell totals for the responses at (1), a, b and ab and adjusting the sum of squares for the effects accordingly (see Example 7.1).

EXAMPLE 7.1. An example of a 2^2 factorial experiment with two replications per cell is considered here, using hypothetical responses to illustrate the principles of the previous section. Consider the data of Table 7.4.

TABLE 7.4 — *2^2 Factorial with Two Replications*

Factor B	Factor A		
	0	1	
0	4 6/10	2 $-2/0$	$+10$
1	3 7/10	-4 $-6/-10$	0
	$+20$	-10	$+10$

Using the general methods of Chapter 6, the sums of squares are

$$SS_{total} = 4^2 + 6^2 + 3^2 + 7^2 + 2^2 + (-2)^2 + (-4)^2 + (-6)^2$$

$$- \frac{(10)^2}{8} = 170 - 12.5 = 157.5$$

$$SS_A = \frac{(20)^2 + (-10)^2}{4} - 12.5 = 112.5$$

$$SS_B = \frac{(10)^2 + (0)^2}{4} - 12.5 = 12.5$$

$$SS_{A \times B \text{ interaction}} = \frac{(10)^2 + (10)^2 + (0)^2 + (-10)^2}{2} - 12.5 - 112.5$$

$$- 12.5 = 12.5$$

$$SS_{error} = 157.5 - 112.5 - 12.5 - 12.5 = 20.0$$

These results could be displayed in an ANOVA table. Using the methods of Sec. 7.2, we get, with the treatment combinations, the total response

$$(1) = 10 \qquad a = 0 \qquad b = 10 \qquad ab = -10$$

and the contrasts

$$4A = -10 + 0 - 10 + (-10) = -30$$

$$4B = -10 - 0 + 10 + (-10) = -10$$

$$4AB = +10 - 0 - 10 + (-10) = -10$$

The coefficient 4 used with each response represents the two individual responses at each level. In general the coefficient of these effects is $r \cdot 2^n$, where r is the number of replications and n the number of factors. Here $r = 2$ and $n = 2$. The sum of squares for these three contrasts are

$$SS_A = \frac{(4A)^2}{r \cdot 2^2} = \frac{(-30)^2}{2 \cdot 4} = \frac{900}{8} = 112.5$$

$$SS_B = \frac{(4B)^2}{r \cdot 2^2} = \frac{(-10)^2}{2 \cdot 4} = \frac{100}{8} = 12.5$$

$$SS_{AB} = \frac{(4AB)^2}{r \cdot 2^2} = \frac{(-10)^2}{2 \cdot 4} = \frac{100}{8} = 12.5$$

since

$$2^2 = \sum_{i=1}^{4} c_{im}^2 = 1 + 1 + 1 + 1 = 4$$

These results are the same as given by the general method. The total sum of squares must be calculated as usual in order to get the error sum of squares by subtraction.

For this special case of a 2^n factorial experiment, Yates [15] developed a rather simple scheme for computing these contrasts. The method can best be illustrated on Example 1.1, using Table 7.5.

TABLE 7.5 — Yates Method on a 2^2 Factorial

Treatment Combination	Response-X	(1)	(2)	SS
(1)	10	10	$10 = $ total	12.5
a	0	0	$-30 = 4A$	112.5
b	10	-10	$-10 = 4B$	12.5
ab	-10	-20	$-10 = 4AB$	12.5

In Table 7.5, list all treatment combinations in the first column. Place the total response to each of these treatment combinations in the second column. For the third column, labeled (1), add the responses in pairs; e.g., $10 + 0 = 10$ for the first two and $10 - 10 = 0$ for the next two; this completes half of column (1). For the second half, subtract the responses in pairs, always subtracting the first from the second; e.g., $0 - 10 = -10$; $-10 - (10) = -20$. This completes column (1). Column (2) is determined in the same manner as column (1) using the column (1) results: $10 + 0 = 10$; $-10 - 20 = -30$; $0 - 10 = -10$; $-20 - (-10) = -10$. Proceed in this same manner until the nth column is reached: (1), (2), (3), $\cdots$ (n). In this case $n = 2$, so there are just two columns, (1) and (2). The values in column n are the contrasts, where the first entry is $r \cdot 2^{n-1}$ times the grand total of all readings; the one corresponding to a is $r \cdot 2^{n-1} \cdot A$, b is $r \cdot 2^{n-1} \cdot B$, and ab is $r \cdot 2^{n-1} \cdot AB$. When the results of the last column (column n) are squared and divided by $r \cdot 2^n$, the results are the sums of squares as shown above. The first sum of squares $(\text{total})^2/8$ is the correction term for the grand mean given in Chapter 6. The Yates method reduces the analysis to simply adding and subtracting numbers. It is very useful provided the experiment is a 2^n factorial with r replications per cell.

As proof for the Yates method on a 2^2 factorial, go through the steps above using the treatment combination symbols for the responses as in Table 7.6.

TABLE 7.6 — Yates Method on a 2² in General;
One Observation per Cell

Treatment Combination	(1)	(2)
(1)	$(1) + a$	$(1) + a + b + ab$ = total
a	$b + ab$	$-(1) + a - b + ab$ = $2A$
b	$a - (1)$	$-(1) - a + b + ab$ = $2B$
ab	$ab - b$	$(1) - a - b + ab$ = $2AB$

It is obvious that the last column does give the proper treatment contrasts.

7.3 2³ Factorial

Considering a third factor C, also at two levels, the experiment will be a $2 \times 2 \times 2$ or 2^3 factorial, again run in a completely randomized manner. The treatment combinations are now (1), a, b, ab, c, ac, bc, abc, and they may be represented as vertices of a cube as in Fig. 7.2.

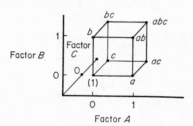

FIG. 7.2   *2³ Factorial Arrangements*

With these $8 = 2^3$ observations, or $8r$ if there are replications, the main effects and each interaction may be expressed by using the proper coefficients (-1 or $+1$) on these eight responses. For the effect of Factor A, consider all responses in the right-hand plane (a, ab, ac, abc) with plus signs and all in the left-hand plane [(1), b, bc, c] with minus signs as these will show the effect of increasing the level of A. Or

$$4A = -(1) + a - b + ab - c + ac - bc + abc$$

For Factor B, consider responses in the lower and higher planes of the cube

$$4B = -(1) - a + b + ab - c - ac + bc + abc$$

The AB interaction is determined by the difference in the A effect from level 0 of B to level 1 of B, regardless of C

$$\text{At } B_0: 2A \text{ effect } a + ac - c - (1)$$

$$B_1: 2A \text{ effect } abc + ab - b - bc$$

The difference in these is the interaction

$$4AB = [abc + ab - b - bc] - [a + ac - c - (1)]$$

$$4AB = abc + ab - b - bc - a - ac + c + (1)$$

or

$$4AB = +(1) - a - b + ab + c - ac - bc + abc$$

which gives the same signs as the products of corresponding signs on $4A$ and $4B$.

For Factor C, compare the responses in the back plane of the cube to those in the front plane of the cube

$$4C = c + bc + ac + abc - (1) - b - a - ab$$

or

$$4C = -(1) - a - b - ab + c + ac + bc + abc$$

The AC and BC interactions can be determined as AB was, and it can be seen that the resulting interaction effects are

$$4AC = +(1) - a + b - ab - c + ac - bc + abc$$

$$4BC = +(1) + a - b - ab - c - ac + bc + abc$$

To determine the ABC interaction, consider the BC interaction at level 0 of A versus the BC interaction at level 1 of A. Any difference in these is an ABC interaction.

$$2BC \text{ interaction at } A_0: +(1) - b - c + bc$$
$$2BC \text{ interaction at } A_1: +a - ab - ac + abc$$

Their difference is

$$4ABC = (a - ab - ac + abc) - [(1) - b - c + bc)]$$

or

$$4ABC = -(1) + a + b - ab + c - ac - bc + abc$$

which can also be obtained from multiplying the coefficients of A and BC, or B and AC, or C and AB. These others can also be used to get the ABC interaction, but the results are the same. Summarizing gives us Table 7.7.

TABLE 7.7 — Coefficients for Effects in a 2^3 Factorial Experiment

Treatment	Effect							
Combination	Total	A	B	AB	C	AC	BC	ABC
(1)	+	−	−	+	−	+	+	−
a	+	+	−	−	−	−	+	+
b	+	−	+	−	−	+	−	+
ab	+	+	+	+	−	−	−	−
c	+	−	−	+	+	−	−	+
ac	+	+	−	−	+	+	−	−
bc	+	−	+	−	+	−	+	−
abc	+	+	+	+	+	+	+	+

Table 7.7 illustrates once again the orthogonality of the effects and can easily be extended to 4, 5, and more factors if each factor is at two levels only. In a 2^3 factorial experiment, the sum of squares is given by

$$SS_{effect} = \frac{(contrast)^2}{r \cdot 2^3} = \frac{(contrast)^2}{8r}$$

and again the Yates method leads to an easy computation of the contrasts.

EXAMPLE 7.2. In Chapters 1 and 6, the problem on power requirements for cutting with ceramic tools was analyzed in detail. It

TABLE 7.8 — Ceramic Tool Data in 2^3 Form

	Tool Type			
	1		2	
Type of cut	Bevel 15°	Angle 30°	Bevel 15°	Angle 30°
Continuous	(1) 2	b 15	a −5	ab 13
Interrupted	c −12	bc −2	ac −17	abc −7

Tool Type = Factor A Bevel = Factor B Cut = Factor C

is readily seen that this is a $2 \times 2 \times 2 = 2^3$ factorial with four replications per cell. This problem could be analyzed by the special methods of this chapter. From Table 6.9 on coded data the treatment combinations might be summarized as in Table 7.8.

In Table 7.8, the totals of the four replications for each treatment combination have been entered in their corresponding cells. By the Yates method we get the entries in Table 7.9.

TABLE 7.9 — Yates Method on Ceramic Tool Data

Treatment Combination	Response	(1)	(2)	(3)	SS
(1)	2	−3	25	−13 = total	5.28
a	−5	28	−38	−19 = 16A	11.28
b	15	−29	−9	51 = 16B	81.28
ab	13	−9	−10	5 = 16AB	0.78
c	−12	−7	31	−63 = 16C	124.03
ac	−17	−2	20	−1 = 16AC	0.03
bc	−2	−5	5	−11 = 16BC	3.78
abc	−7	−5	0	−5 = 16ABC	0.78

These sums of squares are seen to be in substantial agreement with those of Table 6.10. We must resort to the individual readings, however, to determine the total sum of squares and then the error sum of squares. This was done in Table 6.10, and the interpretation of this problem is given in Chapter 6. The purpose of repeating the problem here was merely to show the use of the Yates method on a 2^3 factorial experiment.

7.4 2^n — Remarks

The methods shown for 2^2 and 2^3 factorials above may easily be extended to 2^n factorials where n factors are each considered at two levels. The contrasts are determined from the responses to the treatment combinations by associating plus signs with high levels of a factor and minus signs with low levels; the contrasts for interactions are found by multiplication of corresponding coefficients.

The general relationships for 2^n factorials with r replications per cell are

$$\text{Contrast} = r \cdot 2^{n-1} \text{ (effect)}$$

or

$$\text{Effect} = \frac{1}{r \cdot 2^{n-1}} \text{ [contrast]}$$

and

$$\text{SS}_{\text{contrast}} = \frac{(\text{contrast})^2}{r \cdot 2^n}$$

A general ANOVA would be as in Table 7.10, but not in "normal" order.

TABLE 7.10 — ANOVA for a 2^n Factorial with r Replications

Source		df	
main effects:	A	1	
	B	1	
	C	1	n
	.	.	
	.	.	
	.	.	
2-factor interactions:	AB	1	
	AC	1	
	BC	1	$C(n,2) = \dfrac{n(n-1)}{2}$
	.	.	
	.	.	
	.	.	
3-factor interactions:	ABC	1	
	ABD	1	
	BCD	1	$C(n,3) = \dfrac{n(n-1)(n-2)}{6}$
	.	.	
	.	.	
	.	.	
4-factor, etc.			
Sum of all treatment combinations		$2^n - 1$	
Residual or error		$2^n(r-1)$	
Total		$r \cdot 2^n - 1$	

7.5 Summary

Experiment	*Design*	*Analysis*

I. Single Factor

	1. Completely Randomized $X_{ij} = \mu + T_j + \epsilon_{ij}$	1. One-way ANOVA
	2. Randomized Block $X_{ij} = \mu + B_i + T_j + \epsilon_{ij}$	2.
	a. Complete	a. Two-way ANOVA
	b. Incomplete-Balanced	b. Special ANOVA
	c. Incomplete-General	c. Regression Method
	3. Latin Square $X_{ijk} = \mu + B_i + T_j + \gamma_k + \epsilon_{ijk}$	3.
	a. Complete	a. Three-way ANOVA
	b. Incomplete-Youden Square	b. Special ANOVA [like 2(b)]
	4. Graeco-Latin Square $X_{ijkm} = \mu + B_i + T_j + \gamma_k + W_m + \epsilon_{ijkm}$	4. Four-way ANOVA

II. Two or more Factors
A. Factorial (crossed)

	1. Completely Randomized $X_{ijk} = \mu + A_i + B_j + AB_{ij} + \epsilon_{k(ij)}$ etc. for more factors	1.
	a. General	a. ANOVA with interactions
	b. 2^n Case	b. Yates method, or general *ANOVA*. Use: (1), a, b, ab, etc.

PROBLEMS

7-1.   For the 2^2 factorial with three observations per cell given below (hypothetical data), do an analysis by the method of Chapter 6.

| | Factor A | |
Factor B	A_1	A_2
	0	4
B_1	2	6
	1	2
	-1	-1
B_2	-3	-3
	1	-7

7-2.   Redo Prob. 7-1 by the Yates method and compare results.

7-3.   In an experiment on chemical yield, three factors were studied, each at two levels. The experiment was completely randomized and the factors were known only as A, B, and C. The results were

| A_1 | | | | A_2 | | | |
| B_1 | | B_2 | | B_1 | | B_2 | |
C_1	C_2	C_1	C_2	C_1	C_2	C_1	C_2
1595	1745	1835	1838	1573	2184	1700	1717
1578	1689	1823	1614	1592	1538	1815	1806

Analyze by the methods of Chapter 6.

7-4.   Analyze Prob. 7-3 by the Yates method and compare your results.

7-5.   Plot any results from Prob. 7-3 which might be meaningful from a management point of view.

7-6.   The results of Prob. 7-3 lead to another experiment with four factors each at two levels, with the following data:

A_1							
B_1				B_2			
C_1		C_2		C_1		C_2	
D_1	D_2	D_1	D_2	D_1	D_2	D_1	D_2
1985	2156	1694	2184	1765	1923	1806	1957
1592	2032	1712	1921	1700	2007	1758	1717

A_2							
B_1				B_2			
C_1		C_2		C_1		C_2	
D_1	D_2	D_1	D_2	D_1	D_2	D_1	D_2
1595	1578	2243	1745	1835	1863	1614	1917
2067	1733	1745	1818	1823	1910	1838	1922

Analyze these data by the general methods of Chapter 6.

7-7.   Analyze Prob. 7-6 using the Yates method.

7-8.   Plot from Prob. 7-6 any results you think are meaningful.

Qualitative and Quantitative Factors

8.1 Introduction

In many of the examples used in previous chapters, the levels of the factors considered were qualitative levels. That is, no numerical scale could be attached to the levels such as machines, glass types, or operators. The order of the levels was unimportant and a Duncan procedure was used after an analysis in an attempt to rank the levels of these qualitative factors based on the average response each level produced. Often in experimental work, factor levels are quantitative; i.e., they are set at measured values such as temperatures of 20 °F, 40 °F, or 80 °F, altitudes 0-K, 1-K, 2-K, or 3-K, speeds 1200 rpm, 1400 rpm, or 1600 rpm. In the case where the levels of factors are quantitative, it is often possible to extract more information on how the response variable might vary with the changing levels of the quantitative factor. That is, how does chemical yield vary with temperature? Is there, perhaps, a linear relationship between yield and temperature? How does the power requirement vary with the feed rate of the material? Is there a second degree or quadratic relationship here? In this chapter, quantitative levels of factors will be discussed as well as situations in which one factor is qualitative and the other quantitative or both are quantitative.

To see how to extract linear and quadratic effects, consider a quantitative factor with three levels, and assume that these three levels are equispaced from one another. For example: temperatures at 20 °F, 40 °F, 60 °F, or altitudes of 0-K, 1-K, and 2-K. By equispacing quantitative levels, the analysis can be simplified considerably. If $T_{.1}$, $T_{.2}$, and $T_{.3}$ represent response totals in an experiment where the factor being considered is set at 3 equispaced levels, we might find the results in Fig. 8.1.

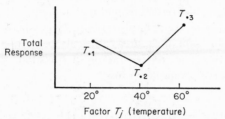

Factor T_j (temperature)

FIG. 8.1   Diagram for Quantitative Levels

If temperature produces a linear response, the linear effect from 20 °F to 40 °F is $T_{.2} - T_{.1}$ and the linear effect from 40 °F to 60 °F is $T_{.3} - T_{.2}$. The total linear effect is then

$$(T_{.2} - T_{.1}) + (T_{.3} - T_{.2})$$
$$C_L = -T_{.1} + T_{.3}$$

which is a contrast.

If temperature produces a quadratic effect on the response, the slope from 20 °F to 40 °F will be different from the slope between 40 °F and 60 °F. This difference in slopes is

$$(T_{.3} - T_{.2}) - (T_{.2} - T_{.1})$$
$$C_Q = T_{.3} - 2T_{.2} + T_{.1}$$

which is also a contrast.

Note that the linear contrast C_L is orthogonal to the quadratic contrast C_Q, so we can determine the sum of squares that is due to both the linear and quadratic contrasts.

If there were four levels of temperature, we could extract a linear, quadratic and cubic effect by proper choice of coefficients for the response totals. In order to expedite the solution of such problems, tables of *orthogonal polynomials* are available which give the proper coefficients, depending on the number of levels of the factor. Such tables appear in Fisher and Yates [8], and a section of this table is reproduced as Appendix Table F. From this Table F, it is seen that the proper coefficients for four levels of a quantitative factor are

Linear:	-3	-1	$+1$	$+3$
Quadratic:	$+1$	-1	-1	$+1$
Cubic:	-1	$+3$	-3	$+1$

The table also gives two quantities, F and K. F is simply the sum of the squares of the coefficients as used with any contrasts, and K is a scale factor useful if we wish to determine the equation of the curve after it is seen to be significant.

The use of tables of orthogonal polynomials is the same as for any contrast. By applying these coefficients to the response totals, a linear, quadratic, or cubic sum of squares can easily be extracted from the sum of squares for the quantitative factor in question. The procedure is illustrated in several examples below.

8.2   Single Factor — Quantitative Levels

An experiment is designed to determine the effect on a TV bulb rating of standing time in minutes after filming. The rating is measured to a base of 100 for a normal bulb, so 100 has been subtracted from all ratings in the data as a simple coding procedure. The standing times were set at 0, 10, 20, and 30 minutes, with eight tubes sampled for each time level. The experiment was completely randomized, with the results shown in Table 8.1.

TABLE 8.1 — Bulb-Rating Data

	Standing Time (Minutes)			
	0	10	20	30
	−7	−5	+5	+5
	−3	−3	+5	−1
	−5	−5	+5	+5
	−5	−1	+5	+5
	−5	−7	+5	+5
	−5	−5	−3	+5
	−3	+5	+5	+5
	+5	−1	+1	+5
$T_{.j}$	−28	−22	28	34
$\sum_{i=1}^{8} X_{ij}^2$	192	160	160	176

$T_{..} = 12$

$$\sum_{j=1}^{4} \sum_{i=1}^{8} X_{ij}^2 = 688$$

As this is a single-factor experiment run as a completely randomized design, the model would be

$$X_{ij} = \mu + T_j + \epsilon_{ij}$$

$$i = 1, 2, \cdots 8$$

$$j = 1, 2, 3, 4$$

Using the analysis technique of Chapter 3 gives

$$SS_{total} = 688 - \frac{(12)^2}{32} = 683.5$$

$$SS_{time} = \frac{(-28)^2 + (-22)^2 + (28)^2 + (34)^2}{8} - \frac{(12)^2}{32} = 396.5$$

$$SS_{error} = 683.5 - 396.5 = 287.0$$

An ANOVA table is shown in Table 8.2.

TABLE 8.2 — Bulb-Rating Analysis

Source	df	SS	MS	EMS
Between times	3	396.5	132.2	$\sigma_e^2 + 8\sigma_t^2$
Error	28	287.0	10.2	σ_e^2
TOTALS	31	683.5		

The F ratio is

$$F_{3,28} = \frac{132.2}{10.2} = 12.96$$

which is significant at the 1 percent level. This indicates that the standing time does affect the tube rating, and since the standing time is quantitative and the levels are equispaced, it may be worthwhile to try and find out *how* tube rating varies with standing time. Since there are four levels of standing time, we might extract a linear, quadratic and cubic effect and test each for significance. Appendix Table F gives the following coefficients of Table 8.3 to be applied to the response totals.

TABLE 8.3 — Orthogonal Polynomial Coefficients for Tube-Rating Problem

	$T_{.1} = -28$	$T_{.2} = -22$	$T_{.3} = 28$	$T_{.4} = 34$	F
Linear	-3	-1	$+1$	$+3$	20
Quadratic	$+1$	-1	-1	$+1$	4
Cubic	-1	$+3$	-3	$+1$	20

Applying these coefficients to the totals gives, for time effects

$$T_{linear} = T_L = -3(-28) - 1(-22) + 1(28) + 3(34) = 236$$

$$T_{quadratic} = T_Q = +1(-28) - 1(-22) - 1(28) + 1(34) = 0$$

$$T_{cubic} = T_C = -1(-28) + 3(-22) - 3(28) + 1(34) = -88$$

The corresponding sums of squares are

$$SS_{TL} = \frac{(236)^2}{8(20)} = 348.1$$

$$SS_{TQ} = \frac{(0)^2}{8(4)} = 0.0$$

$$SS_{TC} = \frac{(-88)^2}{8(20)} = 48.4$$

$$SS_{total} = 396.5$$

which agrees with the SS_{times} in Table 8.2.

This additional information may be summarized in the ANOVA table of Table 8.4.

TABLE 8.4 — ANOVA on Tube-Rating Problem for Quantitative Effects

Source	df	SS	MS
Between times	3	396.5	
T_L	1	348.1	348.1
T_Q	1	0.0	0.0
T_C	1	48.4	48.4
Error (within times)	28	287.0	10.2
TOTALS	31	683.5	

F tests can now be set up with 1 and 28 df to test for significant linear, quadratic and cubic trends.
For linear

$$F_{1,28} = \frac{348.1}{10.2} = 34.1$$

which is highly significant.
For quadratic

$$F_{1,28} = \frac{0}{10.2} = 0$$

which is not significant.
For cubic

$$F_{1,28} = \frac{48.4}{10.2} = 4.75$$

which is also significant at the 1 percent level.

From this analysis, a definite linear trend of tube rating with standing time is observed and also a tendency toward a cubic relationship. A graph of the observed responses along with their means (Fig. 8.2) bears out this result.

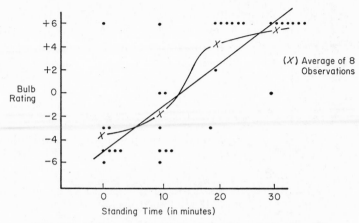

FIG. 8.2   *Bulb Rating Graphed as a Function of Standing Time*

From Fig. 8.2, we see that the linear increase in rating with standing time can be easily observed. A word of caution may be in order about the cubic effect, since a cubic equation can be passed through any four points. In order to verify this cubic trend, we should probably take more standing times (say, at 5, 15, and 25 minutes) and recheck this trend. These data show how we can test for linear, quadratic and cubic trends by the use of orthogonal polynomials.

8.3   Two Factors — One Qualitative, One Quantitative

The case of two-factor, factorial experiments where both factors are qualitative has been discussed in Chapter 6. A problem will now be considered where one factor is set at qualitative levels and the other at quantitative (and equispaced) levels.

We wish to determine the effect of both depth and position in a tank (Fig. 8.3) on the concentration of a cleaning solution in ounces per gallon. Concentrations are measured at three depths from the surface of the tank, 0 in., 15 in., and 30 in. At each depth measurements are taken at five different lateral positions in the tank. These are considered as

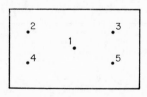

FIG. 8.3

five qualitative positions, although probably some orientation measure might be made on them. At each depth and position, two observations are taken. This is then a 5×3 factorial with two replications per cell (total of 30 observations). The design is a completely randomized design and the model is

$$X_{ijk} = \mu + D_i + P_j + DP_{ij} + \epsilon_{k(ij)}$$

$$i = 1, 2, 3 \qquad j = 1, 2, \cdots 5 \qquad k = 1, 2$$

where D_i represents the depth and P_j the position. The data collected are shown in Table 8.5.

TABLE 8.5 — Cleaning Solution Concentration Data

	Depth from Top of Tank (D_i)		
Position (P_j)	0 in.	15 in.	30 in.
1	5.90	5.90	5.94
	5.91	5.89	5.80
2	5.90	5.89	5.75
	5.91	5.89	5.83
3	5.94	5.91	5.86
	5.90	5.91	5.83
4	5.93	5.94	5.83
	5.91	5.90	5.89
5	5.90	5.94	5.83
	5.87	5.90	5.86

In this case where one factor is set at quantitative levels (D_i) and the other at qualitative levels (P_j), the first step is to run a two-factor analysis of variance just as if both were qualitative factors. Coding the data of Table 8.5 by subtracting 5.90 and multiplying by 100 gives Table 8.6.

From these coded data

$$SS_{total} = 643 - \frac{(-44)^2}{30} = 578.47$$

$$SS_D = \frac{(7)^2 + (7)^2 + (-58)^2}{10} - \frac{(-44)^2}{30} = 281.67$$

$$SS_P = \frac{(-6)^2 + (-23)^2 + (-3)^2 + (0)^2 + (-10)^2}{6}$$
$$- \frac{(-44)^2}{30} = 50.47$$

TABLE 8.6 — Coded Cleaning Solution Concentration Data with Totals

Position (P_j)	Depth from Top of Tank (D_i) 0 in.	15 in.	30 in.	$T_{.j.}$
1	0 1/1	0 $-1/-1$	4 $-10/-6$	-6
2	0 1/1	-1 $-1/-2$	-15 $-7/-22$	-23
3	4 0/4	1 1/2	-4 $-7/-11$	-5
4	3 1/4	4 0/4	-7 $-1/-8$	0
5	0 $-3/-3$	4 0/4	-7 $-4/-11$	-10
$T_{i..}$	7	7	-58	$T_{...} = -44$
$\sum_{k=1}^{2}\sum_{j=1}^{5} X_{ijk}^{2}$	37	37	570	$\sum_{i}^{3}\sum_{j}^{5}\sum_{k}^{2} X_{ijk}^{2} = 644$

$$SS_{D \times P \text{ interaction}} = \frac{(1)^2 + (1)^2 + (4)^2 + \ldots + (-11)^2}{2} - \frac{(-44)^2}{30}$$

$$- 281.67 - 50.47 = 58.33$$

$$SS_{\text{error}} = 579.47 - 281.67 - 50.47 - 58.33 = 189.00$$

giving the ANOVA table in Table 8.7.

TABLE 8.7 — ANOVA Table for Cleaning Solution Problem

Source	df	SS	MS	EMS
Depths: D_i	2	281.67	140.83	$\sigma_e^2 + 10\sigma_D^2$
Positions: P_j	4	50.47	12.62	$\sigma_e^2 + 6\sigma_P^2$
$D \times P$ interaction: DP_{ij}	8	58.33	7.29	$\sigma_e^2 + 2\sigma_{DP}^2$
Error: $\epsilon_{k(ij)}$	15	189.00	12.60	σ_e^2
TOTALS	29	579.47		

From Table 8.7, it is seen that only depth produced a significant effect on concentration of solution as

$$F_{2,15} = \frac{140.83}{12.60} = 11.24$$

which is significant as the 1 percent level of significance. Since the depth effect is significant and since the three depths are equispaced, it may be worthwhile to extract a linear and quadratic depth effect to learn how concentration varies with depth. The coefficients for $k = 3$ levels are shown in Table 8.8.

TABLE 8.8 — *Orthogonal Coefficients*

Linear:	-1	0	$+1$	$F{:}2$
Quadratic:	$+1$	-2	$+1$	$F{:}6$
$T_{i..}$:	7	7	-58	

Applying these coefficients to the depth totals ($T_{i..}$'s) gives

Linear effect of depth $= -1(7) + 0(7) + 1(-58) = -65$

Quadratic effect of depth $= +1(7) - 2(7) + 1(-58) = -65$

Since these are orthogonal contrasts, their sums of squares are

$$\text{SS}_L = \frac{(-65)^2}{10(2)} = 211.25$$

$$\text{SS}_Q = \frac{(-65)^2}{10(6)} = \frac{70.42}{281.67}$$

and their total is the depth sum of squares.

Even though the $D \times P$ interaction is not significant, there may be an interaction between the linear effect of depth and positions or between the quadratic effect of depth and positions. To compute these interactions, the linear effect of depth is determined at each position and these effects are then compared to see whether or not they differ. The same procedure is followed for the quadratic effect of depth at each position.

Applying the linear coefficients of

$$-1 \quad 0 \quad +1$$

at each position gives

$$P_1{:} \ -1(1) + 0(-1) + 1(-6) \ = \ -7$$

$$P_2{:} \ -1(1) + 0(-2) + 1(-22) = \ -23$$

$$P_3{:} \ -1(4) + 0(2) + 1(-11) \ = \ -15$$

$$P_4{:} \ -1(4) + 0(4) + 1(-8) \ = \ -12$$

$$P_5{:} \ -1(-3) + 0(4) + 1(-11) = \ \frac{-8}{-65}$$

To compare these five effects, determine the sum of squares between them

$$\frac{(-7)^2 + (-23)^2 + (-15)^2 + (-12)^2 + (-8)^2}{2(2)} - \frac{(-65)^2}{10(2)} = 41.50$$

Similarly, for the quadratic effect of depth at the five positions, we have

$$P_1: +1(1) - 2(-1) + 1(-6) \quad = \quad -3$$

$$P_2: +1(1) - 2(-2) + 1(-22) = \quad -17$$

$$P_3: +1(4) - 2(2) + 1(-11) \quad = \quad -11$$

$$P_4: +1(4) - 2(4) + 1(-8) \quad = \quad -12$$

$$P_5: +1(-3) - 2(4) + 1(-11) = \quad \underline{-22}$$

$$-65$$

Comparing these five quadratic effects gives

$$\frac{(-3)^2 + (-17)^2 + (-11)^2 + (-12)^2 + (-22)^2}{2(6)} - \frac{(-65)^2}{10(6)} = 16.83$$

Note that the sum of these two sums of squares $(41.50 + 16.83)$ equals the $D \times P$ interaction sum of squares (58.33) as it should. Summarizing for this problem with one quantitative and one qualitative factor, the complete ANOVA breakdown is as shown in Table 8.9.

TABLE 8.9 — Complete ANOVA for Cleaning Solution Problem

Source	df	SS	MS
Depths	2	281.67	
linear	1	211.25	211.25**
quadratic	1	70.42	70.42*
Positions	4	50.47	12.62
$D \times P$ interaction	8	58.33	
$D_{\text{linear}} \times P$	4	41.50	10.38
$D_{\text{quadratic}} \times P$	4	16.83	4.21
Error	15	189.00	12.60
Totals	29	579.47	

The results in Table 8.9 indicate a strong depth effect, with the linear depth effect significant at the 1 percent level (**) and the quadratic depth effect significant at the 5 percent level (*). There is no position effect nor interaction between depth and position. These results seem reasonable from a graph (Fig. 8.4) of cell totals versus depth and positions.

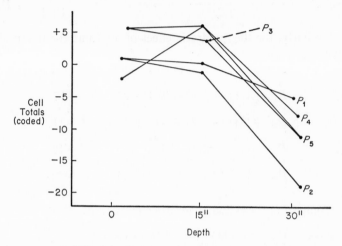

FIG. 8.4   Graph of Cleaning Solution Problem

This graph (Fig. 8.4) shows little interaction, as the curves are quite parallel (statistically speaking) and there is little difference between the five position curves. The depth effect is quite obvious, and concentration is seen to drop off with increasing depth but on more of a curve than a straight line. Further investigation is suggested at depths between those already studied. The lack of any position effect or interaction should mean that this new experiment could be run at only one position; the results should then be the same at all five positions.

8.4   Two Factors — Both Quantitative

If both factors in a two-factor factorial are at quantitative levels, each factor can be broken down into its linear, quadratic, or cubic effects, and all combinations of interaction can be determined, such as linear by linear, linear by quadratic, and quadratic by quadratic. To illustrate the procedure for analyzing a factorial experiment where both factors are at quantitative (and equispaced) levels, consider a problem in which we wish to study the effect of knife-edge radius (R) in inches and feedroll force (F) in pounds per inch on the energy necessary to cut 1-in. lengths of alfalfa. The measured variable (energy) was measured in 100 in.-lb per lb of dry matter. The resulting data are given in Table 8.10.

TABLE 8.10 — Data for Alfalfa Cutting Problem

Feedroll Force (F_j) in lb/in.	Knife-Edge Radius (R_i)				$T_{.j.}$
	0.000 in.	0.005 in.	0.010 in.	0.015 in.	
5	29 30 20/79	98 128 67/293	44 81 77/202	84 100 63/247	821
10	22 26 16/64	35 80 29/144	53 93 59/205	103 90 98/291	704
15	18 17 11/46	49 68 61/178	58 103 128/289	80 91 77/248	761
20	38 31 21/90	68 74 47/189	87 116 90/293	86 113 81/280	852
$T_{i..}$	279	804	989	1066	$T_{...} = 3138$

Here the experiment was run in a completely random order with three replications per cell. The model was

$$X_{ijk} = \mu + R_i + F_j + RF_{ij} + \epsilon_{k(ij)}$$

$$i = 1,2,3,4 \qquad j = 1,2,3,4 \qquad k = 1,2,3$$

Both the knife-edge radius and the feedroll force were set at four equi-spaced, quantitative levels. In analyzing these data, an analysis is first made as if both factors were qualitative. Using the data of Table 8.10, the following statistics are computed

$$SS_{total} = 254{,}656 - \frac{(3138)^2}{48} = 49{,}509.25$$

$$SS_{radius} = \frac{(279)^2 + (804)^2 + (989)^2 + (1066)^2}{12} - \frac{(3138)^2}{48}$$

$$= 31{,}414.42$$

$$SS_{force} = \frac{(821)^2 + (704)^2 + (761)^2 + (852)^2}{12} - \frac{(3138)^2}{48}$$

$$= 1{,}076.75$$

$$SS_{R \times F \text{ interaction}} = \frac{(79)^2 + (64)^2 + \ldots + (280)^2}{3} - \frac{(3138)^2}{48} - 31{,}414.42$$

$$- 1{,}076.75 = 6{,}474.08$$

$$SS_{error} = 49{,}509.25 - 31{,}414.42 - 1{,}076.75 - 6{,}474.08$$

$$= 10{,}544.00$$

The ANOVA is summarized in Table 8.11.

TABLE 8.11 — First ANOVA for Alfalfa Problem

Source	df	SS	MS	F
R_i	3	31,414.42	10,471.47	31.78**
F_j	3	1,076.75	358.92	1.09
$(R \times F)_{ij}$	9	6,474.08	719.34	2.18
$\epsilon_{k(ij)}$	32	10,544.00	329.50	
TOTALS	47	49,509.25		

The results of this first analysis show that the knife-edge radius (R_i) has a highly significant effect on the energy requirements. There is no apparent force effect and the interaction is not quite significant at the 5 percent level of significance.

Since both effects are quantitative, they will be broken down further in an attempt to see how the energy requirement might be related to each factor. Even though feedroll force (F_j) is not significant here, it will nevertheless be broken into its component parts to illustrate the method of analysis. As both factors are at four equispaced, quantitative levels, the proper coefficients for each factor total are given by the orthogonal polynomials of Appendix Table F.

					F
Linear:	-3	-1	$+1$	$+3$	20
Quadratic:	$+1$	-1	-1	$+1$	4
Cubic:	-1	$+3$	-3	$+1$	20

Applying these coefficients to both the radius totals and force totals, linear, quadratic and cubic effects and sums of squares can be determined as follows:

Sum of Squares

$$R_L = -3(279) - 1(804) + 1(989) + 3(1066) = 2546$$
$$\frac{(2546)^2}{12(20)} = 27,008.82$$

$$R_Q = +1(279) - 1(804) - 1(989) + 1(1066) = -448$$
$$\frac{(-448)^2}{12(4)} = 4,181.33$$

$$R_C = -1(279) + 3(804) - 3(989) + 1(1066) = 232$$
$$\frac{(232)^2}{12(20)} = 224.27$$

$$SS_R = 31,414.42$$

$$F_L = -3(821) - 1(704) + 1(761) + 3(852) = 150$$
$$\frac{(150)^2}{12(20)} = \quad 93.75$$

$$F_Q = +1(821) - 1(704) - 1(761) + 1(852) = 208$$
$$\frac{(208)^2}{12(4)} = \quad 901.33$$

$$F_C = -1(821) + 3(704) - 3(761) + 1(852) = -140$$
$$\frac{(-140)^2}{12(20)} = \quad 81.67$$

$$SS_F = \quad 1{,}076.75$$

Each of these effects has 1 df, and each may be tested for significance. The $R \times F$ interaction with its 9 df can be broken down into 9 single df components as follows:

$R_L \times F_L$	$R_Q \times F_L$	$R_C \times F_L$
$R_L \times F_Q$	$R_Q \times F_Q$	$R_C \times F_Q$
$R_L \times F_C$	$R_Q \times F_C$	$R_C \times F_C$

In practice, it is often difficult to interpret some of these higher polynomial interactions, and sometimes only the linear by linear, linear by quadratic, and quadratic by linear are computed and the remaining ones lumped into a residual interaction. Since the objective of this problem is to illustrate the method of analysis, all nine components will be computed. A simple computing scheme for these single degree-of-freedom interactions involves only the cell totals and proper coefficients, since cell totals form the basis for interaction effects. The proper coefficients for these cell totals can be found by multiplying the corresponding coefficients of the main effects. To illustrate this, consider the $R_L \times F_L$ interaction arrayed as in Table 8.12.

TABLE 8.12 — Linear-by-Linear Interaction

F_L	$R_L \rightarrow$ -3		-1		$+1$		$+3$	
$\downarrow$ -3	9	79	3	293	-3	202	-9	247
-1	3	64	1	144	-1	205	-3	291
$+1$	-3	46	-1	178	$+1$	289	$+3$	248
$+3$	-9	90	-3	189	$+3$	293	$+9$	280

Multiplying the coefficients of R_L by those of F_L gives the coefficients in the upper left-hand corners of the cells in Table 8.12. These coefficients are then applied to the corresponding cell totals. The results give a contrast.

$$R_L \times F_L = 9(79) + 3(64) - 3(46) - 9(90) + 3(293) + 1(144)$$

$$- 1(178) - 3(189) - 3(202) - 1(205) + 1(289)$$

$$+ 3(293) - 9(247) - 3(291) + 3(248) + 9(280) = 758$$

The sum of squares due to $R_L \times F_L$ is then

$$\text{SS}_{R_L \times F_L} = \frac{(758)^2}{3[9^2 + 3^2 + (-3)^2 + \ldots + 9^2]} = \frac{(758)^2}{3(400)} = 478.80$$

For the $R_L \times F_Q$, use the linear coefficients on R multiplied by the quadratic coefficients on F as in Table 8.13.

TABLE 8.13 — Linear by Quadratic Interaction

F_Q ↓	$R_L \to -3$	-1	$+1$	$+3$	
$+1$	-3	-1	$+1$	$+3$	
-1	$+3$	$+1$	-1	-3	$\sum_{i,j} c_{ij}^2 = 80$
-1	$+3$	$+1$	-1	-3	
$+1$	-3	-1	$+1$	$+3$	

These cell coefficients are then applied to the cell totals

$$R_L \times F_Q = -3(79) + 3(64) + \ldots + 3(280) = -372$$

$$\text{SS}_{R_L \times F_Q} = \frac{(-372)^2}{3(80)} = 576.60$$

For $R_L \times F_C$, the cell coefficients are those in Table 8.14.

TABLE 8.14 — Linear by Cubic Interaction

F_C ↓	$R_L \to -3$	-1	$+1$	$+3$	
-1	3	1	-1	-3	
$+3$	-9	-3	3	9	$\sum_{i,j} c_{ij}^2 = 400$
-3	9	3	-3	-9	
$+1$	-3	-1	1	3	

$$R_L \times F_C = 3(79) - 9(64) + \ldots + 3(280) = 336$$

$$\text{SS}_{R_L \times F_C} = \frac{(336)^2}{3(400)} = 94.08$$

For $R_Q \times F_L$, the cell coefficients are those in Table 8.15.

TABLE 8.15 — Quadratic by Linear

F_L/R_Q	+1	−1	−1	+1	
−3	−3	3	3	−3	
−1	−1	1	1	−1	$\sum_{i,j} c_{ij}^2 = 80$
+1	+1	−1	−1	1	
+3	+3	−3	−3	3	

$$R_Q \times F_L = -3(79) + 3(64) + \ldots + 3(280) = -8$$

$$\mathrm{SS}_{R_Q \times F_L} = \frac{(-8)^2}{3(80)} = 0.27$$

For $R_Q \times F_Q$, cell coefficients are those in Table 8.16.

TABLE 8.16 — Quadratic by Quadratic

F_Q/R_Q	+1	−1	−1	+1	
+1	1	−1	−1	+1	
−1	−1	1	1	−1	$\sum_{i,j} c_{ij}^2 = 16$
−1	−1	1	1	−1	
+1	1	−1	−1	1	

$$R_Q \times F_Q = 1(79) - 1(64) + \ldots + 1(280) = -114$$

$$\mathrm{SS}_{R_Q \times F_Q} = \frac{(-114)^2}{3(16)} = 270.75$$

For $R_Q \times F_C$, cell coefficients are as shown in Table 8.17.

TABLE 8.17 — Quadratic by Cubic

F_C/R_Q	+1	−1	−1	+1	
−1	−1	1	1	−1	
+3	3	−3	−3	3	$\sum_{i,j} c_{ij}^2 = 80$
−3	−3	3	3	−3	
+1	1	−1	−1	1	

$$R_Q \times F_C = -1(79) + 3(64) + \ldots + 1(280) = 594$$

$$\mathrm{SS}_{R_Q \times F_C} = \frac{(594)^2}{3(80)} = 1470.15$$

For $R_C \times F_L$, cell coefficients are as shown in Table 8.18.

TABLE 8.18 — Cubic by Linear

F_L/R_C	-1	$+3$	-3	$+1$
-3	3	-9	9	-3
-1	1	-3	3	-1
$+1$	-1	3	-3	1
$+3$	-3	9	-9	3

$$\sum_{i,j} c_{ij}^2 = 400$$

$$R_C \times F_L = 3(79) + 1(64) \times \ldots + 3(280) = -1864$$

$$\text{SS}_{R_C \times F_L} = \frac{(-1864)^2}{3(400)} = 2895.41$$

For $R_C \times F_Q$, cell coefficients are as shown in Table 8.19.

TABLE 8.19 — Cubic by Quadratic

F_Q/R_C	-1	$+3$	-3	$+1$
$+1$	-1	3	-3	1
-1	$+1$	-3	3	-1
-1	1	-3	3	-1
$+1$	-1	3	-3	1

$$\sum_{i,j} c_{ij}^2 = 80$$

$$R_C \times F_Q = -1(79) + 1(64) + \ldots + 1(280) = 406$$

$$\text{SS}_{R_C \times F_Q} = \frac{(406)^2}{3(80)} = 686.82$$

For $R_C \times F_C$, cell coefficients are those in Table 8.20.

TABLE 8.20 — Cubic by Cubic

F_C/R_C	-1	$+3$	-3	$+1$
-1	1	-3	3	-1
$+3$	-3	9	-9	3
-3	3	-9	9	-3
$+1$	-1	3	-3	1

$$\sum_{i,j} c_{ij}^2 = 400$$

$$R_C \times F_C = 1(79) - 3(64) + \ldots + 1(280) = -38$$

$$\text{SS}_{R_C \times F_C} = \frac{(-38)^2}{3(400)} = 1.20$$

If all of these single degree-of-freedom, interaction sums of squares are added, the sum of the overall $R \times F$ interaction sum of squares is

$$\begin{aligned}
\text{SS for } R_L \times F_L &= 478.80 \\
R_L \times F_Q &= 576.60 \\
R_L \times F_C &= 94.08 \\
R_Q \times F_L &= 00.27 \\
R_Q \times F_Q &= 270.75 \\
R_Q \times F_C &= 1470.15 \\
R_C \times F_L &= 2895.41 \\
R_C \times F_Q &= 686.82 \\
R_C \times F_C &= 1.20 \\
\hline
\text{SS}_{\text{overall}} \, R \times F &= 6474.08
\end{aligned}$$

Summarizing all of the above results in a complete ANOVA table along with the significance tests, we get Table 8.21.

TABLE 8.21 — Complete ANOVA for Alfalfa Problem

Source	df	SS	MS	F
Radius (R_i)	3	31,414.42		
R_L	1	27,008.82	27,008.82	81.97***
R_Q	1	4181.33	4181.33	12.69**
R_C	1	224.27	224.27	<1
Force (F_j)	3	1076.75		
F_L	1	93.75	93.75	<1
F_Q	1	901.33	901.33	2.74
F_C	1	81.67	81.67	<1
$R \times F$ interaction	9	6474.08		
$R_L \times F_L$	1	478.80	478.80	1.45
$R_L \times F_Q$	1	576.60	576.60	1.75
$R_L \times F_C$	1	94.08	94.08	<1
$R_Q \times F_L$	1	0.27	0.27	<1
$R_Q \times F_Q$	1	270.75	270.75	<1
$R_Q \times F_C$	1	1470.15	1470.15	4.46*
$R_C \times F_L$	1	2895.41	2895.41	8.79**
$R_C \times F_Q$	1	686.82	686.82	2.08
$R_C \times F_C$	1	1.20	1.20	<1
Error	32	10,544.00	329.50	
TOTALS	47	49,509.25		

The complete analysis of Table 8.21 shows a highly significant linear effect and a significant quadratic effect for the knife-edge radius. No force effects are found to be significant, but there is a highly significant interaction between the cubic component of radius and the linear component of force, and there is also a significant interaction between the quadratic component of radius and the cubic component of force. This $R_C \times F_L$ interaction may mean that linear changes in force produce different cubic trends, because of the radius. Also, the $R_Q \times F_C$ may

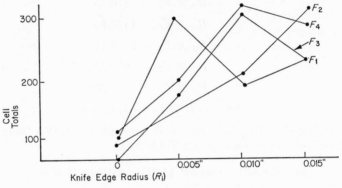

FIG. 8.5   Graph I of Alfalfa Problem

mean that quadratic changes in the radius produce different cubic trends, because of the force. Some of these conclusions can be seen in Fig. 8.5, a graph of cell totals versus radius for the four (4) force levels.

Figure 8.5 shows the strong linear effect and the over-all quadratic effect of radius. The closeness of the lines also shows a lack of force effect.

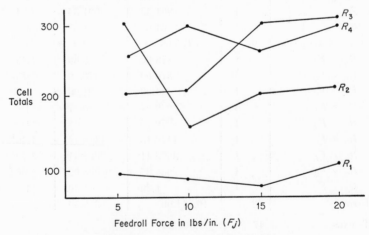

FIG. 8.6   Graph II of Alfalfa Problem

Some sort of interaction may be indicated, as the curves are not parallel. Replotting with cell totals versus force at 4 radius levels gives Fig. 8.6. Figure 8.6 also shows the strong radius effect, indicated by the gaps between most of the curves. It may also help to show the different curvilinear effect of radius for linear shifts in force.

8.5   Summary

The examples of this chapter may easily be extended to higher order factorials whenever one or more factors is considered at quantitative levels. The use of orthogonal polynomials makes the analysis rather simple, provided the experiment is designed with equispaced quantitative levels. The summary of designs at the end of Chapter 7 has not been changed by this chapter, as these methods can be used on all experiments where quantitative levels are involved.

PROBLEMS

8-1.   In Prob. 3-1, assume that the five levels of Factor A are quantitative and equispaced. Using orthogonal polynomials, determine the sum of squares for linear, quadratic, cubic, and quartic effects of Factor A and test for significance.

8-2.   In Prob. 4-1, assume that the three days are equispaced in time from their date of manufacture, and extract the quantitative effects and interactions (or error).

8-3.   Data on screen quality for lacquer concentrations and standing times effect only are as follows:

Standing Times	Lacquer Concentrations			
	$\frac{1}{2}$	1	$1\frac{1}{2}$	2
30	16	12	17	13
	14	11	19	11
20	15	14	15	12
	15	17	18	14
10	10	7	10	9
	9	6	14	13

Assuming a completely randomized design, do an ANOVA on these data using the general methods of Chapter 6.

8-4.   Since both factors in Prob. 8-3 are quantitative and equispaced, set up orthogonal polynomials and pull out all possible effects and their interactions.

8-5.   Show graphically the reasonableness of your results in Prob. 8-4.

CHAPTER

9 | 3^n Factorial Experiments

9.1 Introduction

As 2^n factorial experiments represent an interesting special case of factorial experimentation, so also do 3^n factorial experiments. 3^n factorials consider n factors each at three levels; thus there are 2 df between the levels of each of these factors. If the three levels are quantitative and equispaced, the methods of Chapter 8 may be used to extract linear and quadratic effects and to test these for significance. 3^n factorials also play an important role in more complicated design problems which will be discussed in subsequent chapters. For this chapter, it will be assumed that the design is a completely randomized design and that the levels of the factors considered are fixed levels. Such levels may be either qualitative or quantitative.

9.2 3^2 Factorial

If just two factors are crossed in an experiment and each of the two are set at three levels, there are $3 \times 3 = 9$ treatment combinations. Since each factor is at three levels, the notation of Chapter 7 will no longer suffice. There is now a low, intermediate and high level for each factor which may be designated as 0, 1 and 2. A model for this arrangement would be

$$X_{ij} = \mu + A_i + B_j + AB_{ij} + \epsilon_{ij}$$

where $i = 1, 2, 3$; $j = 1, 2, 3$; and the error term is confounded with the AB interaction unless there are some replications in the nine cells, in which case

$$X_{ijk} = \mu + A_i + B_j + AB_{ij} + \epsilon_{k(ij)}$$

and $k = 1, 2, \cdots r$ for r replications.

To introduce some notation for treatment combinations when three levels are involved, consider the data layout in Fig. 9.1.

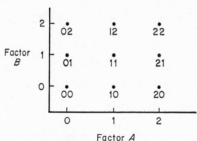

FIG. 9.1 3^2 *Data Layout*

In Fig. 9.1, two digits are used to describe each of the nine treatment combinations. The first digit indicates the level of Factor A, and the second digit, the level of Factor B. Thus, 12 means A at its intermediate level and B at its highest level. This notation can easily be extended to more factors and as many levels as are necessary. It could have been used for 2^n factorials as 00, 10, 01 and 11, corresponding respectively to (1), a, b, and ab. The only reason for not using this digital notation on 2^n factorials is that so much of the literature includes this (1), a, b, etc. notation. By proper choice of coefficients on these treatment combinations, the linear and quadratic effects of both A and B can be determined, as well as their interactions, such as $A_L \times B_L$, $A_L \times B_Q$, $A_Q \times B_L$ and

TABLE 9.1 — 3^2 Factorial with Responses and Totals

| Factor B | Factor A | | | |
	0	1	2	$T_{.j}$
0	00 1	10 -2	20 3	2
1	01 0	11 4	21 1	5
2	02 2	12 -1	22 2	3
$T_{i.}$	3	1	6	10

$A_Q \times B_Q$. The methods of analysis will be illustrated on a simple hypothetical example.

Suppose the responses in Table 9.1 were recorded for the treatment combinations indicated in the upper left-hand corner of each cell.

Analyzing the data of Table 9.1 by the general methods of Chapter 6 gives

$$\text{SS}_{\text{total}} = 1^2 + 0^2 + 2^2 + \ldots + 2^2 - \frac{(10)^2}{9} = 28.89$$

$$\text{SS}_A = \frac{3^2 + 1^2 + 6^2}{3} - \frac{(10)^2}{9} = 4.22$$

$$\text{SS}_B = \frac{2^2 + 5^2 + 3^2}{3} - \frac{(10)^2}{9} = 1.56$$

$$\text{SS}_{\text{error}} = 28.89 - 4.22 - 1.56 = 23.11$$

and the ANOVA table is Table 9.2.

TABLE 9.2 — ANOVA for 3² Factorial of Table 9.1

Source	df	SS	MS
A_i	2	4.22	2.11
B_j	2	1.56	0.78
AB_{ij}	4	23.11	5.77
TOTALS	8	28.89	

A further breakdown of this analysis is now possible by recalling that coefficients of -1, 0, $+1$ applied to the responses at low, intermediate and high levels of a factor will measure its linear effect; whereas, coefficients of $+1$, -2, $+1$ applied to these same responses will measure the

TABLE 9.3 — Coefficients for a 3² Factorial with Quantitative Levels

Trt. Comb →	00	01	02	10	11	12	20	21	22	Σc_i^2
Factors A_L	-1	-1	-1	0	0	0	$+1$	$+1$	$+1$	6
↓ A_Q	$+1$	$+1$	$+1$	-2	-2	-2	$+1$	$+1$	$+1$	18
B_L	-1	0	$+1$	-1	0	$+1$	-1	0	$+1$	6
B_Q	$+1$	-2	$+1$	$+1$	-2	$+1$	$+1$	-2	$+1$	18
$A_L B_L$	$+1$	0	-1	0	0	0	-1	0	$+1$	4
$A_L B_Q$	-1	$+2$	-1	0	0	0	$+1$	-2	$+1$	12
$A_Q B_L$	-1	0	$+1$	$+2$	0	-2	-1	0	$+1$	12
$A_Q B_Q$	$+1$	-2	$+1$	-2	$+4$	-2	$+1$	-2	$+1$	36
Responses: X_{ij}	1	0	2	-2	4	-1	3	1	2	

quadratic effect of this factor. As in the case of 2^n factorials, products of coefficients will give the proper coefficients for various interactions. This can best be shown by a table (Table 9.3) which indicates the coefficients for each effect to be used with the nine treatment combinations.

From Table 9.3, it can be seen that A_L compares all highest levels of $A(+1)$ with all lowest levels of $A(-1)$. A_Q compares the extreme levels with twice the intermediate levels. Both of these effects are taken across *all* levels of B. Now B_L compares the highest versus the lowest level of B at the 0 level of A, then at level 1 of A, then at level 2 of A, reading from left to right across B_L. Similarly B_Q compares the extreme levels of B with twice the intermediate level at all three levels of A. The coefficients for interaction are found by multiplying corresponding main-effect coefficients. An examination of these coefficients in the light of what interactions there are should make the coefficients seem quite plausible. The sums of squares of the coefficients are given at the right of Table 9.3.

Applying these coefficients to the responses for each treatment combination gives

$$A_L = -1(1) - 1(0) - 1(2) + 0(-2) + 0(4) \\ + 0(-1) + 1(3) + 1(1) + 1(2) = 3$$

$$A_Q = +1(1) + 1(0) + 1(2) - 2(-2) - 2(4) \\ - 2(-1) + 1(3) + 1(1) + 1(2) = 7$$

$$B_L = -1(1) + 0(0) + 1(2) - 1(-2) + 0(4) \\ + 1(-1) - 1(3) + 0(1) + 1(2) = 1$$

$$B_Q = +1(1) - 2(0) + 1(2) + 1(-2) - 2(4) \\ + 1(-1) + 1(3) - 2(1) + 1(2) = -5$$

$$A_L B_L = +1(1) + 0(0) - 1(2) + 0(-2) + 0(4) \\ + 0(-1) - 1(3) + 0(1) + 1(2) = -2$$

$$A_L B_Q = -1(1) + 2(0) - 1(2) + 0(-2) + 0(4) \\ + 0(-1) + 1(3) - 2(1) + 1(2) = 0$$

$$A_Q B_L = -1(1) + 0(0) + 1(2) + 2(-2) + 0(4) \\ - 2(-1) - 1(3) + 0(1) + 1(2) = -2$$

$$A_Q B_Q = +1(1) - 2(0) + 1(2) - 2(-2) + 4(4) \\ - 2(-1) + 1(3) - 2(1) + 1(2) = 28$$

the corresponding sums of squares become

$$SS_{AL} = \frac{(3)^2}{6} = 1.50 \qquad\qquad SS_{ALBL} = \frac{(-2)^2}{4} = 1.00$$

$$SS_{AQ} = \frac{(7)^2}{18} = 2.72 \qquad\qquad SS_{ALBQ} = \frac{0^2}{12} = 0.00$$

$$SS_{BL} = \frac{(1)^2}{6} = 0.17 \qquad\qquad SS_{AQBL} = \frac{(-2)^2}{12} = 0.33$$

$$SS_{BQ} = \frac{(-5)^2}{18} = 1.39 \qquad\qquad SS_{AQBQ} = \frac{(28)^2}{36} = 21.78$$

Summarizing, we obtain Table 9.4.

TABLE 9.4 — ANOVA Breakdown for 3^2 Factorial

Source		df	SS	
A_i		2	4.22	
	A_L	1		1.50
	A_Q	1		2.72
B_j		2	1.56	
	B_L	1		0.17
	B_Q	1		1.39
AB_{ij}		4	23.11	
	$A_L B_L$	1		1.00
	$A_L B_Q$	1		0.00
	$A_Q B_L$	1		0.33
	$A_Q B_Q$	1		21.78
TOTALS		8	28.89	

The results of this analysis will not be tested, as there is no separate measure of error and the interaction effect is obviously large compared to other effects. As the numbers used here are purely hypothetical, the purpose has been only to show how such data can be analyzed and how the notation can be used.

Before leaving this problem, reconsider the data of Table 9.1. Add the data by diagonals rather than by rows or columns. First consider the diagonals downward from left to right where the main diagonal is $1 + 4 + 2 = 7$, the next one to the right is $-2 + 1 + 2 = 1$, and the last $+2$ is found by repeating the table again on the right of the present one as in Table 9.5.

TABLE 9.5 — *Diagonal Computations*

Factor B	Factor A			Factor A		
	0	1	2	0	1	2
0	1	−2	3	1	−2	3
1	0	4	1	0	4	1
2	2	−1	2	2	−1	2

Similarly, the next downward diagonal gives $3 + 0 + (-1) = 2$. The sum of squares between these three diagonal terms is then

$$\frac{(7)^2 + (1)^2 + (2)^2}{3} - \frac{(10)^2}{9} = 6.89$$

If the diagonals are now considered downward and to the left, their totals are

$$3 + 4 + 2 = 9$$

$$1 + 1 - 1 = 1$$

$$-2 + 0 + 2 = 0$$

and their sum of squares is

$$\frac{(9)^2 + (1)^2 + (0)^2}{3} - \frac{(10)^2}{9} = 16.22$$

These two somewhat artificial sums of squares of 6.89 and 16.22 are seen to add up to the interaction sum of squares

$$6.89 + 16.22 = 23.11$$

These two components of interaction have no physical significance, but simply illustrate another way to extract two orthogonal components of interaction. Testing each of these separately for significance has no meaning, but this arbitrary breakdown is very useful in more complex designs. Some authors refer to these two components as the I and J components of interaction

$$I\,(AB) = 6.89 \qquad 2\ \text{df}$$

$$J\,(AB) = 16.22 \qquad 2$$

$$\text{Total } A \times B = 23.11 \qquad 4\ \text{df}$$

Each such component carries 2 df. These are sometimes referred to as the AB and AB^2 components of $A \times B$ interaction. In this notation, effects can be multiplied together using a modulus of 3, since this is a 3^n factorial A *modulus* of 3 means that the resultant number is equal to the remainder when the number in the usual base of 10 is divided by 3. Thus $4 = 1$ in modulus 3, as 1 is the remainder when 4 is divided by 3. The following associations also hold

$$\text{Numbers: } 0 \quad 3 = 0 \quad 6 = 0 \quad 9 = 0$$
$$1 \quad 4 = 1 \quad 7 = 1 \quad 10 = 1$$
$$2 \quad 5 = 2 \quad 8 = 2 \quad 11 = 2 \text{ etc.}$$

When using the form $A^p B^q$, it is postulated that the only exponent allowed on the first letter in the expression is a 1. To make it a 1, the expression can be squared and reduced, modulus 3. For example

$$A^2 B = (A^2 B)^2 = A^4 B^2 = AB^2$$

Hence, AB and AB^2 are the only components of the $A \times B$ interaction with 2 df each. Here the two types of notation are related as follows

$$I(AB) = AB^2$$
$$J(AB) = AB$$

To summarize this simple experiment, all effects can be expressed with 2 df, each as in Table 9.6.

TABLE 9.6 — 3² Factorial by 2 df Analysis

Source	df	SS
A_i	2	4.22
B_j	2	1.56
$I(AB) = AB^2$	2	6.89
$J(AB) = AB$	2	16.22
TOTALS	8	28.89

It will be found very useful to break such an experiment down into 2 df effects when more complex designs are considered. Here, this breakdown is presented merely to show another way to partition the interaction effect.

9.3 3³ Factorial

If an experimenter has three factors each at three levels, or a $3 \times 3 \times 3 = 3^3$ factorial, there are several ways to break down the effects of Factors A, B and C and their associated interactions. If the order of experimentation is completely randomized, the model for such an experiment is

$$X_{ijk} = \mu + A_i + B_j + AB_{ij} + C_k + AC_{ik} + BC_{jk} + ABC_{ijk} + \epsilon_{ijk}$$

with the last two terms confounded unless there is replication within the cells. In this model, $i = 1, 2, 3$; $j = 1, 2, 3$; and $k = 1, 2, 3$; making 27 treatment combinations. These 27 treatment combinations may be as shown in Table 9.7.

TABLE 9.7 — 3³ Factorial Treatment Combinations

		Factor A		
Factor B	Factor C	0	1	2
	0	000	100	200
0	1	001	101	201
	2	002	102	202
	0	010	110	210
1	1	011	111	211
	2	012	112	212
	0	020	120	220
2	1	021	121	221
	2	022	122	222

Association of the proper coefficients on these 27 treatment combinations would allow the Table 9.8 breakdown of an ANOVA if all effects were set at quantitative levels.

TABLE 9.8 — 3³ Factorial Analysis for Linear and Quadratic Effects

Source		df		
A_i		2	$A_L C_Q$	1
	A_L	1	$A_Q C_L$	1
	A_Q	1	$A_Q C_Q$	1
B_j		2	BC_{jk}	4
	B_L	1	$B_L C_L$	1
	B_Q	1	$B_L C_Q$	1
AB_{ij}		4	$B_Q C_L$	1
	$A_L B_L$	1	$B_Q C_Q$	1
	$A_L B_Q$	1	ABC_{ijk}	8
	$A_Q B_L$	1	$A_L B_L C_L$	1
	$A_Q B_Q$	1	$A_L B_L C_Q$	1
C_k		2	$A_L B_Q C_L$	1
	C_L	1	$A_L B_Q C_Q$	1
	C_Q	1	$A_Q B_L C_L$	1
AC_{ik}		4	$A_Q B_L C_Q$	1
	$A_L C_L$	1	$A_Q B_Q C_L$	1
			$A_Q B_Q C_Q$	1
			TOTAL	26 df

In an actual problem, these three-way interactions would be hard to explain, and quite often the ABC interaction is left with its 8 df for use as an error term to test the main effects A, B, C and the two-way interactions.

Another possible partitioning of these effects is in terms of 2 df effects using I and J components on AB, AC, and BC interactions. These could be designated as AB, AB^2, AC, AC^2, and BC, BC^2, each with 2 df. However, the three-way interaction with its 8 df may need a further breakdown. Sometimes ABC is broken into four 2-df components called $X(ABC)$, $Y(ABC)$, $Z(ABC)$ and $W(ABC)$; or, using the notation of the last section: ABC, ABC^2, AB^2C, and AB^2C^2. Here again no first letter is squared, and $A^2BC = (A^2BC)^2 = A^4B^2C^2 = AB^2C^2$ modulus 3. Such a partitioning would yield Table 9.9.

TABLE 9.9 — 3³ Factorial in 2 df Analyses

Source	df	
A	2	
B	2	
AB	2	⎱ 4
AB^2	2	⎰
C	2	
AC	2	⎱ 4
AC^2	2	⎰
BC	2	⎱ 4
BC^2	2	⎰
ABC	2	⎫
ABC^2	2	⎬ 8
AB^2C	2	⎪
AB^2C^2	2	⎭
TOTAL	26 df	

EXAMPLE 9.1. A problem involving the effect of three factors, each at three levels, was proposed by Professor Burr of Purdue University. Here the measured variable was yield and the factors which might affect this response were days, operators and concentrations of solvent. Three days, three operators, and three concentrations were chosen. Days and operators were qualitative effects; concentrations were quantitative and set at 0.5, 1.0, 2.0. Although these are not equispaced, the logarithms of these three levels are equispaced, and the logarithms can then be used if a curve-fitting is warranted. For the purposes of this chapter, all levels

of all factors will be considered as fixed and the design will be considered as completely randomized. It was decided to take three replications of each of the $3^3 = 27$ treatment combinations. The data, after coding by subtracting 20.0, are presented in Table 9.10.

TABLE 9.10 — Example Data on 3³ Factorial with Three Replications

Concentrations (C_k)	Days (D_i)								
	5/14			5/15			5/16		
	Operator (O_j)								
	A	B	C	A	B	C	A	B	C
0.5	1.0	0.2	0.2	1.0	1.0	1.2	1.7	0.2	0.5
	1.2	0.5	0.0	0.0	0.0	0.0	1.2	0.7	1.0
	1.7	0.7	−0.3	0.5	0.0	0.5	1.2	1.0	1.7
1.0	5.0	3.2	3.5	4.0	3.2	3.7	4.5	3.7	3.7
	4.7	3.7	3.5	3.5	3.0	4.0	5.0	4.0	4.5
	4.2	3.5	3.2	3.5	4.0	4.2	4.7	4.2	3.7
2.0	7.5	6.0	7.2	6.5	5.2	7.0	6.7	7.5	6.2
	6.5	6.2	6.5	6.0	5.7	6.7	7.5	6.0	6.5
	7.7	6.2	6.7	6.2	6.5	6.8	7.0	6.0	7.0

If these data are analyzed on a purely qualitative basis, the methods of Chapter 6, Sec. 6.4 can be used. The resulting ANOVA is shown in Table 9.11.

TABLE 9.11 — First ANOVA for Example 9-1

Source	df	SS	MS
D_i	2	3.48	1.74**
O_j	2	6.14	3.07**
DO_{ij}	4	4.07	1.02**
C_k	2	468.99	234.49***
DC_{ik}	4	0.59	0.15
OC_{jk}	4	0.89	0.22
DOC_{ijk}	8	1.09	0.14
$\epsilon_{m(ijk)}$	54	9.98	0.18
TOTALS	80	495.23	

The model for this example is merely $X_{ijkm} = \mu$ plus the sum of the terms in the Source column in Table 9.11. From this analysis, the concentration effect is tremendous, and the days, operators and day $\times$ operator interaction are all significant at the 1 percent level of significance.

Since concentrations are at quantitative levels, the linear and quadratic effects of concentrations may be computed, as well as the interactions between linear effect of concentration and days, quadratic effect of concentration and days, linear effect of concentration and operators, and quadratic effect of concentration and operators. It is not usually worthwhile to extract three-way interaction in this way. To calculate these quantitative effects, it is usually helpful to construct some two-way tables for the interactions which are being computed. Two of these are shown as Table 9.12(a) and Table 9.12(b).

TABLE 9.12 — Cell Totals for D $\times$ C and O $\times$ C Interactions

(a) Concentrations				(b) Concentrations			
Days	0.5	1.0	2.0	Operators	0.5	1.0	2.0
5/14	5.2	34.5	60.5	A	9.5	39.1	61.6
5/15	4.2	33.1	56.6	B	4.3	32.5	55.3
5/16	9.2	38.0	60.4	C	4.8	34.0	60.6
TOTALS 18.6	105.6	177.5	301.7	TOTALS 18.6	105.6	177.5	301.7

From Table 9.12(a), applying the linear and quadratic coefficients to the concentration totals, we have

$$C_L = -1(18.6) + 0(105.6) + 1(177.5) = 158.9; \quad \frac{\text{SS}}{\frac{(158.9)^2}{27(2)}} = 467.58$$

$$C_Q = +1(18.6) - 2(105.6) + 1(177.5) = -15.1; \quad \frac{(-15.1)^2}{27(6)} = 1.41$$

$$\text{SS}_c = 468.99$$

For the $D \times C$ interactions, consider each level of days separately. At

$$5/14: C_L = -1(5.2) + 0(34.5) + 1(60.5) = 55.3$$

$$5/15: C_L = -1(4.2) + 0(33.1) + 1(56.6) = 52.4$$

$$5/16: C_L = -1(9.2) + 0(38.0) + 1(60.4) = 51.2$$

The $D \times C_L$ SS$_{\text{interaction}}$ is then

$$\frac{(55.3)^2 + (52.4)^2 + (51.2)^2}{9(2)} - \frac{(158.9)^2}{27(2)} = 0.49$$

For quadratic effects, at

$$5/14: \quad C_Q = +1(5.2) - 2(34.5) + 1(60.5) = -3.3$$

$$5/15: \quad C_Q = +1(4.2) - 2(33.1) + 1(56.6) = -5.4$$

$$5/16: \quad C_Q = +1(9.2) - 2(38.0) + 1(60.4) = -6.4$$

The $D \times C_Q$ SS$_{\text{interaction}}$ is then

$$\frac{(-3.3)^2 + (-5.4)^2 + (-6.4)^2}{9(6)} - \frac{(-15.1)^2}{27(6)} = 0.09$$

$$SS_{D \times C} = 0.58$$

If the same procedure is now applied to the data of Table 9.12(*b*) we have

$$SS_{O \times C_L} = \frac{(52.1)^2 + (51.0)^2 + (55.8)^2}{9(2)} - \frac{(158.9)^2}{27(2)} = 0.70$$

$$SS_{O \times C_Q} = \frac{(-7.1)^2 + (-5.4)^2 + (-2.6)^2}{9(6)} - \frac{(-15.1)^2}{27(6)} = 0.19$$

$$SS_{O \times C} = 0.89$$

The resulting ANOVA can now be shown as in Table 9.13.

TABLE 9.13 — Second ANOVA for Example 9-1

Source	df	SS	MS
D_i	2	3.48	1.74**
O_j	2	6.14	3.07**
DO_{ij}	4	4.07	1.02**
C_L	1	467.58	467.58***
C_Q	1	1.41	1.41**
$D \times C_L$	2	0.49	0.24
$D \times C_Q$	2	0.09	0.04
$O \times C_L$	2	0.70	0.35
$O \times C_Q$	2	0.19	0.09
DOC_{ijk}	8	1.09	0.14
$\epsilon_{m(ijk)}$	54	9.98	0.18
TOTALS	80	495.22	

This second analysis shows that the linear effect and the quadratic effect of concentration are extremely significant. Two plots [Fig. 9.2(*a*) and 9.2(*b*)] may help in picturing what is really happening in this experiment.

The left-hand plot (9.2*a*) shows the effect of operators, days and $D \times O$ interaction. The right-hand plot (9.2*b*) indicates that the linear

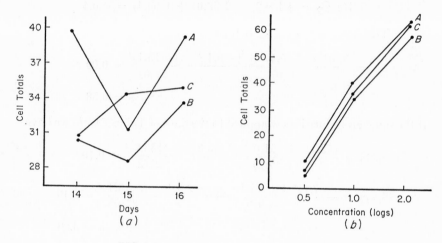

FIG. 9.2   Plots of 3^3 Example of Table 9.10

effect of concentration far outweighs the quadratic effect and there is no significant interaction. If a straight line or three straight lines were fit to these data, the logs of the concentrations would be used, as the logs are equispaced.

Although this would usually conclude the analysis of this problem, each interaction will be broken down into its diagonal, or I and J, components in order to illustrate the technique. To compute the two diagonal components of the two-factor interactions, the two parts of Table 9.12 can be used, along with a similar table for the $D \times O$ cells (see Table 9.14.)

TABLE 9.14 — Cell Totals for $D \times O$ Interactions

	Operators		
Days	A	B	C
5/14	39.5	30.2	30.5
5/15	31.2	28.6	34.1
5/16	39.5	33.3	34.8

From Table 9.14, the diagonal components of the $D \times O$ interaction are

$$I(D \times O) =$$

$$\frac{(39.5 + 28.6 + 34.8)^2 + (30.2 + 34.1 + 39.5)^2 + (30.5 + 33.3 + 31.2)^2}{27}$$

$$- \frac{(301.7)^2}{81} = 1.74$$

call it DO^2.

$$J(D \times O) = \frac{(30.5 + 28.6 + 39.5)^2 + (96.2)^2 + (106.9)^2}{27} - \frac{(301.7)^2}{81}$$

$$= 2.33$$

call it DO. These total $1.74 + 2.33 = 4.07$, the $D \times O$ interaction sum of squares.

Applying the same technique to the two parts of Table 9.12 gives

$$I(DC) = DC^2 = \frac{(98.7)^2 + (102.7)^2 + (100.3)^2}{27} - \frac{(301.7)^2}{81} = 0.30$$

$$J(DC) = DC = \frac{(102.8)^2 + (99.8)^2 + (99.1)^2}{27} - \frac{(301.7)^2}{81} = 0.29$$

$$D \times C = 0.59$$

$$I(OC) = OC^2 = \frac{(102.6)^2 + (99.9)^2 + (99.2)^2}{27} - \frac{(301.7)^2}{81} = 0.24$$

$$J(OC) = OC = \frac{(98.9)^2 + (104.0)^2 + (98.8)^2}{27} - \frac{(301.7)^2}{81} = 0.65$$

$$O \times C = 0.89$$

To break down the 8 df of the DOC interaction, form an $O \times D$ table showing each of the three levels of concentration C as in Table 9.15.

TABLE 9.15 — *Cell Totals for $D \times O$ Interaction at Each Level of Concentration*

O_i	D_i at C_1			D_i at C_2			D_i at C_3		
A	3.9	1.5	4.1	13.9	11.0	14.2	21.7	18.7	21.2
B	1.4	1.0	1.9	10.4	10.2	11.9	18.4	17.4	19.5
C	−0.1	1.7	3.2	10.2	11.9	11.9	20.4	20.5	19.7

For each of these concentration levels, find the I and J effect totals; e.g., at C_1:

I components are: 8.1, 3.3, 7.2

J components are: 5.0, 6.1, 7.5

Now form a table with these I and J components at each level of C (see Table 9.16).

TABLE 9.16 — *Diagonal Totals for Each Level of Concentration*

C_k	$I(DO)$			$J(DO)$		
	i_0	i_1	i_2	j_0	j_1	j_2
0.5	8.1	3.3	7.2	5.0	6.1	7.5
1.0	36.0	33.1	36.5	34.6	33.3	37.7
2.0	58.8	58.6	60.1	59.0	56.8	61.7

Treat each half of Table 9.16 as a simple interaction and compute the I and J components. Thus

$$DOC = I[C \times I(DO)] = \frac{(101.3)^2 + (98.6)^2 + (101.8)^2}{27} - \frac{(301.7)^2}{81}$$
$$= 0.22$$

$$DOC^2 = J[C \times I(DO)] = \frac{(99.1)^2 + (99.4)^2 + (103.2)^2}{27} - \frac{(301.7)^2}{81}$$
$$= 0.39$$

$$DO^2C = I[C \times J(DO)] = \frac{(100.0)^2 + (102.8)^2 + (98.9)^2}{27} - \frac{(301.7)^2}{81}$$
$$= 0.30$$

$$DO^2C^2 = J[C \times J(DO)] = \frac{(99.8)^2 + (102.4)^2 + (99.5)^2}{27} - \frac{(301.7)^2}{81}$$
$$= 0.19$$

Total $D \times O \times C = 1.10$

TABLE 9.17 — *Third ANOVA for 3³ Experiment*

Source	df	SS
D_i	2	3.48
O_j	2	6.14
DO	2	2.33
DO^2	2	1.74
C_k	2	468.99
DC	2	0.29
DC^2	2	0.30
OC	2	0.65
OC^2	2	0.24
DOC	2	0.22
DOC^2	2	0.39
DO^2C	2	0.30
DO^2C^2	2	0.19
$\epsilon_{m(ijk)}$	54	9.98
TOTALS	80	495.24

compared to 1.09 in Table 9.13. This last breakdown into four parts could also have been accomplished by considering the $C \times O$ interaction at three levels of D_i, or the $C \times D$ interaction at three levels of O_j.

The resulting analysis is summarized in Table 9.17.

This analysis is in substantial agreement with Tables 9.11 and 9.13. No new tests would be performed on the data in Table 9.17, as they represent only an arbitrary breakdown of the interactions into 2 df components. The purpose of such a breakdown will be discussed in subsequent chapters. For testing hypotheses on interaction, these components are added together again.

9.4 Summary

The summary at the end of Chapter 7 (Sec. 7.5) may now be extended for Part II.

Experiment	*Design*	*Analysis*
II. Two or More Factors		
A. Factorial (crossed)		
	1. Completely Randomized $X_{ijk} = \mu + A_i + B_j + AB_{ij} + \epsilon_{k(ij)}$ etc. for more factors.	1.
	a. General Case.	*a.* ANOVA with interactions.
	b. 2^n case.	*b.* Yates Method or general ANOVA use: (1), *a,b,ab*, etc.
	c. 3^n case.	*c.* General ANOVA use: 00,10,20,01,11 etc. and $A \times B = AB + AB^2$ etc. for interaction.

PROBLEMS

9-1. Pull-off force in pounds on glued boxes at three temperatures and three humidities with two observations per treatment combination in a completely randomized experiment gives

Humidity (B)	Temperature (A)		
	Cold	Ambient	Hot
50%	0.8	1.5	2.5
	2.8	3.2	4.2
70%	1.0	1.6	1.8
	1.6	1.8	1.0
90%	2.0	1.5	2.5
	2.2	0.8	4.0

Do a complete analysis of this problem by the general methods of Chapter 6.

9-2. Assuming the temperatures in Prob. 9-1 are equispaced, extract linear and quadratic effects of both temperature and humidity as well as all components of interaction.

9-3. From Prob. 9-1, extract the AB and AB^2 components of interaction.

9-4. Develop a "Yates Method" for this 3^2 experiment and check the results with those above.

9-5. A behavior variable on concrete pavements was measured for three surface thicknesses: 3 in., 4 in., and 5 in.; three base thicknesses: 0 in., 3 in. and 6 in., and three sub-base thicknesses: 4 in., 8 in., and 12 in. Two observations were made under each of the 27 pavement conditions and complete randomization performed. The results were

Sub-base Thickness	Surface Thickness								
	3″			4″			5″		
	Base Thickness			Base Thickness			Base Thickness		
	0″	3″	6″	0″	3″	6″	0″	3″	6″
4″	2.8	4.3	5.7	4.1	5.4	6.7	6.0	6.3	7.1
	2.6	4.5	5.3	4.4	5.5	6.9	6.2	6.5	6.9
8″	4.1	5.7	6.9	5.3	6.5	7.7	6.1	7.2	8.1
	4.4	5.8	7.1	5.1	6.7	7.4	5.8	7.1	8.4
12″	5.5	7.0	8.1	6.5	7.7	8.8	7.0	8.0	9.1
	5.3	6.8	8.3	6.7	7.5	9.1	7.2	8.3	9.0

Do a complete ANOVA of this experiment by the methods of Chapter 6.

9-6. Since all three factors are quantitative and equispaced, determine linear and quadratic effects for each factor and all interaction breakdowns. Test for significance.

9-7. Break down the interactions of Prob. 9-5 into 2 df components such as AB, AB^2, ABC, AB^2C, etc.

9-8. Use a Yates Method to solve Prob. 9-5 and check the results.

9-9. Plot any significant results of Prob. 9-5.

CHAPTER 10 | Fixed, Random and Mixed Models

10.1 Introduction

In Chapter 1 it was pointed out that, in the planning stages of an experiment, the experimenter must decide whether the levels of factors considered are to be set at fixed values or are to be chosen at random from many possible levels. In the intervening chapters, it has always been assumed that the factor levels were fixed. In practice it may be desirable to choose the levels of some factors at random, depending on the objectives of the experiment. Are the results to be judged for these levels alone or are they to be extended to more levels of which those in the experiment are but a random sample? In the case of some factors such as temperature, time, or pressure, it is usually desirable to pick fixed levels, often near the extremes and at some intermediate points, because a random choice might not cover the range in which the experimenter is interested. In such cases of fixed, quantitative levels, we often feel safe in interpolating between the fixed levels chosen. Other factors such as operators, days, or batches may often be only a small sample of all possible operators, days, or batches. In such cases, the particular operator, day or batch may not be very important but only whether or not operators, days or batches in general increase the variability of the experiment.

It is not reasonable to decide after the data have been collected whether the levels are to be considered fixed or random. This decision must be made prior to the running of the experiment, and if random levels are to be used, they must be chosen from all possible levels by a random process. In the case of random levels, it will be assumed that the levels are chosen from an infinite population of possible levels. Bennett and Franklin [2] discuss a case in which the levels chosen are from a finite set of possible levels.

When all levels are fixed, the mathematical model of the experiment is called a *fixed model*. When all levels are chosen at random, the model is called a *random model*. When several factors are involved, some at fixed levels and others at random levels, the model is called a *mixed model*.

10.2 Single-Factor Models

In the case of a single-factor experiment, the factor may be referred to as a *treatment effect*, as in Chapter 3; and if the design is completely randomized, the model is

$$X_{ij} = \mu + T_j + \epsilon_{ij} \tag{10.1}$$

Whether the treatment levels are fixed or random, it is assumed in this model that μ is a fixed constant and the errors are normally and independently distributed with a zero mean and the same variance; i.e., ϵ_{ij} are $NID(0, \sigma_e^2)$. The decision as to whether the levels of the treatments are fixed or random will affect the assumptions about the treatment term, T_j. The different assumptions and other differences will be compared in parallel columns.

Fixed Model	*Random Model*
1. Assumptions: T_j's are fixed constants. $$\sum_{j=1}^{k} T_j = \sum_{j=1}^{k} (\mu_{.j} - \mu) = 0$$ (These add to zero as they are the only treatment means being considered.)	1. Assumptions: T_j's are random variables and are $$NID\ (0, \sigma_T^2)$$ (Here σ_T^2 represents the variance among the T_j's or among the true treatment means, μ_j's. The T_j's average to zero when averaged over all possible levels, but for the k levels of the experiment they usually will not average 0.)
2. Analysis: Procedures as given in Chapter 3 for computing SS.	2. Analysis: Same as for fixed model.
3. EMS:	3. EMS:

Source	df	EMS
T_j	$k-1$	$\sigma_e^2 + n\dfrac{\sum\limits^{k} T_j^2}{k-1}$
ϵ_{ij}	$k(n-1)$	σ_e^2

Source	df	EMS
T_j	$k-1$	$\sigma_e^2 + n\sigma_T^2$
ϵ_{ij}	$k(n-1)$	σ_e^2

4. Hypothesis tested:

$$H_0: T_j = 0 \text{ (for all } j)$$

4. Hypothesis tested:

$$H_0: \sigma_T^2 = 0$$

The EMS (expected mean square) column turns out to be extremely important in more complex experiments as an aid in deciding how to set up an F test for significance. The expected mean square for any term in the model is the long-range average of the calculated mean square when the X_{ij} from the model is substituted in algebraic form into the Mean Square computation. The derivation of these EMS values is often complicated, but some of the simpler ones will be derived in a later section. Here the expressions will be assumed correct.

For the fixed model, if the hypothesis is true that $T_j = 0$ for all j; i.e., all the k fixed treatment means are equal, then $\Sigma_j T_j^2 = 0$ and the EMS for T_j and ϵ_{ij} are both σ_e^2. Hence, the observed mean squares for treatments and error mean square are both estimates of the error variance, and they can be compared by means of an F test. If this F test shows a significantly high value, it must mean that $n\,\Sigma_j\, T_j^2/k - 1$ is not zero and the hypothesis is to be rejected.

For the random model, if the hypothesis is true that $\sigma_T^2 = 0$, i.e., the variance among all treatment means is zero, then again each mean square is an estimate of the error variance. Again an F test between the two mean squares is appropriate.

From the two tables in Step 3 above, it is seen that for a single-factor experiment there is no difference in the test to be made after the analysis, and the only difference is in the generality of the conclusions. If H_0 is rejected, there is probably a difference between the k fixed treatment means for the fixed model; for the random model there is a difference between all treatments of which the k examined are but a random sample.

Because of the similarities between the two models, the EMS for the treatment effect is often written as $\sigma_e^2 + n\sigma_T^2$ whether the model is fixed or random. Of course, it is understood that for the fixed case $\sigma_T^2 = \Sigma_j T_j^2/k - 1$ which is really not a variance estimate, as there are only k treatment means. Some authors use $\phi(T)$ for $\Sigma_j T_j^2 / k - 1$ in the fixed case.

10.3   Two-factor Models

For two factors, A and B, the model in the general case is

$$X_{ijk} = \mu + A_i + B_j + AB_{ij} + \epsilon_{k(ij)}$$

$$i = 1, 2, \cdots a \qquad j = 1, 2, \cdots b \qquad k = 1, 2, \cdots n$$

provided the design is completely randomized. In this model, it is again assumed that μ is a fixed constant and $\epsilon_{k(ij)}$'s are $NID(0, \sigma_e^2)$. If both A and B are at fixed levels, the model is a fixed model. If both are at random levels, the model is a random model, and if one is at fixed levels and the other at random levels, the model is a mixed model. Comparing each of these models gives

Fixed	*Random*	*Mixed*
1. Assumptions A_i's are fixed constants and $$\sum_{i=1}^{a} A_i = 0$$	1. Assumptions A_i's are $NID(0, \sigma_A^2)$	1. Assumptions A_i's fixed $$\sum_i^a A_i = 0$$
B_j's are fixed constants and $$\sum_{j=1}^{b} B_j = 0$$	B_j's are $NID(0, \sigma_B^2)$	B_j are $NID(0, \sigma_B^2)$
AB_{ij} are fixed constants and $$\sum_i^a \sum_j^b AB_{ij} = 0$$	AB_{ij}'s are $NID(0, \sigma_{AB}^2)$	AB_{ij} are $NID(0, \sigma_{AB}^2)$ but $$\sum_i^a AB_{ij} = 0$$ $$\sum_j^b AB_{ij} \neq 0.$$ [For A fixed, B random]
2. Analysis Procedures of Chapter 6 for sums of squares	2. Same	2. Same
3. EMS:	3. EMS:	3. EMS:

Source	df	EMS (Fixed)	EMS (Random)	EMS (Mixed)
A_i	$a - 1$	$\sigma_e^2 + nb\dfrac{\sum_i^a A_i^2}{a - 1}$	$\sigma_e^2 + n\sigma_{AB}^2 + nb\sigma_A^2$	$\sigma_e^2 + n\sigma_{AB}^2 + nb\dfrac{\sum_i^a A_i^2}{a - 1}$
B_j	$b - 1$	$\sigma_e^2 + na\dfrac{\sum_j^b B_j^2}{b - 1}$	$\sigma_e^2 + n\sigma_{AB}^2 + na\sigma_B^2$	$\sigma_e^2 + na\sigma_B^2$
AB_{ij}	$(a - 1)(b - 1)$	$\sigma_e^2 + \dfrac{n\sum_i\sum_j AB_{ij}^2}{(a - 1)(b - 1)}$	$\sigma_e^2 + n\sigma_{AB}^2$	$\sigma_e^2 + n\sigma_{AB}^2$
$\epsilon_{k(ij)}$	$ab(n - 1)$	σ_e^2	σ_e^2	σ_e^2

4. Hypotheses tested:

H_1: $A_i = 0$ for all i

H_2: $B_j = 0$ for all j

H_3: $AB_{ij} = 0$ for all i and j

4. Hypotheses tested:

H_1: $\sigma_A^2 = 0$

H_2: $\sigma_B^2 = 0$

H_3: $\sigma_{AB}^2 = 0$

4. Hypotheses tested:

H_1: $A_i = 0$ all i

H_2: $\sigma_B^2 = 0$

H_3: $\sigma_{AB}^2 = 0$

In the assumptions for the mixed model, the fact that summing the interaction term over the fixed factor (Σ_i) is zero but summing it over the random factor (Σ_j) is not zero affects the expected mean squares, as seen in item 3 above.

For the fixed model, the mean squares for A, B and AB are each compared to the error mean square to test the respective hypotheses, as should be clear from an examination of the EMS column when the hypotheses are true. For the random model, the third hypothesis of no interaction is tested by comparing the mean square for interaction to the mean square for error, but the first and second hypotheses are each tested by comparing the mean square for the main effect $(A_i$ or $B_j)$ with the mean square for the interaction as seen by their expected mean square values. For a mixed model, the interaction hypothesis is tested by comparing the interaction mean square with the error mean square. The random effect (B_j) is also tested by comparing its mean square with the error mean square. The fixed effect (A_i), however, is tested by comparing its mean square with the interaction mean square.

From these observations on a two-factor experiment, the importance of the EMS column is evident, as this column can be used to see how the tests of hypotheses should be run. It is also important to note that these EMS expressions can be determined prior to the running of the experiment. This will indicate whether or not a good test of a hypothesis exists. In some cases, the proper test indicated by the EMS column will have insufficient degrees of freedom to be sufficiently sensitive; in which case, the investigator might wish to change the experiment. This would involve such changes as a choice of more levels of some factors, or changing from random to fixed levels of some factors.

10.4   EMS Rules

The two examples above have shown the importance of the EMS column in determining what tests of significance are to be run after the analysis is completed. Because of the importance of this EMS column in these and more complex models, it is often useful to have some simple method of determining these values from the model for the given experiment. A set of rules can be stated which will determine the EMS column very rapidly, without recourse to their derivation. The rules will be illustrated on the two-factor mixed model of Sec. 10.3. To determine the EMS column for any model:

1. Write the variable terms in the model as row headings in a two-way table.

A_i
B_j
AB_{ij}
$\epsilon_{k(ij)}$

2. Write the subscripts in the model as column headings; over each subscript write F if the factor levels are fixed, R if random. Also write the number of observations each subscript is to cover.

	a	b	n
	F	R	R
	i	j	k
A_i			
B_j			
AB_{ij}			
$\epsilon_{k(ij)}$			

3. For each row (each term in the model) copy the number of observations under each subscript, providing the subscript does not appear in the row heading.

	a F i	b R j	n R k
A_i		b	n
B_j	a		n
AB_{ij}			n
$\epsilon_{k(ij)}$			

4. For any bracketed subscripts in the model, place a 1 under those subscripts which are inside the brackets.

	a F i	b R j	n R k
A_i		b	n
B_j	a		n
AB_{ij}			n
$\epsilon_{k(ij)}$	1	1	

5. Fill the remaining cells with a 0 or a 1, depending upon whether the subscript represents a fixed (F) or a random (R) factor.

	a F i	b R j	n R k
A_i	0	b	n
B_j	a	1	n
AB_{ij}	0	1	n
$\epsilon_{k(ij)}$	1	1	1

6. To find the expected mean square for any term in the model:

Cover the entries in the column (or columns) which contain nonbracketed subscript letters in this term in the model (e.g., for A_i, cover column i; for $\epsilon_{k(ij)}$, cover column k).

Multiply the remaining numbers in each row. Each of these products is the coefficient for its corresponding term in the model, provided the subscript on the term is also a subscript on the term whose expected mean square is being determined. The sum of these coefficients multiplied by the variance of their corresponding terms is the expected mean square of the term being considered (e.g., for A_i, cover column i. The products of the remaining coefficients are bn, n, n, and 1, but the first n is not used, as there is no i in its term (B_j). The resulting expected mean square is then $bn\sigma_A^2 + n\sigma_{AB}^2 + 1 \cdot \sigma_e^2$). For all terms, these rules give

	a F i	b R j	n R k	EMS
A_i	0	b	n	$\sigma_e^2 + n\sigma_{AB}^2 + nb\sigma_A^2$
B_j	a	1	n	$\sigma_e^2 + na\sigma_B^2$
AB_{ij}	0	1	n	$\sigma_e^2 + n\sigma_{AB}^2$
$\epsilon_{k(ij)}$	1	1	1	σ_e^2

These results are seen to be in agreement with the expected mean square values for the mixed model in Sec. 10.3. Here, σ_A^2 is, of course, a fixed type of variance

$$\sigma_A^2 = \frac{\sum_i A_i^2}{a - 1}$$

Although the rules seem rather involved, they become very easy to use with a bit of practice. A more complex example will illustrate the point.

EXAMPLE 10.1. An industrial engineering student wished to determine the effect of five different clearances on the time required to position and assemble mating parts. As all such experiments involve operators, it was natural to consider a random sample of operators to perform the experiment. He also decided the part should be assembled directly in front of the operator and at arm's length from the operator. He also tried four different angles, from zero deg directly in front of the operator through 30, 60 and 90 deg from this position. Thus, four factors were involved, any one of which might affect the time required to position and assemble the part. The experimenter decided to replicate each setup six times and to completely randomize the order of experimentation. Here operators (O_i) were at random levels (6 being chosen), angles (A_j) at four fixed levels (0 deg, 30 deg, 60 deg, 90 deg), clearances (C_k) at five fixed levels, and locations (L_m) fixed either in front of or at arm's length from the operator. This is a $6 \times 4 \times 5 \times 2$ factorial experiment with six replications, run in a completely randomized design. The expected mean square values can be determined from the rules given in Sec. 10.4 as shown in Table 10.1.

TABLE 10.1 — EMS For Clearance Problem

Model	6 R i	4 F j	5 F k	2 F m	6 R q	EMS
O_i	1	4	5	2	6	$\sigma_e^2 + 240\sigma_O^2$
A_j	6	0	5	2	6	$\sigma_e^2 + 60\sigma_{OA}^2 + 360\sigma_A^2$
OA_{ij}	1	0	5	2	6	$\sigma_e^2 + 60\sigma_{OA}^2$
C_k	6	4	0	2	6	$\sigma_e^2 + 48\sigma_{OC}^2 + 288\sigma_C^2$
OC_{ik}	1	4	0	2	6	$\sigma_e^2 + 48\sigma_{OC}^2$
AC_{jk}	6	0	0	2	6	$\sigma_e^2 + 12\sigma_{OAC}^2 + 72\sigma_{AC}^2$
OAC_{ijk}	1	0	0	2	6	$\sigma_e^2 + 12\sigma_{OAC}^2$
L_m	6	4	5	0	6	$\sigma_e^2 + 120\sigma_{OL}^2 + 720\sigma_L^2$
OL_{im}	1	4	5	0	6	$\sigma_e^2 + 120\sigma_{OL}^2$
AL_{jm}	6	0	5	0	6	$\sigma_e^2 + 30\sigma_{OAL}^2 + 180\sigma_{AL}^2$
OAL_{ijm}	1	0	5	0	6	$\sigma_e^2 + 30\sigma_{OAL}^2$
CL_{km}	6	4	0	0	6	$\sigma_e^2 + 24\sigma_{OCL}^2 + 144\sigma_{CL}^2$
OCL_{ikm}	1	4	0	0	6	$\sigma_e^2 + 24\sigma_{OCL}^2$
ACL_{jkm}	6	0	0	0	6	$\sigma_e^2 + 6\sigma_{OACL}^2 + 36\sigma_{ACL}^2$
$OACL_{ijkm}$	1	0	0	0	6	$\sigma_e^2 + 6\sigma_{OACL}^2$
$\epsilon_{q(ijkm)}$	1	1	1	1	1	σ_e^2

From this table it is easily seen that all interactions involving operators and the operator main effect are tested against the error mean square at the bottom of the table. All interactions and main effects involving fixed factors are tested by the mean square just below them in the table.

The rules given in this section are general enough to be applied to the most complex designs, as will be seen in later chapters.

10.5   EMS Derivations

Introduction

In order to derive the expected mean square from the model of a given problem, it is necessary to define some terms concerning expected values. The expected value of a random variable, X, can be thought of as its long range, average value, written as

$$E(X) = \mu_X$$

where μ_X is the true mean of all X's in the population. μ_X can also be considered as the weighted value of each X_i where the weights are taken as the probabilities that each X_i occurs. Thus

$$E(X) = \sum_{i=1}^{n} X_i p(X_i) = \mu_X \text{ (for } X \text{ discrete)}$$

$$= \int_{-\infty}^{\infty} x f(x) dx \text{ (for } X \text{ continuous)}$$

As variance is merely the long-range average of squared deviations from the mean, we may write

$$\sigma_X^2 = \sum_{i=1}^{n} (X_i - \mu_X)^2 p(X_i) = E[(X - \mu_X)^2] \text{(for } X \text{ discrete)}$$

$$= \int_{-\infty}^{\infty} (x - \mu_x)^2 f(x) dx \text{ (for } X \text{ continuous)}$$

As s^2 defined in Chapter 2 is unbiased, it follows that

$$E(s^2) = E\left[\sum_{i} (X_i - \bar{X})^2/(n - 1)\right] = \sigma_X^2 \qquad (10.1)$$

which relates the expected value of the sum of squared deviations from a sample mean, $\bar{X}$, to the variance of the population sampled. From this last expression

$$E\left[\sum_{i} (X_i - \bar{X})^2\right] = (n - 1)\sigma_X^2 \qquad (10.2)$$

and in general

$$E\left[\sum_{i} (Q_i - \bar{Q})^2\right] = [\text{df on SS}]\sigma_Q^2 \qquad (10.3)$$

where the coefficient on the right is the degrees of freedom associated with the sum of squares on the left.

Here are a few basic theorems involving expected values that will be useful later

$$E(k) \quad = k \text{ (where } k \text{ is a constant)} \qquad (10.4)$$

$$E(kx) = kE(x) \text{ (where } k \text{ is a constant)} \qquad (10.5)$$

$$E(X_1 + X_2) = E(X_1) + E(X_2) \qquad (10.6)$$

and this may be extended to many variables.

$$E[(X - \mu_X)^2] = E(X^2) - \mu_X^2 = \sigma_X^2 \qquad (10.7)$$

All of these expressions will be used in deriving the expected mean square values by applying the expected value operator E to the mean square of a given term in the model.

Single-Factor Experiment

For a single-factor experiment

$$X_{ij} = \mu + T_j + \epsilon_{ij} \tag{10.8}$$

and it is necessary to determine the expected mean square values for T_j and for ϵ_{ij}.

From Chapter 3, Sec. 3.3, the sum of squares for the treatment effect is given by

$$SS_T = \sum_{j=1}^{k} n(\bar{X}_{.j} - \bar{X}_{..})^2$$

where the number of observations per treatment will be considered constant and equal to n. Using the model of Eq. (10.8)

$$\bar{X}_{.j} = \sum_{i=1}^{n} X_{ij}/n = \sum_{i=1}^{n} \frac{(\mu + T_j + \epsilon_{ij})}{n}$$

$$\bar{X}_{.j} = \frac{n\mu}{n} + \frac{nT_j}{n} + \sum_{i=1}^{n} \epsilon_{ij}/n$$

$$\bar{X}_{.j} = \mu + T_j + \sum_{i=1}^{n} \epsilon_{ij}/n \tag{10.9}$$

Also

$$\bar{X}_{..} = \sum_{j=1}^{k} \sum_{i=1}^{n} X_{ij}/nk = \sum_{j}^{k} \sum_{i}^{n} (\mu + T_j + \epsilon_{ij})/nk$$

$$\bar{X}_{..} = \frac{nk\mu}{nk} + \left(n\sum_{j}^{k} T_j/nk \right) + \left(\sum_{j}^{k} \sum_{i}^{k} \epsilon_{ij}/nk \right)$$

$$= \mu + \left(\sum_{j}^{k} T_j/k \right) + \left(\sum_{j}^{k} \sum_{i}^{n} \epsilon_{ij}/nk \right) \tag{10.10}$$

Subtracting Eq. (10.10) from Eq. (10.9) gives

$$\bar{X}_{.j} - \bar{X}_{..} = T_j - \left(\sum_{j=1}^{k} T_j/k \right) + \left(\sum_{i=1}^{n} \epsilon_{ij}/n \right) - \left(\sum_{i}^{n} \sum_{j}^{k} \epsilon_{ij}/nk \right)$$

Squaring gives

$$(\bar{X}_{.j} - \bar{X}_{..})^2 = \left[T_j - \left(\sum_{j=1}^{k} T_j/k \right) \right]^2 + \frac{1}{n^2}\left[\sum_{i}^{n} \epsilon_{ij} - \left(\sum_{i}^{n} \sum_{j}^{k} \epsilon_{ij}/k \right) \right]^2$$

$(+ \text{ cross products})$

Multiplying by n and summing over j gives

$$\text{SS}_T = \sum_{j=1}^{k} n(\bar{X}_{.j} - \bar{X}_{..})^2 = n\sum_{j}^{k}\left[T_j - \left(\sum_{j}^{k} T_j/k\right)\right]^2 + \frac{n}{n^2}\sum_{j}\left[\sum_{i}^{n}\epsilon_{ij}\right.$$

$$\left. - \left(\sum_{i}^{n}\sum_{j}^{k}\epsilon_{ij}/k\right)\right]^2 + n\sum_{j}\ (\text{cross product})$$

The expected value operator may now be applied to this SS_T

$$E(\text{SS}_T) = nE\left\{\sum_{j}^{k}\left[T_j - \left(\sum_{j}^{k} T_j/k\right)\right]^2\right\} + \frac{1}{n}E\left\{\sum_{j}^{k}\left[\sum_{i}^{n}\epsilon_{ij}\right.\right.$$

$$\left.\left. - \left(\sum_{i}^{n}\sum_{j}^{k}\epsilon_{ij}/k\right)\right]^2\right\}$$

as it can be shown that the expected value of the cross product term equals zero.

If the treatment levels are fixed

$$\sum_{j=1}^{k} T_j = 0$$

and the $E(\text{SS}_T)$ becomes

$$E(\text{SS}_T) = n\sum_{j=1}^{k} T_j^2 + \frac{1}{n}(nk - n)\sigma_e^2$$

since errors are random and $\Sigma_{j=1}^{k} T_j^2$ is a constant. The $E(\text{MS}_T) = E(\text{SS}_T/k - 1)$, so

$$E(\text{MS}_T) = \left(n\sum_{j=1}^{k} T_j^2/k - 1\right) + \frac{n(k-1)}{n(k-1)}\sigma_e^2$$

which agrees with the value in Sec. 10.2. If, however, the treatment levels are random

$$\sum_{j=1}^{k} T_j \neq 0$$

and, using Eq. (10.3)

$$E(\text{MS}_T) = \frac{n(k-1)\sigma_T^2}{(k-1)} + \sigma_e^2$$

which again agrees with the random case in Sec. 10.2.

For the error mean square, from Chapter 3

$$\text{SS}_{\text{error}} = \sum_{j=1}^{k}\sum_{i=1}^{n}(X_{ij} - \bar{X}_{.j})^2$$

Subtracting Eq. (10.9) from Eq. (10.8) gives

$$X_{ij} - \bar{X}_{.j} = \epsilon_{i:} - \sum_{i=1}^{n}\epsilon_{ij}/n$$

Squaring and adding gives

$$\sum_j^k \sum_i^n (X_{ij} - \bar{X}_{.j})^2 = \sum_j^k \sum_i^n \left[\epsilon_{ij} - \left(\sum_i \epsilon_{ij}/n \right) \right]^2$$

Taking the expected value, we have

$$E(\text{SS}_{\text{error}}) = E \sum_j^k \sum_i^n \left[\epsilon_{ij} - \left(\sum_i \epsilon_{ij}/n \right) \right]^2$$

$$= \sum_j^k E \sum_i \left[\epsilon_{ij} - \left(\sum_i \epsilon_{ij}/n \right) \right]^2$$

$$= \sum_j^k (n-1)\sigma_e^2$$

$$= k(n-1)\sigma_e^2$$

and

$$E(\text{MS}_e) = E\left(\frac{\text{SS}_e}{k[n-1]} \right) = \sigma_e^2$$

as expected.

Two-Factor Experiment

For a two-factor experiment, the model is

$$X_{ijk} = \mu + A_i + B_j + AB_{ij} + \epsilon_{k(ij)} \qquad (10.11)$$

and $i = 1, 2, \ \cdot \ a; \ j = 1, 2, \ \cdot \ b; \ k = 1, 2, \cdot \cdot \cdot n.$

The sum of squares for Factor A is

$$\text{SS}_A = \sum_{i=1}^a nb(\bar{X}_{i..} - \bar{X}_{...})^2$$

From the model in Eq. (10.11)

$$\bar{X}_{i..} = \left(\sum_j^b \sum_k^n X_{ijk}/bn \right) = \left(\sum_j^b \sum_k^n [\mu + A_i + B_j + AB_{ij} + \epsilon_{k(ij)}]/bn \right)$$

$$\bar{X}_{i..} = \mu + A_i + \left(\sum_j^b B_j/b \right) + \left(\sum_j^b AB_{ij}/b \right) + \left(\sum_j^b \sum_k^n \epsilon_{k(ij)}/bn \right)$$

$$\bar{X}_{...} = \left(\sum_i^a \sum_j^b \sum_k^n X_{ijk}/abn \right) = \left(\sum_i^a \sum_j^b \sum_k^n [\mu + A_i + B_j + AB_{ij} \right.$$
$$\left. + \epsilon_{k(ij)}]/abn \right)$$

$$\bar{X}_{...} = \mu + \left(\sum_i^a A_i/a \right) + \left(\sum_j^b B_j/b \right) + \left(\sum_i^a \sum_j^b AB_{ij}/ab \right)$$
$$+ \left(\sum_i^a \sum_j^b \sum_k^n \epsilon_{k(ij)}/nab \right)$$

Subtracting gives

$$\bar{X}_{i..} - \bar{X}_{...} = \left[A_i - \left(\sum_i^a A_i/a \right) \right] + \left[\left(\sum_j^b AB_{ij}/b \right) \right.$$

$$\left. - \left(\sum_i^a \sum_j^b AB_{ij}/ab \right) \right] + \left[\left(\sum_j^b \sum_k^n \epsilon_{k(ij)}/bn \right) - \left(\sum_i^a \sum_j^b \sum_k^n \epsilon_{k(ij)}/abn \right) \right]$$

note that the B effect cancels out of the A sum of squares as it should, since A and B are orthogonal effects in a factorial experiment. Squaring and adding gives

$$SS_A = nb \sum_{i=1}^a \left[A_i - \left(\sum_i^a A_i/a \right) \right]^2 + nb \sum_{i=1}^a \left[\left(\sum_j^b AB_{ij}/b \right) \right.$$

$$\left. - \left(\sum_i^a \sum_j^b AB_{ij}/ab \right) \right]^2 + nb \sum_{i=1}^a \left[\left(\sum_j^b \sum_k^n \epsilon_{k(ij)}/bn \right) \right. \qquad (10.12)$$

$$\left. - \left(\sum_i^a \sum_j^b \sum_k^n \epsilon_{k(ij)}/abn \right) \right]^2 + \text{(cross product terms)}$$

Taking the expected value for a fixed model where

$$\sum_i A_i = 0 \qquad \sum_{i \, \text{or} \, j} AB_{ij} = 0$$

the result is

$$E(SS_A) = nb \sum_i^a A_i^2 + 0 + \frac{nb}{n^2 b^2}(abn - bn)\sigma_e^2$$

$$E(MS_A) = E(SS_A/a-1) = \left(nb \sum_{i=1}^a A_i^2/a - 1 \right) + \sigma_e^2$$

which agrees with Sec. 10.3 for the fixed model.
    If now the levels of A and B are random

$$\sum_i A_i \neq 0 \qquad \sum_{i \, \text{or} \, j} AB_{ij} \neq 0$$

$$E(SS_A) = nb(a - 1)\sigma_A^2 + \frac{nb}{b^2}(ab - b)\sigma_{AB}^2 + \frac{nb}{n^2 b^2}(abn - bn)\sigma_e^2$$

$$E(MS_A) = nb \, \sigma_A^2 + n\sigma_{AB}^2 + \sigma_e^2$$

as stated in Sec. 10.3 for a random model.

If the model is mixed with A fixed and B random

$$\sum_i^a A_i = 0 \qquad \sum_i^a AB_{ij} = 0$$

but

$$\sum_j^b AB_{ij} \neq 0$$

then

$$E(SS_A) = nb\sum_i^a A_i^2 + \frac{nb}{b^2}(ab - b)\sigma_{AB}^2 + \frac{nb}{n^2b^2}(nab - nb)\sigma_e^2$$

$$E(MS_A) = \left(nb\sum_i^a A_i^2/a - 1\right) + n\,\sigma_{AB}^2 + \sigma_e^2$$

which agrees with the value stated in Sec. 10.3 for a mixed model.

Using these expected value methods, one can derive all expected mean square values given in Sec. 10.3. It might be noted that if A were random in the mixed model

$$\sum_j^b AB_{ij} = 0$$

then the interaction term would not appear in the Factor A sum of squares. This is true of B in the mixed model of Sec. 10.3.

These few derivations should be sufficient to show the general method of derivation and to demonstrate the advantages of the simple rules in Sec. 10.4 in determining these EMS values.

10.6   Remarks

The examples in this chapter should be sufficient to show the importance of the EMS column in deciding just what mean squares should be compared in an F test of a given hypothesis. This EMS column is also useful (usually in random models) to solve for components of variance as illustrated in Chapter 3, Sec. 3.5.

One special case is of interest. In a two-factor factorial when there is but one observation per cell [$k = 1$], the EMS columns of Sec. 10.3 reduce to those in Table 10.2.

TABLE 10.2 — EMS for One Observation per Cell

Model	EMS (Fixed)	EMS (Random)	EMS (Mixed)
A_i	$\sigma_e^2 + b\sigma_A^2$	$\sigma_e^2 + \sigma_{AB}^2 + b\sigma_A^2$	$\sigma_e^2 + \sigma_{AB}^2 + b\sigma_A^2$
B_j	$\sigma_e^2 + a\sigma_B^2$	$\sigma_e^2 + \sigma_{AB}^2 + a\sigma_B^2$	$\sigma_e^2 + a\sigma_B^2$
AB_{ij} or ϵ_{ij}	$\sigma_e^2 + \sigma_{AB}^2$	$\sigma_e^2 + \sigma_{AB}^2$	$\sigma_e^2 + \sigma_{AB}^2$

where σ^2 is used whether fixed or random. A glance at these expected mean square values will show that there is no test for the main effects A and B in a fixed model, as interaction and error are hopelessly confounded. The only test possible is to assume that there is no interaction; then $\sigma_{AB}^2 = 0$, and the main effects are tested against the error. If a no-interaction assumption is not reasonable from information outside the experiment, the investigator should not run one observation per cell but should replicate the data in a fixed model.

For a random model, both main effects can be tested whether interaction is present or not. For a mixed model, there is a test for the fixed effect A but no test for the random effect B. This may not be a serious drawback, since the fixed effect is often the most important; the B effect is included chiefly for reduction of the error term. Such a situation is seen in a randomized block design where treatments are fixed, but blocks may be chosen at random.

In the discussion of the single-factor experiment, it was assumed that there were equal sample sizes (n's) for each treatment. If this is not the case, it can be shown that the expected treatment mean square is

$$\sigma_e^2 + n_0 \sigma_T^2$$

and

$$n_0 = \frac{N^2 - \sum_{j=1}^{k} n_j^2}{(k-1)N}$$

where

$$N = \sum_{j=1}^{k} n_j$$

The test for treatment effect is to compare the treatment mean square to the error mean square; the use of n_0 is primarily for computing components of variance.

PROBLEMS

10-1.   An experiment is run on the effects of three randomly selected operators and five fixed aluminizers on the aluminum thickness of a TV tube. Two readings are made for each operator-aluminizer combination. The following ANOVA table is compiled:

Source	df	SS	MS
Operators	2	107,540	53,770
Aluminizers	4	139,805	34,951
$O \times A$ interaction	8	84,785	10,598
Error	15	230,900	15,393
TOTALS	29	563,030	

Assuming complete randomization, determine the EMS column for this problem and make the indicated significance tests.

10-2. Consider a three-factor experiment where Factor A is at a levels, Factor B at b levels, and Factor C at c levels. The experiment is to be run in a completely randomized manner with n observations for each treatment combination. If Factor A is run at a random levels and both B and C at fixed levels, determine the EMS column and indicate what tests would be made after the analysis.

10-3. Repeat Prob. 10-2 with A and B at random levels, but C at fixed levels.

10-4. Repeat Prob. 10-2 with all three factors at random levels.

10-5. Consider the completely randomized design of a four-factor experiment similar to Example 10.1. If Factors A and B are at fixed levels and C and D are at random levels, set up the EMS column and indicate the tests to be made.

10-6. If three factors are at random levels and one is at fixed levels in Prob. 10-5, work out the EMS column and the tests to be run.

10-7. Determine the EMS column for Prob. 3-6 and solve for components of variance.

10-8. Derive the expression for n_0 in the EMS column of a single-factor completely randomized experiment, where the n's are unequal.

CHAPTER 11

Nested and Nested-Factorial Experiments

11.1 Introduction

In a recent in-plant training course, the members of the class were assigned a final problem. Each class member was to go into the plant and set up an experiment using the techniques that had been discussed in class. One engineer wanted to study the strain readings of glass cathode supports from five different machines. Each machine had four "heads" on which the glass was formed, and he decided to take four samples from each head. He treated this experiment as a 5 × 4 factorial with four replications per cell. Complete randomization of the testing for strain readings presented no problem. His model was

$$X_{ijk} = \mu + M_i + H_j + MH_{ij} + \epsilon_{k(ij)}$$

where $i = 1, 2, \cdots 5$; $j = 1, \cdots 4$; $k = 1, \cdots 4$. His data and analysis appear in Table 11.1.

In this model, he assumed that both machines and heads were fixed, and he used the 10 percent significance level. The results indicated no significant machine or head effect on strain readings, but there was a significant interaction at the 10 percent level of significance.

The question was raised whether the four heads were actually removed from machine A and mounted on machine B, then on C, etc. Of course, the answer was "no" as each machine had its own four heads. So machines and heads did not form a factorial experiment, as the heads

TABLE 11.1 — Data and ANOVA for Strain Readings

		Machines			
Heads	A	B	C	D	E
1	6	10	0	11	1
	2	9	0	0	4
	0	7	5	6	7
	8	12	5	4	9
2	13	2	10	5	6
	3	1	11	10	7
	9	1	6	8	0
	8	10	7	3	3
3	1	4	8	1	3
	10	1	5	8	0
	0	7	0	9	2
	6	9	7	4	2
4	7	0	7	0	3
	4	3	2	8	7
	7	4	5	6	4
	9	1	4	5	0

Source	df	SS	MS	EMS	F	$F_{0.90}$
M_i	4	45.08	11.27	$\sigma_e^2 + 16\sigma_M^2$	1.05	2.04
H_j	3	46.45	15.48	$\sigma_e^2 + 20\sigma_H^2$	1.45	2.18
MH_{ij}	12	236.42	19.70	$\sigma_e^2 + 4\sigma_{MH}^2$	1.84	1.66
$\epsilon_{k(ij)}$	60	642.00	10.70	σ_e^2		
TOTALS	79	969.95				

on each machine were unique for that particular machine. In such a case, the experiment is called a *nested experiment:* levels of one factor are nested within, or are subsamples of, levels of another factor. Such experiments are also sometimes called *hierarchical* experiments.

11.2   Nested Experiments

The above example can now be reanalyzed by treating it as a nested experiment, since heads are nested within machines. Such a factor may be represented in the model as $H_{j(i)}$, where j covers all levels $1, 2 \cdots$ within the ith level of M_i. The number of levels of the nested factor need not be the same for all levels of the other factor. They are all equal in this problem; i.e., $j = 1, 2, 3, 4$ for all i. The errors, in turn, are nested within the levels of i and j; $\epsilon_{k(ij)}$ and $k = 1, 2, 3, 4$ for all i and j.

In order to emphasize the fact that the heads on each machine are different heads, the data layout in Table 11.2 shows heads 1, 2, 3 and 4 on machine A; heads 5, 6, 7 and 8 on machine B; etc.

TABLE 11.2 — Data for Strain-Reading Problem in a Nested Arrangement

Machines	A				B				C				D				E			
Heads	1	2	3	4	5	6	7	8	9	10	11	12	13	14	15	16	17	18	19	20
	6	13	1	7	10	2	4	0	0	10	8	7	11	5	1	0	1	6	3	3
	2	3	10	4	9	1	1	3	0	11	5	2	0	10	8	8	4	7	0	7
	0	9	0	7	7	1	7	4	5	6	0	5	6	8	9	6	7	0	2	4
	8	8	6	9	12	10	9	1	5	7	7	4	4	3	4	5	9	3	2	0
Head Totals	16	33	17	27	38	14	21	8	10	34	20	18	21	26	22	19	21	16	7	14
Machine Totals	93				81				82				88				58			

As the heads which are mounted on the machine can be chosen from many possible heads, we might consider the four heads as a random sample of heads that might be used on a given machine. If such heads are selected at random for the machines, the model would be

$$X_{ijk} = \mu + M_i + H_{j(i)} + \epsilon_{k(ij)}$$

where $i = 1, \cdots 5; \; j = 1, \cdots 4; \; k = 1, \cdots 4$.

This nested model has no interaction present, as the heads are not crossed with the five machines. If heads are considered random and machines fixed, the proper expected mean square values can be determined by the rules given in Chapter 10, as shown in Table 11.3.

TABLE 11.3 — EMS for Nested Experiment

Model	5 F i	4 R j	4 R k	EMS
M_i	0	4	4	$\sigma_e^2 + 4\sigma_H^2 + 16\sigma_M^2$
$H_{j(i)}$	1	1	4	$\sigma_e^2 + 4\sigma_H^2$
$\epsilon_{k(ij)}$	1	1	1	σ_e^2

This breakdown shows that the head effect is to be tested against the error, and the machine effect is to be tested against the heads-within-machines effect.

To analyze the data for a nested design, first determine the total sum of squares

$$SS_{total} = 6^2 + 2^2 + \cdots + 4^2 + 0^2 - \frac{(402)^2}{80} = 969.95$$

and for machines

$$SS_M = \frac{(93)^2 + (81)^2 + (82)^2 + (88)^2 + (58)^2}{16} - \frac{(402)^2}{80} = 45.08$$

To determine the sum of squares between heads within machines, consider each machine separately:

Machine A:

$$SS_H = \frac{(16)^2 + (33)^2 + (17)^2 + (27)^2}{4} - \frac{(93)^2}{16} = 50.19$$

Machine B:

$$SS_H = \frac{(38)^2 + (14)^2 + (21)^2 + (8)^2}{4} - \frac{(81)^2}{16} = 126.18$$

Machine C:

$$SS_H = \frac{(10)^2 + (34)^2 + (20)^2 + (18)^2}{4} - \frac{(82)^2}{16} = 74.75$$

Machine D:

$$SS_H = \frac{(21)^2 + (26)^2 + (22)^2 + (19)^2}{4} - \frac{(88)^2}{16} = 6.50$$

Machine E:

$$SS_H = \frac{(21)^2 + (16)^2 + (7)^2 + (14)^2}{4} - \frac{(58)^2}{16} = 25.25$$

Total $SS_H = 282.87$

The error sum of squares by subtraction is then

$$969.95 - 45.08 - 282.87 = 642.00$$

The degrees of freedom between heads within machine A are $4 - 1 = 3$; for all five machines, the degrees of freedom will be $5 \times 3 = 15$. The analysis follows in Table 11.4.

TABLE 11.4 — ANOVA for Nested Strain-Reading Problem

Source	df	SS	MS	EMS	F	$F_{0.90}$
M_i	4	45.08	11.27	$\sigma_e^2 + 4\sigma_H^2 + 16\sigma_M^2$	<1	2.36
$H_{j(i)}$	15	282.87	18.85	$\sigma_e^2 + 4\sigma_H^2$	1.76	1.60
$\epsilon_{k(ij)}$	60	642.00	10.70	σ_e^2		
TOTALS	79	969.95				

From this analysis, machines appear to have no significant effect on strain readings, but there is a slightly significant (10 percent level) effect of heads within machines on the strain readings. Note that what the experimenter took as head effect (3 df) and interaction effect (12 df) is really heads-within-machines effect (15 df). These results might suggest a more careful adjustment between heads on the same machine. In a nested model, it is also seen that the 5 SS between heads within each machine are "pooled," or added, to give 282.87. This assumes that these sums of squares (which are proportional to variances) within each machine are of about the same magnitude. This might be questioned, as these sums of squares are 50.19, 126.18, 74.75, 6.50, and 25.25. If these five are really different, it appears as if the greatest variability is in machine B. This should indicate the need for work on each machine with an aim toward more homogeneous strain readings between heads on each machine. This example shows the importance of recognizing the difference between a nested experiment and a factorial experiment.

11.3 ANOVA Rationale

To see that the sums of squares computed in Sec. 11.2 were correct, consider the nested model

$$X_{ijk} = \mu + A_i + B_{j(i)} + \epsilon_{k(ij)}$$

or

$$X_{ijk} \equiv \mu + (\mu_{i..} - \mu) + (\mu_{ij.} - \mu_{i..}) + (X_{ijk} - \mu_{ij.})$$

which is an identity.

Using the best estimates of these population means from the sample data, the sample model is

$$X_{ijk} \equiv \bar{X}_{...} + (\bar{X}_{i..} - \bar{X}_{...}) + (\bar{X}_{ij.} - \bar{X}_{i..}) + (X_{ijk} - \bar{X}_{ij.})$$

where $i = 1, 2, \cdots a; j = 1, 2, \cdots b; k = 1, 2, \cdots n$. Transposing $\bar{X}_{...}$ to the left of this expression, squaring both sides, and adding over i, j and k gives

$$\sum_i^a \sum_j^b \sum_k^n (X_{ijk} - \bar{X}_{...})^2 = \sum_{i=1}^a nb(\bar{X}_{i..} - \bar{X}_{...})^2 + \sum_i^a \sum_j^b n(\bar{X}_{ij.} - \bar{X}_{i..})^2$$
$$+ \sum_i^a \sum_j^b \sum_k^n (X_{ijk} - \bar{X}_{ij.})^2$$

as the sums of cross products equal zero. This expresses the idea that the total sum of squares is equal to the sum of squares between levels of A, plus the sum of squares between levels of B within each level of A, plus the sum of the squares of the errors. The degrees of freedom are

$$(abn - 1) \equiv (a - 1) + a(b - 1) + ab(n - 1)$$

Dividing each independent sum of squares by its corresponding degrees of freedom gives estimates of population variance as usual. For computing purposes, the sum of squares as given above should be expanded in terms of totals, with the general results shown in Table 11.5.

TABLE 11.5 — General ANOVA for a Nested Experiment

Source	df	SS	MS
A_i	$a - 1$	$\sum_i^a \dfrac{T_{i..}^2}{nb} - \dfrac{T_{...}^2}{nab}$	$\dfrac{SS_A}{a - 1}$
$B_{j(i)}$	$a(b - 1)$	$\sum_i^a \sum_j^b \dfrac{T_{ij.}^2}{n} - \sum_i^a \dfrac{T_{i..}^2}{nb}$	$\dfrac{SS_B}{a(b - 1)}$
$\epsilon_{k(ij)}$	$ab(n - 1)$	$\sum_i^a \sum_j^b \sum_k^n X_{ijk}^2 - \sum_i^a \sum_j^b \dfrac{T_{ij.}^2}{n}$	$\dfrac{SS_e}{ab(n - 1)}$
TOTALS	$abn - 1$	$\sum_i^a \sum_j^b \sum_k^n X_{ijk}^2 - \dfrac{T_{...}^2}{nab}$	

This is essentially the form followed in the problem of the last section. Note that the

$$SS_{Bj(i)} = \sum_i^a \sum_j^b \frac{T_{ij.}^2}{n} - \sum_i^a \frac{T_{i..}^2}{nb}$$
$$= \sum_i^a \left(\sum_j^b \frac{T_{ij.}^2}{n} - \frac{T_{i..}^2}{nb} \right)$$

which shows the way in which the sum of squares was calculated in the last section: by getting the sum of squares between levels of B for each level of A, and then pooling over all levels of A.

11.4   Nested-Factorial Experiments

In many experiments where several factors are involved, some may be factorial or crossed with others; some may be nested within levels of the others. When both factorial and nested factors appear in the same experiment, it is known as a *nested-factorial experiment*. The analysis of such an experiment is simply an extension of the methods of Chapter 6 and this chapter. Care must be exercised, however, in computing some of the interactions. Levels of both factorial and nested factors may be either fixed or random. The methods of Chapter 10 can be used to determine the expected mean square values and the proper tests to be run.

The nested-factorial is best explained by an example. An investigator wished to improve the number of rounds per minute that could be fired from a Navy gun. He devised a new loading method which he hoped would increase the number of rounds per minute when compared to the existing method of loading. To test his hypothesis, he needed teams of men to operate the equipment. As the general physique of a man might affect the speed with which he could handle the loading of the gun, he chose teams of men in three general groupings — slight, average, and heavy or rugged men. The classification of such men was on the basis of an Armed Services Classification table. He chose three teams at random to represent each of the three physique groupings. Each team was presented with the two methods of gun loading in a random order and each team used each method twice. The model for this experiment was

$$X_{ijkm} = \mu + M_i + G_j + MG_{ij} + T_{k(j)} + MT_{ik(j)} + \epsilon_{m(ijk)}$$

where M_i represents methods: $i = 1, 2$
G_j represents groups: $j = 1, 2, 3$
$T_{k(j)}$ represents teams within groups: $k = 1, 2, 3$ for all j
$\epsilon_{m(ijk)}$ represents random error: $m = 1, 2$ for all i, j, k.

The EMS values are shown in Table 11.6.

TABLE 11.6 — EMS for Gun-Loading Problem

Model	2 F i	3 F j	3 R k	2 R m	EMS
M_i	0	3	3	2	$\sigma_e^2 + 2\sigma_{MT}^2 + 18\sigma_M^2$
G_j	2	0	3	2	$\sigma_e^2 + 4\sigma_T^2 + 12\sigma_G^2$
MG_{ij}	0	0	3	2	$\sigma_e^2 + 2\sigma_{MT}^2 + 6\sigma_{MG}^2$
$T_{k(j)}$	2	1	1	2	$\sigma_e^2 + 4\sigma_T^2$
$MT_{ik(j)}$	0	1	1	2	$\sigma_e^2 + 2\sigma_{MT}^2$
$\epsilon_{m(ijk)}$	1	1	1	1	σ_e^2

which indicates the proper F tests to run.

The data and analysis of this experiment appear in Table 11.7.

TABLE 11.7 — Data and ANOVA for Gun-Loading Problem

Groups	I			II			III		
Teams	1	2	3	4	5	6	7	8	9
Method	20.2	26.2	23.8	22.0	22.6	22.9	23.1	22.9	21.8
I	24.1	26.9	24.9	23.5	24.6	25.0	22.9	23.7	23.5
Method	14.2	18.0	12.5	14.1	14.0	13.7	14.1	12.2	12.7
II	16.2	19.1	15.4	16.1	18.1	16.0	16.1	13.8	15.1

Source	df	SS	MS	EMS
M_i	1	651.95	651.95	$\sigma_e^2 + 2\sigma_{MT}^2 + 18\sigma_M^2$
G_j	2	16.05	8.02	$\sigma_e^2 + 4\sigma_T^2 + 12\sigma_G^2$
MG_{ij}	2	1.19	0.60	$\sigma_e^2 + 2\sigma_{MT}^2 + 6\sigma_{MG}^2$
$T_{k(j)}$	6	39.23	6.54	$\sigma_e^2 + 4\sigma_T^2$
$MT_{ik(j)}$	6	10.75	1.79	$\sigma_e^2 + 2\sigma_{MT}^2$
$\epsilon_{m(ijk)}$	18	41.59	2.31	σ_e^2
TOTALS	35	760.76		

It would be well for the reader to verify that the sums of squares of this table are correct. The only term that is somewhat different in this model than those previously handled is $MT_{ik(j)}$ — the interaction between methods and teams within groups. The safest way to compute this term is to compute the $M \times T$ interaction sums of squares within each of the three groups separately and then pool these sums of squares. (See Table 11.8 through Table 11.10.)

TABLE 11.8 — Data on Gun-Loading Problem for Group I

Teams	1	2	3	Method Totals
Method I	20.2 24.1 / / 44.3	26.2 26.9 / / 53.1	23.8 24.9 / / 48.7	146.1
Method II	14.2 16.2 / / 30.4	18.0 19.1 / / 37.1	12.5 15.4 / / 27.9	95.4
TEAM TOTALS	74.7	90.2	76.6	241.5

To compute the $M \times T$ interaction for Group I, we have

$$SS_{cell} = \frac{(44.3)^2 + (53.1)^2 + (48.7)^2 + (30.4)^2 + (37.1)^2 + (27.9)^2}{2}$$
$$- \frac{(241.5)^2}{12} = 5{,}116.39 - 4{,}860.21 = 256.18$$

$$SS_{method} = \frac{(146.1)^2 + (95.4)^2}{6} - 4860.21 = 214.19$$

$$SS_{team} = \frac{(74.7)^2 + (90.2)^2 + (76.6)^2}{4} - 4860.21 = 35.71$$

$$SS_{M \times T \text{ (interaction)}} = 256.18 - 214.19 - 35.71 = 6.28$$

TABLE 11.9 — Gun-Loading Data for Group II

Teams	4	5	6	Method Totals
Method I	22.0 23.5 / 45.5	22.6 24.6 / 47.2	22.9 25.0 / 47.9	140.6
Method II	14.1 16.1 / 30.2	14.0 18.1 / 32.1	13.7 16.0 / 29.7	92.0
TEAM TOTALS	75.7	79.3	77.6	232.6

$$SS_{cell} = \frac{(45.5)^2 + (47.2)^2 + (47.9)^2 + (30.2)^2 + (32.1)^2 + (29.7)^2}{2}$$
$$- \frac{(232.6)^2}{12} = 199.96$$

$$SS_{method} = \frac{(140.6)^2 + (92.0)^2}{6} - 4508.56 = 196.83$$

$$SS_{team} = \frac{(75.7)^2 + (79.3)^2 + (77.6)^2}{4} - 4508.56 = 1.62$$

$$SS_{M \times T \text{ interaction}} = 199.96 - 196.83 - 1.62 = 1.51$$

TABLE 11.10 — Gun-Loading Data for Group III

Teams	7	8	9	Method Totals
Method I	23.1 22.9 / 46.0	22.9 23.7 / 46.6	21.8 23.5 / 45.3	137.9
Method II	14.1 16.1 / 30.2	12.2 13.8 / 26.0	12.7 15.1 / 27.8	84.0
TEAM TOTALS	76.2	72.6	73.1	221.9

$$SS_{cell} = \frac{(46.0)^2 + (46.6)^2 + (45.3)^2 + (30.2)^2 + (26.0)^2 + (27.8)^2}{2}$$
$$- \frac{(221.9)^2}{12} = 246.96$$

$$SS_{method} = \frac{(137.9)^2 + (84.0)^2}{6} - 4103.30 = 242.10$$

$$SS_{team} = \frac{(76.2)^2 + (72.6)^2 + (73.1)^2}{4} - 4103.30 = 1.90$$

$$SS_{M \times T \text{ interaction}} = 246.96 - 242.10 - 1.90 = 2.96$$

Pooling for all three groups gives

$$SS_{M \times T} = 6.28 + 1.51 + 2.96 = 10.75$$

which is recorded in Table 11.7.

The results of this experiment show a very significant method effect (the new method averaged 23.58 rounds per min, and the old method averaged only 15.08 rounds per min). The results also show a significant difference between teams within groups at the 5 percent significance level. This points up individual differences in the men. No other effects or interactions were significant.

11.5 Summary

The summary at the end of Chapter 7 (Sec. 7.5) may now be extended for Part II.

Experiment	*Design*	*Analysis*
II. Two or More Factors		
A. Factorial (crossed)		
	1. Completely Randomized $X_{ijk} = \mu + A_i + B_j + AB_{ij} + \epsilon_{k(ij)}$, etc., for more factors	1.
	a. General Case	*a.* ANOVA with interactions
	b. 2^n case	*b.* Yates Method or general ANOVA Use: (1) a,b,ab, etc.
	c.	*c.* General ANOVA Use: 00,10,20,01,11, etc. and, $A \times B = AB + AB^2$ etc., for interaction

B. Nested
(Hierarchical)

        1. Completely   1. ANOVA (nested)
        Randomized
        $X_{ijk} = \mu + A_i + B_{j(i)}$
        $+ \epsilon_{k(ij)}$

C. Nested-
  Factorial

        1. Completely   1. ANOVA
        Randomized   (nested-factorial)
        $X_{ijkm} = \mu + A_i + B_{j(i)}$
        $+ C_k + AC_{ik} + BC_{jk(i)}$
        $+ \epsilon_{m(ijk)}$ etc.

PROBLEMS

11-1.   Porosity readings on condenser paper were recorded for paper from four rolls taken at random from each of three lots. The results were as follows. Analyze these data, assuming lots are fixed and rolls random.

Lot	I				II				III			
Roll	1	2	3	4	5	6	7	8	9	10	11	12
	1.5	1.5	2.7	3.0	1.9	2.3	1.8	1.9	2.5	3.2	1.4	7.8
	1.7	1.6	1.9	2.4	1.5	2.4	2.9	3.5	2.9	5.5	1.5	5.2
	1.6	1.7	2.0	2.6	2.1	2.4	4.7	2.8	3.3	7.1	3.4	5.0

11-2.   In Prob. 11.1, how do the results change (if they change) if the lots were chosen at random?

11-3.   Set up the EMS column and indicate the proper tests to make if A is a fixed factor at five levels, B is nested within A at four random levels for each level of A, C is nested within B at three random levels, and two observations are made in each "cell."

11-4.   Repeat Prob. 11-3 for A and B crossed or factorial and C nested within the A, B cells.

11-5.   Two types of machines are used to wind coils. One type is hand-operated; two machines of this type are available. The other type is power-operated; two machines of this type are available. Three coils are wound on each machine from two different wiring stocks. Each coil is then measured for the outside diameter of the wire at a middle position on the coil. The results were as follows. (Units are 10^{-5} in.)

Machine Type	Hand		Power	
Machine No.	2	3	5	8
Stock 1	3279	3527	1904	2464
	3262	3136	2166	2595
	3246	3253	2058	2303
Stock 2	3294	3440	2188	2429
	2974	3356	2105	2410
	3157	3240	2379	2685

Set up the model for this problem and determine what tests can be run.

11-6. Do a complete analysis of Prob. 11-5.

11-7. If the outside diameter readings in Prob. 11-5 were taken at three fixed positions on the coil (tip, middle, and end), what model would now be appropriate and what tests could be run?

11-8. Some research on the abrasive resistance of filled epoxy plastics was carried out by molding blocks of plastic using five fillers: iron oxide, iron filings, copper, alumina, and graphite. Two concentration ratios were used for the ratio of filler to epoxy resin: 1/2 : 1, and 1 : 1. Three sample blocks were made up of each of the 10 combinations above. These blocks were then subjected to a reciprocating motion where gritcloth was used as the abrasive material in all tests. After 10,000 cycles, each sample block was measured in three places at each of three fixed positions on the plates: I, II, and III. These blocks had been measured before cycling so that the difference in thickness was used as the measured variable. Measurements were made to the nearest 0.0001 in. Assuming complete randomization of the order of testing of the 30 blocks, set up a mathematical model for this situation and set up the ANOVA table with an EMS column. We are interested in the effect of concentration ratio, fillers, and positions on the block. The three observations at each position will be considered as error, and there may well be differences between the average of the three sample blocks within each treatment combination.

11-9. Data for Prob. 11-8 were found to be as follows here and on the next page. Complete an ANOVA for these data and state your conclusions.

11-10. From the results of Prob. 11-9, what filler-concentration combination would you recommend if you were interested in a minimum amount of wear? The 1 : 1 ratio is cheaper than 1/2 : 1.

Concentration	Alumina						Graphite					
	1/2 : 1			1 : 1			1/2 : 1			1 : 1		
Position	I	II	III	I	II	III	I	II	III	I	II	III
Sample 1	7.0	5.4	6.4	7.1	5.0	6.4	8.8	5.5	9.0	18.0	14.4	18.5
	7.3	5.1	5.7	6.9	5.7	6.6	8.3	5.9	11.0	17.6	12.4	19.2
	6.6	5.0	7.7	6.5	4.0	6.2	6.9	4.7	11.3	18.4	12.6	19.4
	20.9	15.5	19.8	20.5	14.7	19.2	24.0	16.1	31.3	54.0	39.4	57.1
Sample 2	6.8	5.1	4.6	6.8	4.0	7.5	7.7	6.8	10.1	15.6	11.6	17.6
	6.9	5.5	5.8	7.2	5.2	7.8	6.5	7.0	11.2	14.6	12.8	18.7
	6.2	4.8	5.8	4.8	4.4	6.0	5.9	7.2	10.8	15.1	13.4	19.3
	19.9	15.4	16.2	18.8	13.6	21.3	20.1	21.0	32.1	45.3	37.8	55.6
Sample 3	7.3	6.3	5.1	6.2	4.4	5.7	7.2	7.0	7.7	13.3	11.7	15.5
	7.6	5.3	6.5	6.6	4.8	6.6	6.8	6.9	9.3	13.8	13.4	18.0
	5.6	4.8	7.1	4.4	3.8	5.6	6.2	5.2	9.8	13.6	12.1	19.6
	20.5	16.4	18.7	17.2	13.0	17.9	20.2	19.1	26.8	40.7	37.2	53.1
TOTALS	163.3			156.2			210.7			420.2		

	Iron Filings						Iron Oxide						Copper					
	1/2 : 1			1 : 1			1/2 : 1			1 : 1			1/2 : 1			1 : 1		
Concentration																		
Position	I	II	III	I	II	III	I	II	III	I	II	III	I	II	III	I	II	III
Sample 1	2.1	1.1	1.3	3.6	1.6	2.3	3.0	1.1	3.2	1.8	1.3	2.4	2.7	1.4	2.8	2.8	1.5	2.4
	2.1	1.1	1.7	3.8	1.0	2.5	3.8	1.8	4.1	2.1	1.0	1.9	2.9	2.2	3.8	2.6	1.1	2.1
	1.0	0.9	1.7	2.9	1.6	2.4	3.0	1.1	3.3	1.9	1.6	1.8	3.0	1.8	3.4	1.9	1.4	2.0
	5.2	3.1	4.7	10.3	4.2	7.2	9.8	4.0	10.6	5.8	3.9	6.1	8.6	5.4	10.0	7.3	4.0	6.5
Sample 2	1.7	1.1	1.7	2.1	1.1	1.7	3.1	1.6	2.2	2.1	1.0	1.5	2.5	1.8	2.4	2.1	1.0	1.5
	1.8	1.0	2.0	2.6	1.1	1.0	3.0	1.7	3.0	2.0	0.8	2.0	3.0	2.6	3.3	2.5	1.0	1.6
	1.3	0.8	2.0	1.6	0.9	1.4	2.7	1.2	2.7	2.3	1.0	2.0	2.0	2.1	2.4	1.5	1.2	1.7
	4.8	2.9	5.7	6.3	3.1	4.1	8.8	4.5	7.9	6.4	2.8	5.5	7.5	6.5	8.1	6.1	3.2	4.8
Sample 3	3.2	0.8	1.4	2.3	1.1	1.8	2.1	1.5	2.0	1.6	1.2	1.6	3.3	2.1	3.4	2.6	1.3	2.6
	2.8	0.8	2.0	2.6	1.2	2.0	2.9	1.9	2.5	1.6	1.1	1.4	3.2	2.0	4.1	2.9	1.5	3.3
	2.0	0.5	1.9	2.1	0.7	2.4	1.6	2.5	2.4	1.9	1.2	2.1	3.2	2.0	3.8	2.8	1.2	2.7
	8.0	2.1	5.3	7.0	3.0	6.2	6.6	4.9	6.9	5.1	3.5	5.1	9.7	6.1	11.3	8.3	4.0	8.6
Totals	41.8			51.4			64.0			44.2			73.2			52.8		

CHAPTER
12

Experiments of Two or More Factors
—Restrictions on Randomization

12.1 Introduction

In the discussion of factorial and nested experiments, it was assumed that the whole experiment was performed in a completely randomized manner. In practice, however, it may not be feasible to run the whole experiment several times in one day, or by one experimenter, etc. It then becomes necessary to restrict this complete randomization and block the experiment in the same manner that a single-factor experiment was blocked in Chapter 4. Instead of running several replications of the experiment all at one time, it may be possible to run one complete replication on one day, a second complete replication on another day, a third replication on a third day, etc. In this case, each replication is a block, and the design is a randomized block design with a complete factorial or nested experiment randomized within each block.

Occasionally a second restriction on randomization is necessary, in which case a Latin Square design might be used, with the treatments in the square representing a complete factorial or nested experiment.

12.2 Factorial Experiment in a Randomized Block Design

Just as the factorial arrangements were extracted from the treatment effect in Eqs. (6.1) and (6.2), so can these arrangements be extracted from the treatment effect in the randomized complete block design of Chapter 4 (Sec. 4.2). For the completely randomized design, you will recall that

$$X_{ij} = \mu + T_j + \epsilon_{ij}$$

can be subdivided into

$$X_{ijk} = \mu + A_i + B_j + AB_{ij} + \epsilon_{k(ij)}$$

where $A_i + B_j + AB_{ij} = T_j$ of the first model.

When a complete experiment is replicated several times and R_k represents the blocks or replications, the randomized block model would be

$$X_{ij} = \mu + R_k + T_m + \epsilon_{km}$$

where R_k represents the blocks or replications and T_m represents the treatments. If the treatments are formed from a two-factor factorial experiment, then

$$T_m = A_i + B_j + AB_{ij}$$

and the complete model is

$$X_{ijk} = \mu + R_k + A_i + B_j + AB_{ij} + \epsilon_{ijk} \tag{12.1}$$

Here it is assumed that there is no interaction between replications (blocks) and treatments, which is the usual assumption underlying a randomized block design. Any such interaction is confounded in the error term ϵ_{ijk}.

To get a more concrete picture of this type of design, consider three levels of Factor A, two levels of B and four replications. The treatment combinations may be written as A_1B_1, A_1B_2, A_2B_1, A_2B_2, A_3B_1 and A_3B_2. Such a design assumes that all six of these treatment combinations can be run on a given day, if days are the replications or blocks. A layout in which these six treatment combinations are randomized within each replication might be

Rep. I: $\quad A_1B_2 \quad A_3B_1 \quad A_3B_2 \quad A_2B_1 \quad A_1B_1 \quad A_2B_2$

Rep. II: $\quad A_2B_2 \quad A_1B_1 \quad A_3B_2 \quad A_2B_1 \quad A_1B_2 \quad A_3B_1$

Rep. III: $\quad A_2B_1 \quad A_3B_2 \quad A_1B_2 \quad A_3B_1 \quad A_2B_2 \quad A_1B_1$

Rep. IV: $\quad A_1B_1 \quad A_3B_1 \quad A_3B_2 \quad A_2B_1 \quad A_1B_2 \quad A_2B_2$

An analysis breakdown would be that shown in Table 12.1.

TABLE 12.1 — *Two-Factor Experiment in a Randomized Block Design*

Source		df
Replications (R_k)		3
Treatments (T_m)		5
	A_i	2
	B_j	1
	AB_{ij}	2
Error	(ϵ_{ijk})	15
TOTAL		23

To see how the interaction of replications and treatments is used as error, consider the expanded model and the corresponding EMS terms exhibited in Table 12.2. Here the factors are fixed and replications are considered as random.

TABLE 12.2 — *EMS Terms for Two-Factor Experiment in a Randomized Block*

Source	df	3 F i	2 F j	4 R k	1 R m	EMS
R_k	3	3	2	1	1	$\sigma_e^2 + 6\sigma_R^2$
A_i	2	0	2	4	1	$\sigma_e^2 + 2\sigma_{RA}^2 + 8\sigma_A^2$
RA_{ik}	6	0	2	4	1	$\sigma_e^2 + 2\sigma_{RA}^2$
B_j	1	3	0	4	1	$\sigma_e^2 + 3\sigma_{RB}^2 + 12\sigma_B^2$
RB_{jk}	3	3	0	1	1	$\sigma_e^2 + 3\sigma_{RB}^2$
AB_{ij}	2	0	0	4	1	$\sigma_e^2 + \sigma_{RAB}^2 + 4\sigma_{AB}^2$
RAB_{ijk}	6	0	0	1	1	$\sigma_e^2 + \sigma_{RAB}^2$
$\epsilon_{m(ijk)}$	0	1	1	1	1	σ_e^2(not retrievable)
TOTAL	23					

Since the degrees of freedom are quite low for the tests indicated above, and since there is no separate estimate of error variance, it is customary to assume that $\sigma_{RA}^2 = \sigma_{RB}^2 = \sigma_{RAB}^2 = 0$ and to pool these three terms to serve as the error variance. The reduced model is then as shown in Table 12.3.

TABLE 12.3 — EMS Terms for Two-Factor Experiment,
Randomized Block, Reduced Model

Source	df	EMS
R_k	3	$\sigma_e^2 + 6\sigma_R^2$
A_i	2	$\sigma_e^2 + 8\sigma_A^2$
B_j	1	$\sigma_e^2 + 12\sigma_B^2$
AB_{ij}	2	$\sigma_e^2 + 4\sigma_{AB}^2$
ϵ_{ijk}	15	σ_e^2
TOTAL	23	

Here all effects are tested against the 15 df error term. Although we usually pool the interactions of replications with treatment effects for the error term, this is not always necessary. It will depend upon the degrees of freedom available for testing various hypotheses in Table 12.2, and also whether or not any repeat measurements can be taken within a replication. If this latter is possible, a separate estimate of σ_e^2 is available and all tests in Table 12.2 may be made.

EXAMPLE 12.1. At Purdue, a researcher was interested in determining the effect of both nozzle types and operators on the rate of fluid flow in cubic centimeters through these nozzles. He considered three fixed nozzle types and five randomly chosen operators. Each of these 15 combinations was to be run in a random order on each of three days. These three days will be considered as three replications of the complete 3×5 factorial experiment. After subtracting 96.0 cm^3 from each reading and multiplying all readings by 10, the data layout and observed readings (in cubic centimeters) are as recorded in Table 12.4.

TABLE 12.4 — Nozzle Example Data

Operators	1			2			3			4			5		
Nozzles	A	B	C	A	B	C	A	B	C	A	B	C	A	B	C
Rep. I	6	13	10	26	4	−35	11	17	11	21	−5	12	25	15	−4
Rep. II	6	6	10	12	4	0	4	10	−10	14	2	−2	18	8	10
Rep. III	−15	13	−11	5	11	−14	4	17	−17	7	−5	−16	25	1	24

The model for this example is

$$X_{ijk} = \mu + R_k + N_i + O_j + NO_{ij} + \epsilon_{ijk}$$

where $k = 1, 2, 3$; $i = 1, 2, 3$; $j = 1, 2, \cdots 5$, the R_k levels are random, O_j levels are random and N_i levels are fixed. If m repeat measurements are considered in the model, but $m = 1$, the EMS values are those appearing in Table 12.5.

TABLE 12.5 — EMS For Nozzle Example

Source	df	3 F i	5 R j	3 R k	1 R m	EMS
R_k	2	3	5	1	1	$\sigma_e^2 + 15\sigma_R^2$
N_i	2	0	5	3	1	$\sigma_e^2 + 3\sigma_{NO}^2 + 15\sigma_N^2$
O_j	4	3	1	3	1	$\sigma_e^2 + 9\sigma_O^2$
NO_{ij}	8	0	1	3	1	$\sigma_e^2 + 3\sigma_{NO}^2$
$\epsilon_{m(ijk)}$	28	1	1	1	1	σ_e^2
TOTAL	44					

These EMS values indicate that all main effects and the interaction can be tested with reasonable precision (df). The sums of squares are computed in the usual manner from the subtotals in Table 12.6.

TABLE 12.6 — Subtotals in Nozzle Example

	Totals	Nozzles	Operators 1	2	3	4	5	Nozzle Totals
Rep. I	127	A	-3	43	19	42	68	169
Rep. II	92	B	32	19	44	-8	24	111
Rep. III	29	C	9	-49	-16	-6	30	-32
TOTAL	248	TOTALS	38	13	47	28	122	248

Using these subtotals, the usual sums of squares can easily be computed and the results displayed as in Table 12.7.

TABLE 12.7 — ANOVA for Nozzle Example

Source	df	SS	MS	EMS	F	$F_{0.95}$
R_k	2	328.84	164.42	$\sigma_e^2 + 15\sigma_R^2$	1.70	3.34
N_i	2	1426.97	713.48	$\sigma_e^2 + 3\sigma_{NO}^2 + 15\sigma_N^2$	3.13	4.46
O_j	4	798.79	199.70	$\sigma_e^2 + 9\sigma_O^2$	2.06	2.71
NO_{ij}	8	1821.48	227.68	$\sigma_e^2 + 3\sigma_{NO}^2$	2.35	2.29
ϵ_{ijk}	28	2709.16	96.76	σ_e^2		
TOTALS	44	7085.24				

The results of tests of hypotheses on this model show only a significant Nozzle $\times$ Operator interaction at the 5 percent level of significance. The plot in Fig. 12.1 of all totals for the right-hand data of Table 12.6 shows this interaction graphically.

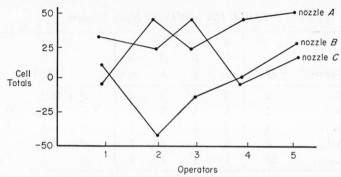

FIG. 12.1   *Interaction Plot for Nozzles* × *Operators in Nozzle Example*

If desirable, the model of this example could be expanded to include an estimate of replication by operator and replication by nozzle interactions, using the three-way interaction (N × O × Rep) as the error. The results of such a breakdown are recorded in Table 12.8.

TABLE 12.8 — *ANOVA for Nozzle Example with Replication Interactions*

Source	df	SS	MS	EMS	F
R_k	2	328.84	164.42	$\sigma_e^2 + 3\sigma_{RO}^2 + 15\sigma_R^2$	1.86
N_i	2	1426.97	713.48	$\sigma_e^2 + 3\sigma_{NO}^2 + 5\sigma_{NR}^2 + 15\sigma_N^2$	(*)
NR_{ik}	4	272.23	68.06	$\sigma_e^2 + 5\sigma_{NR}^2$	<1
O_j	4	798.79	199.70	$\sigma_e^2 + 3\sigma_{RO}^2 + 9\sigma_O^2$	2.26
RO_{jk}	8	705.60	88.20	$\sigma_e^2 + 3\sigma_{RO}^2$	<1
NO_{ij}	8	1821.48	227.68	$\sigma_e^2 + 3\sigma_{NO}^2$	2.10
NRO_{ijk} or ϵ_{ijk}	16	1731.33	108.21	σ_e^2	
TOTALS	44	7085.24			

| | Operators | | | | | | Nozzles | | | |
Replications	1	2	3	4	5	Totals	A	B	C	Totals
I	29	−5	39	28	36	127	89	44	−6	127
II	22	16	4	14	36	92	54	30	8	92
III	−13	2	4	−14	50	29	26	37	−34	29
TOTALS	38	13	47	28	122	248	169	111	−32	248

(*) The nozzle mean square is seen to have no exact test by examining the expected mean squares below it. However, if σ_{NR}^2 is assumed to be zero, the test of H_o: $\sigma_N^2 = 0$ is

$$F_{2,8} = \frac{713.48}{227.68} = 3.13$$

which is not significant at the 5 percent level $(F_{0.95})$ (2,8) = 4.46).

The F tests indicate no significant effects. The $N \times O$ Interaction does not show significance as it did in Table 12.7, because the test is less sensitive due to the reduction in degrees of freedom from 28 to 16 in the error mean square. Since both the $N \times R$ and $R \times O$ interaction F tests are less than one, we are probably justified in assuming that σ_{NR}^2 and σ_{RO}^2 are zero and in pooling these with σ_{NRO}^2 for a 28 df error mean square as in Table 12.7.

12.3 Factorial Experiment in a Latin Square Design

If there are two restrictions on the randomization, and an equal number of restriction levels and treatment levels are used, Chapter 5 has shown that a Latin Square design may be used. The model for this design is

$$X_{ijk} = \mu + R_i + T_j + \gamma_k + \epsilon_{ijk}$$

where T_j represents the treatments, and both R_i and γ_k represent restrictions on the randomization. If a 4×4 Latin Square is used for a given experiment, such as the one in Sec. 5.2, the four treatments A, B, C, and D could represent the four treatment combinations of a 2×2 factorial. (See Table 12.9.) Here

$$T_j = A_m + B_q + AB_{mq}$$

TABLE 12.9 — 4 × 4 Latin Square (Same as Table 5.1)

Positions	Cars			
	I	II	III	IV
1	C	D	A	B
2	B	C	D	A
3	A	B	C	D
4	D	A	B	C

with its 3 df. Thus, a factorial experiment $(A \times B)$ is run in a Latin Square design. For the problem of Sec. 5.2, instead of four tire brands, the four treatments could consist of two brands (A_1 and A_2) and two types (B_1 and B_2). The types might be black- and white-walled tires. The complete model would then be

$$X_{ikmq} = \mu + R_i + \gamma_k + A_m + B_q + AB_{mq} + \epsilon_{ikmq}$$

and the degrees-of-freedom breakdown would be that shown in Table 12.10.

TABLE 12.10 — Degrees-of-Freedom Breakdown for Table 12.9

Source	df
R_i	3
γ_k	3
A_m	1 ⎫
B_q	1 ⎬ 3 df for T_j
AB_{mq}	1 ⎭
ϵ_{ikmq}	6
TOTAL	15

This idea could be extended to running a factorial in a Graeco–Latin Square, etc.

12.4 Remarks

In the sections above, factorial experiments have been considered where the design of the experiment was a randomized block or a Latin Square. It is also possible to run a nested experiment or a nested-factorial experiment in a randomized block or Latin Square design. In the case of a nested experiment, the treatment effect might be broken down as

$$T_m = A_i + B_{j(i)}$$

and when this experiment has one restriction on the randomization, the model is

$$X_{ijk} = \mu + R_k + \underbrace{A_i + B_{j(i)}}_{T_m} + \epsilon_{ijk}$$

If a nested-factorial is repeated on several different days, the model would be

$$X_{ijkm} = \mu + R_k + \underbrace{A_i + B_{j(i)} + C_m + AC_{im} + BC_{mj(i)}}_{T_q} + \epsilon_{ijkm}$$

where the whole nested-factorial is run in a randomized block design.

The analysis of such designs follow from the methods of Chapter 11.

12.5 Summary

The summary at the end of Chapter 11 may now be extended.

Experiment	*Design*	*Analysis*
II. Two or More Factors		
A. Factorial		
	1. Completely Randomized	1.
	$X_{ijk} = \mu + A_i + B_j + AB_{ij} + \epsilon_{k(ij)}$	
	a. General Case	a. ANOVA with interactions
	b. 2^n	b. Yates Method
	c. 3^n	c. General ANOVA
	2. Randomized Block (Complete)	2. Factorial ANOVA
	$X_{ijk} = \mu + R_k + A_i + B_j + AB_{ij} + \epsilon_{ijk}$	
	3. Latin Square (Complete)	3.
	$X_{ijkm} = \mu + R_k + \gamma_m + A_i + B_j + AB_{ij} + \epsilon_{ijkm}$	
		a. Factorial ANOVA
B. Nested		
	1. Completely Randomized	1. Nested ANOVA
	$X_{ijk} = \mu + A_i + B_{j(i)} + \epsilon_{k(ij)}$	
	2. Randomized Block (Complete)	2. Nested ANOVA
	$X_{ijk} = \mu + R_k + A_i + B_{j(i)} + \epsilon_{ijk}$	
	3. Latin Square (Complete)	3. Nested ANOVA
	$X_{ijkm} = \mu + R_k + \gamma_m + A_i + B_{j(i)} + \epsilon_{ijkm}$	

C. Nested-
   Factorial

1. Completely
   Randomized
   $X_{ijkm} = \mu + A_i + B_{j(i)}$
   $+ C_k + AC_{ik} + BC_{kj(i)}$
   $+ \epsilon_{m(ijk)}$

1. Nested-Factorial
   ANOVA

2. Randomized Block
   (Complete)
   $X_{ijkm} = \mu + R_k + A_i$
   $+ B_{j(i)} + C_m + AC_{im}$
   $+ BC_{mj(i)} + \epsilon_{ijkm}$

2. Nested-Factorial
   ANOVA

3. Latin Square
   (Complete)
   $X_{ijkmg} = \mu + R_k + \gamma_m$
   $+ A_i + B_{j(i)} + C_g$
   $+ AC_{ig} + BC_{gj(i)}$
   $+ \epsilon_{ijkmg}$

3. Nested-Factorial
   ANOVA

PROBLEMS

12-1.   Data on the glass rating of tubes taken from two fixed stations and three shifts are recorded each week for three weeks. Considering the weeks as blocks, the six treatment combinations (two stations by three shifts) were tested in a random order each week, with results as follows:

	Station 1			Station 2		
Shifts	1	2	3	1	2	3
	3	3	3	6	3	6
Week 1	6	4	6	8	9	8
	6	7	7	11	11	13
	14	8	11	4	15	4
Week 2	16	8	12	6	15	7
	19	9	17	7	17	10
	2	2	2	2	2	10
Week 3	3	3	4	5	4	12
	6	4	6	7	6	13

Analyze these data as a factorial run in a randomized block design.

12-2.   In the example of Sec. 5.2 (Table 5.2) consider Tire brands A, B, C, D as four combinations of two factors, ply of tires and type of tread, where

$$A = P_1 T_1 \qquad B = P_1 T_2 \qquad C = P_2 T_1 \qquad D = P_2 T_2$$

representing the four combinations of two ply values and two tread types. Analyze the data for this revised design — a 2^2 factorial run in a Latin Square design.

12-3.   If, in Prob. 11-5, the stock factor is replaced by "days," considered random, and the rest of the experiment is performed in a random manner on each of the two days, use the same numerical results and reanalyze with this restriction.

12-4.   Again, in Prob. 11-5, assume that the whole experiment (24 readings) was repeated on five randomly selected days. Set up an outline of this experiment, including the EMS column, df, etc.

12-5.   Discuss the similarities and differences between a nested experiment with two factors and a randomized block design with one factor.

CHAPTER

13

Factorial Experiment— Split-Plot Design

13.1 Introduction

In many experiments where a factorial arrangement is desired, it may not be possible to completely randomize the order of experimentation. In the last chapter, restrictions on randomization were considered, and both randomized block and Latin Square designs were discussed. There are still many practical situations in which it is not at all feasible to even randomize within a block. Under certain conditions, these restrictions will lead to a split-plot design. An example will show why such designs are quite common.

EXAMPLE 13.1. The data in Table 13.1 were compiled on the effect of oven temperature (T) and baking time (B) on the life (X) of an electrical component.*

Looking only at this table of data, we might think of this as a 4×3 factorial with three replications per cell and proceed to the analysis in Table *13.1*.

Here only the temperature has a significant effect on the life of the component at the 1 percent significance level.

We might go on now and seek linear, quadratic and cubic effects of temperature; but, before proceeding, a few questions on design

---

*Taken from a problem on p. 112 of [14].

TABLE 13.1 — Electrical-Component Life Test Data

Baking	Oven Temperature (T)			
Time (B)	580°	600°	620°	640°
	217	158	229	223
5 min	188	126	160	201
	162	122	167	182
	233	138	186	227
10 min	201	130	170	181
	170	185	181	201
	175	152	155	156
15 min	195	147	161	172
	213	180	182	199

TABLE 13.2 — ANOVA for Life-Test Data as a Factorial

Source	df	SS	MS	EMS
T_i	3	12,494	4,165	$\sigma_e^2 + 9\sigma_T^2$
B_j	2	566	283	$\sigma_e^2 + 12\sigma_B^2$
BT_{ij}	6	2,601	434	$\sigma_e^2 + 3\sigma_{BT}^2$
$\epsilon_{k(ij)}$	24	13,670	570	σ_e^2
TOTALS	35	29,331		

should be raised. What was the order of experimentation? The data analysis above assumes a completely randomized design. This means that one of the four temperatures was chosen at random and the oven was heated to this temperature, then a baking time was chosen at random and an electrical component was inserted in the oven and baked for the time selected. After this run, the whole procedure was repeated until the data were compiled. Now, was the experiment really conducted in this manner? Of course the answer is "no." Once an oven is heated to temperature, all nine components are inserted; three are baked for five minutes, three for 10 minutes, and three for 15 minutes. We would argue that this is the only practical way to run the experiment. Complete randomization is too impractical as well as too expensive. Fortunately, this restriction on the complete randomization can be handled in a design called a *split-plot* design.

The four temperature levels are called *plots*. They could be called blocks, but, in the previous chapter, blocks and replications have been used for a complete rerun of the whole experiment. (The word "plots" has been inherited from agricultural applications.) In such a setup, temperature — a main effect — is confounded with these plots. If conditions change from one oven temperature to another, these changes will show up as temperature differences. Thus, in such a design, a main effect is confounded with plots. This is necessary because it is often the most practical way to order the experiment. Now once a temperature has been set up by choosing one of the four temperatures at random, three components can be placed in the oven and one component can be baked for five minutes, another for 10 minutes, and the third one for 15 minutes. The specific component which is to be baked for 5, 10 and 15 minutes is again decided by a random selection. These three baking time levels may be thought of as a splitting of the plot into three parts, one part for each baking time. This defines the three parts of a main plot that are called split-plots. Note here that only three components were placed in the oven, not nine. The temperature is then changed to another level and three more components are placed in the oven for 5, 10 and 15 minutes baking time. This same procedure is followed for all four temperatures; after this the whole experiment may be replicated. These replications may be run several days after the initial experiment; in fact, it is often desirable to collect data from two or three replications and then decide if more replications are necessary.

The experiment conducted above was actually run as a split-plot experiment and laid out as shown in Table 13.3.

TABLE 13.3 — Split-Plot Layout for Electrical Component-Life Test Data

Rep (R)	Baking Time (B)	Oven Temperature (T)			
		580°	600°	620°	640°
	5 min.	217	158	229	223
I	10 min.	233	138	186	227
	15 min.	175	152	155	156
	5 min.	188	126	160	201
II	10 min.	201	130	170	181
	15 min.	195	147	161	172
	5 min.	162	122	167	182
III	10 min.	170	185	181	201
	15 min.	213	180	182	199

Here temperatures are confounded with plots and the $R \times T$ cells are called whole plots. Inside a whole plot, the baking times are applied to one third of the material. These plots associated with the three baking times are called split-plots. Since one main effect is confounded with plots and the other main effect is not, it is usually desirable to place in the split the main effect we are most concerned about testing, as this factor is not confounded.

We might think that Factor B (baking time) is nested with the main plots, but this is not the case, as the same levels of B are used in all plots. A model for this experiment would be

$$X_{ijk} = \mu + \underbrace{R_i + T_j + RT_{ij}}_{\text{whole plot}} + \underbrace{B_k + RB_{ik} + TB_{jk} + RTB_{ijk}}_{\text{split plot}}$$

The first three variable terms in this model represent the whole plot, and the RT interaction is often referred to as the *whole plot error*. The usual assumption is that this interaction does not exist, that this term is really an estimate of the error within the main plot. The last four terms represent the split plot, and the RTB interaction is referred to as the *split-plot error*. Sometimes the RB term is also considered non-existent and is combined with RTB as an error term. A separate error term might be obtained if it were feasible to repeat some observations within the split plot. The proper EMS values can be found by considering m repeat measurements where $m = 1$. (See Table 13.4.)

TABLE 13.4 — *EMS for Split-Plot Electrical Component Data*

	Source	df	3 R i	4 F j	3 F k	1 R m	EMS
Whole	R_i	2	1	4	3	1	$\sigma_e^2 + 12\sigma_R^2$
Plot	T_j	3	3	0	3	1	$\sigma_e^2 + 3\sigma_{RT}^2 + 9\sigma_T^2$
	TR_{ij}	6	1	0	3	1	$\sigma_e^2 + 3\sigma_{RT}^2$
Split	B_k	2	3	4	0	1	$\sigma_e^2 + 4\sigma_{RB}^2 + 12\sigma_B^2$
Plot	RB_{ik}	4	1	4	0	1	$\sigma_e^2 + 4\sigma_{RB}^2$
	TB_{jk}	6	3	0	0	1	$\sigma_e^2 + \sigma_{RTB}^2 + 3\sigma_{TB}^2$
	RTB_{ijk}	12	1	0	0	1	$\sigma_e^2 + \sigma_{RTB}^2$
	$\epsilon_{m(ijk)}$	—	1	1	1	1	σ_e^2 (not retrievable)
	TOTAL	35					

Since the error mean square cannot be isolated in this experiment, σ_{RTB}^2 is taken as the split-plot error, and σ_{RT}^2 is taken as the whole-plot error. The main effects and interaction of interest (TB) can be tested, as seen from the EMS column, although no exact tests exist for the replication effect nor for interactions involving the replications. This is not a serious disadvantage for this design, since tests on replication effects are not of interest but are isolated only to reduce the error variance. The analysis of the data from Table 13.3 follows the methods given in Chapter 6. The results are shown in Table 13.5.

TABLE 13.5 — ANOVA for Split-Plot Electrical Component Data

Source	df	SS	MS	EMS
R_i	2	1963	982	$\sigma_e^2 + 12\sigma_R^2$
T_j	3	12494	4165	$\sigma_e^2 + 3\sigma_{RT}^2 + 9\sigma_T^2$
RT_{ij}	6	1774	296	$\sigma_e^2 + 3\sigma_{RT}^2$
B_k	2	566	283	$\sigma_e^2 + 4\sigma_{RB}^2 + 12\sigma_B^2$
RB_{ik}	4	7021	1755	$\sigma_e^2 + 4\sigma_{RB}^2$
TB_{jk}	6	2601	434	$\sigma_e^2 + \sigma_{RTB}^2 + 3\sigma_{TB}^2$
RTB_{ijk}	12	2912	243	$\sigma_e^2 + \sigma_{RTB}^2$
TOTALS	35	29331		

Testing the hypothesis of no temperature effect gives

$$F_{3,6} = \frac{4165}{296} = 14.1 \text{ (significant at the 1 percent level)}$$

Testing for baking time gives

$$F_{2,4} = \frac{283}{1755} < 1 \text{ (not significant)}$$

Testing for TB interaction gives

$$F_{6,12} = \frac{434}{243} = 1.79 \text{ (not significant at the 5 percent level)}$$

No exact tests are available for testing the replication effect or replication interaction with other factors, but these effects are present only to reduce the experimental error in this split-plot design.

The results of this split-plot analysis are not too different from the results using the incorrect method of Table 13.2, but this split-plot design shows the need for careful consideration of the method of randomization before starting an experiment. This split-plot design represents a restriction on the randomization over a complete randomization in a factorial experiment.

Since this type of design is encountered often in industrial experiments, another example will be considered.

EXAMPLE 13.2. A defense-related organization was to study the pulloff force necessary to separate boxes of chaff from a tape on which they are affixed. These boxes are made of a cardboard material, approximately 3 in. by 3 in. by 1 in., and are mounted on a strip of cloth tape that has an adhesive backing. The tape is 2 in. wide, and the boxes are placed 7 in. center-to-center on the strip. There are 75 boxes mounted on each strip.

The tape is pulled from the box at a 90-deg angle as it is wound onto a drum. During this separation process, the portion of the tape still adhering to the box carries the box onto a platform. The box trips a microswitch, which energizes a plunger. The plunger then kicks the box out of the machine.

After this problem was discussed with the plant engineers, several factors were listed which might affect this pulloff force. The most important factors were temperature and humidity. It was agreed to use three fixed temperature levels, $-55\,°C$, $25\,°C$, and $55\,°C$, and three fixed humidity levels, 50 percent, 70 percent, and 90 percent. These gave nine basic treatment combinations. Since there might be differences in pulloff force as a result of the strip selected, it was decided to choose five different strips at random for use in this experiment. There might also be differences within a strip, so two boxes were chosen at random and cut from each strip for the test.

The test in the laboratory was accomplished by hand-holding the package, attaching a spring scale to the strip by means of a hole previously punched in the strip, and pulling the tape from the package in a direction perpendicular to the package.

In discussing the design of this experiment, it seemed best to set the climatic condition (a combination of temperature and humidity) at random from one of the $3 \times 3 = 9$ conditions, and then test two boxes from each of the five strips while these conditions were maintained. Then another of the nine conditions is set, and the results again determined on 2 boxes from each of the 5 strips. This is, then, a restriction on the randomization, and the resulting design is a split-plot design. It was agreed to replicate the complete experiment four times. A layout for this experiment is shown in Table 13.6.

TABLE 13.6 — Split-Plot Design of Chaff Experiment

			Temperature (T)								
			$-55°$			$25°$			$55°$		
			Humidity Percentage (H)								
Strip (S)	Box	50	70	90	50	70	90	50	70	90
	1	1									
		2									
	2	3									
		4									
Rep I	3	5									
(R)		6									
	4	7									
		8									
	5	9									
		10									

Rep II (Repeat as above)
Rep III (Repeat as above)

In Table 13.6, each replication is a repeat of Replication I, but a new order of randomizing the nine atmospheric conditions is taken in each replication. In this design, atmospheric conditions and replications form the whole plot, and strips are in the split-plot.

The model for this design and its associated EMS relations are set up in Table 13.7.

TABLE 13.7 — EMS for Chaff Experiment

	Source	df	4 R i	3 F j	3 F k	5 R m	2 R q	EMS
	R_i	3	1	3	3	5	2	$\sigma_e^2 + 18\sigma_{RS}^2 + 90\sigma_R^2$
	T_j	2	4	0	3	5	2	$\sigma_e^2 + 6\sigma_{RTS}^2 + 24\sigma_{TS}^2 + 30\sigma_{RT}^2 + 120\sigma_T^2$
Whole	RT_{ij}	6	1	0	3	5	2	$\sigma_e^2 + 6\sigma_{RTS}^2 + 30\sigma_{RT}^2$
Plot	H_k	2	4	3	0	5	2	$\sigma_e^2 + 6\sigma_{RHS}^2 + 24\sigma_{HS}^2 + 30\sigma_{RH}^2 + 120\sigma_H^2$
	RH_{ik}	6	1	3	0	5	2	$\sigma_e^2 + 6\sigma_{RHS}^2 + 30\sigma_{RH}^2$
	TH_{jk}	4	4	0	0	5	2	$\sigma_e^2 + 2\sigma_{RTHS}^2 + 8\sigma_{THS}^2 + 10\sigma_{RTH}^2 + 40\sigma_{TH}^2$
	RTH_{ijk}	12	1	0	0	5	2	$\sigma_e^2 + 2\sigma_{RTHS}^2 + 10\sigma_{RTH}^2$
	S_m	4	4	3	3	1	2	$\sigma_e^2 + 18\sigma_{RS}^2 + 72\sigma_S^2$
	RS_{im}	12	1	3	3	1	2	$\sigma_e^2 + 18\sigma_{RS}^2$
Split	TS_{jm}	8	4	0	3	1	2	$\sigma_e^2 + 6\sigma_{RTS}^2 + 24\sigma_{TS}^2$
Plot	RTS_{ijm}	24	1	0	3	1	2	$\sigma_e^2 + 6\sigma_{RTS}^2$
	HS_{km}	8	4	3	0	1	2	$\sigma_e^2 + 6\sigma_{RHS}^2 + 24\sigma_{HS}^2$
	RHS_{ikm}	24	1	3	0	1	2	$\sigma_e^2 + 6\sigma_{RHS}^2$
	THS_{jkm}	16	4	0	0	1	2	$\sigma_e^2 + 2\sigma_{RTHS}^2 + 8\sigma_{THS}^2$
	$RTHS_{ijkm}$	48	1	0	0	1	2	$\sigma_e^2 + 2\sigma_{RTHS}^2$
	$\epsilon_{q(ijkm)}$	180	1	1	1	1	1	σ_e^2
	TOTAL	359						

From the EMS column tests can be made on the effects of replications, replications by temperature interaction, replications by humidity interaction, replications by temperature by humidity interaction, strips, and strips by all other factor interactions. Unfortunately no exact tests are available for the factors of chief importance: temperature, humidity and temperature by humidity interaction. Of course, we could first test the hypotheses that can be tested, and if some of these are not significant at a reasonably high level (say 25 percent), assume they are nonexistent and then remove these terms from the EMS column. For example, if the RT interaction can be assumed as zero ($\sigma_{RT}^2 = 0$), the temperature mean square can be tested against the TS interaction mean square with 2 and 8 df. Or, if the TS interaction can be assumed as zero $(\sigma_{TS}^2 = 0)$, the temperature mean square may be tested against the RT interaction with 2 and 6 df. If neither of these assumptions is reasonable, a special method for testing the mean squares can be used, which is discussed in the next section.

Unfortunately, data were available only for the first replication of this experiment, so its complete analysis cannot be given. The method of analysis is the same as given in Chapter 6, even though this experiment is rather complicated. It is presented here only to show another actual example of a split-plot design.

13.2 A Pseudo F Test

Occasionally the EMS column for a given experiment indicates that there is no exact F test for one or more of the factors in the design model. Such a situation was observed in Table 13.7, where no exact F test is available for temperature, humidity or TH interaction. One method for testing hypotheses in such situations was developed by Satterthwaite and is given in Bennett and Franklin [2], pp. 367–368.

The scheme consists of constructing a mean square as a linear combination of the mean squares in the experiment, where the expected mean square for this mean square includes the same terms as in the expected mean square of the term being tested, except for the variance of that term. For example, to test the temperature effect in Table 13.7, a mean square is to be constructed whose expected value is

$$\sigma_e^2 + 6\sigma_{RTS}^2 + 24\sigma_{TS}^2 + 30\sigma_{RT}^2$$

This can be found by the linear combination

$$\mathrm{MS} = \mathrm{MS}_{RT} + \mathrm{MS}_{TS} - \mathrm{MS}_{RTS}$$

as its expected value is

$$E(\mathrm{MS}) = \sigma_e^2 + 6\sigma_{RTS}^2 + 30\sigma_{RT}^2 + \sigma_e^2 + 6\sigma_{RTS}^2 + 24\sigma_{TS}^2 - \sigma_e^2 - 6\sigma_{RTS}^2$$

$$= \sigma_e^2 + 6\sigma_{RTS}^2 + 24\sigma_{TS}^2 + 30\sigma_{RT}^2$$

An F test can now be constructed using the mean square for temperature as the numerator and this mean square as the denominator. Such a test is called a Pseudo-F test or F' test. The real problem here is to determine the degrees of freedom for the denominator mean square. According to Bennett and Franklin, if

$$\mathrm{MS} = a_1(\mathrm{MS})_1 + a_2(\mathrm{MS})_2 + \cdots$$

and $(MS)_1$ is based on v_1 df, $(MS)_2$ is based on v_2 df, etc., then the degrees of freedom for MS are

$$v = \frac{(MS)^2}{a_1^2 \dfrac{(MS)_1^2}{v_1} + a_2^2 \dfrac{(MS)_2^2}{v_2} + \cdots}$$

In the case of testing for temperature effect above, $a_1 = 1$, $a_2 = 1$ and $a_3 = -1$ and the degrees of freedom are $v_1 = 6$, $v_2 = 8$ and $v_3 = 24$. To complete the Pseudo-F test, we would need the computed mean squares, which are not available in this example. The Pseudo-F test can be illustrated in Example 12.1 (Table 12.8). We could test the nozzle effect by combining the mean squares

$$MS = MS_{NR} + MS_{NO} - MS_{NRO}$$

Here the coefficients are 1, 1 and -1, and the corresponding mean squares and degrees of freedom are

$$MS_{NR} = 68.06 \text{ with } v_1 = 4 \text{ df}$$

$$MS_{NO} = 227.68 \text{ with } v_2 = 8 \text{ df}$$

$$MS_{NRO} = 108.21 \text{ with } v_3 = 16 \text{ df}$$

The F' test is then

$$F' = \frac{MS_N}{MS_{NR} + MS_{NO} - MS_{NRO}}$$

$$= \frac{713.48}{68.06 + 227.68 - 108.21}$$

$$= \frac{713.48}{187.53} = 3.80$$

and

$$v = \frac{(187.53)^2}{(1)^2 \dfrac{(68.06)^2}{4} + (1)^2 \dfrac{(227.68)^2}{8} + (-1)^2 \dfrac{(108.21)^2}{16}}$$

$$v = 4.2$$

With 2 and 4 df the 5 percent F value is 6.94, and with 2 and 5 df it is 5.79; hence, the $F' = 3.80$ is not significant at the 5 percent level.

13.3 Summary

The summary of Chapter 12 may now be extended.

Experiment	*Design*	*Analysis*
II. Two or More Factors		
A. Factorial		
	1. Completely Randomized	
	2. Randomized Block	2.
	a. Complete $X_{ijk} = \mu + R_k + A_i + B_j + AB_{ij} + \epsilon_{ijk}$	a. Factorial ANOVA
	b. Incomplete — Confounding of (1) Main Effect — Split Plot	b. (1) Split-Plot ANOVA

$$X_{ijk} = \mu + \underbrace{R_i + A_j + RA_{ij}}_{\text{whole plot}}$$

$$\underbrace{+ B_k + RB_{ik} + AB_{jk} + RAB_{ijk}}_{\text{split plot}}$$

PROBLEMS

13-1. As part of the experiment discussed in Example 13.2, a chamber was set at 50 percent relative humidity and two boxes from each of three strips were inserted and the pull-off force determined. This was repeated for 70 percent and 90 percent, the order of humidities being randomized. Two replications of the whole experiment were made and the results follow:

	Strips	Humidity 50%		70%		90%	
	1	1.12	1.75	3.50	0.50	1.00	0.75
Rep I	2	1.13	3.50	0.75	1.00	0.50	0.50
	3	2.25	3.25	1.75	1.88	1.50	0.00
	1	1.75	1.88	1.75	0.75	1.50	0.75
Rep II	2	5.25	5.25	0.75	2.25	1.50	1.50
	3	1.50	3.50	1.62	2.50	0.75	0.50

Set up a split-plot model for this experiment and outline the ANOVA table, including EMS.

13-2. Analyze Prob. 13-1.

13-3. In Prob. 12-3, perform a psuedo-F test on the type effect.

13-4. Set up F' tests for the effects in Prob. 12-4 that cannot be tested directly.

13-5. In a time-study two types of stimuli are used — two- and three-dimensional film — and combinations of stimuli and job are repeated once to give eight strips of film. The order of these eight is completely randomized on one long film and presented to five analysts for rating at one sitting. Since this latter represents a restriction on the randomization, the whole experiment is repeated at three sittings (four in all) and the experiment is considered as a split-plot design. Set up a model for this experiment and indicate the tests to be made. (Consider analysts as random).

13-6. Determine an F' test for any effects in Prob. 13-5 that cannot be run directly.

13-7. Three replications are made of an experiment to determine the effect of days of the week and operators on screen-color difference of a TV tube in deg K. On a given day, each of four operators measured the screen-color difference on a given tube. The order of measuring by the four operators is randomized each day for five days of the week. The results are

	Operator	Mon.	Tues.	Wed.	Thurs.	Fri.
	A	800	950	900	740	880
Rep I	B	760	900	820	740	960
	C	920	920	840	900	1020
	D	860	940	820	940	980
	A	780	810	880	960	920
Rep II	B	820	940	900	780	820
	C	740	900	880	840	880
	D	800	900	800	820	900
	A	800	1030	800	840	800
Rep III	B	900	920	880	920	1000
	C	800	1000	920	760	920
	D	900	980	900	780	880

Set up the model and outline the ANOVA table for this problem.

13-8. Considering days as fixed, operators as random, and replications as random, analyze Prob. 13-7.

13-9. Explain how a split-plot design differs from a nested design, since both have a factor within levels of another factor.

CHAPTER 14

Factorial Experiment—
Confounding in Blocks

14.1 Introduction

As seen in Chapter 13, there are many situations in which randomization is restricted. The split-plot design is an example of a restriction on randomization where a main effect is confounded with blocks. Sometimes these restrictions are necessary because the complete factorial cannot be run in one day, or in one environmental chamber, etc. When such restrictions are imposed on the experiment, a decision must be made as to what information may be sacrificed and thus on what is to be confounded. A simple example may help to illustrate this point.

A chemist was studying the disintegration of a chemical in solution. He had a beaker of the mixture and wished to determine whether or not the depth in the beaker would affect the amount of disintegration and whether material from the center of the beaker would be different than material from near the edge. He decided on a 2^2 factorial experiment — one factor being depth, the other radius. A cross-section of the beaker (Fig. 14.1) shows the four treatment combinations to be considered.

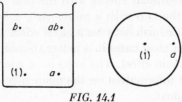

FIG. 14.1

In Fig. 14.1 (1) represents radius zero, depth at lower level (near bottom of beaker). *a* represents the radius at near maximum (near the edge of the beaker) and a low depth level. *b* is radius zero, depth at a higher level, and *ab* is both radius and depth at higher levels. In order to get a reading on the amount of disintegration of material, samples of solution must be drawn from these four positions. This was accomplished by dipping into the beaker with an instrument designed to "capture" a small amount of solution. The only problem was that the experimenter had only two hands and could get only two samples at the same time. By the time he returned for the other two samples, conditions might have changed and the amount of disintegration would probably be greater. Thus there is a physical restriction on this 2^2 factorial experiment; only two observations can be made at one time. The question is, which two treatment combinations should be taken on the first dip? Considering the two dips as blocks, we are forced to use an incomplete block design, as the whole factorial cannot be performed in one dip.

Three possible block patterns are shown in Table 14.1.

TABLE 14.1 — Three Possible Blockings of a 2^2 Factorial

	I	II	III
Dip 1:	(1) *b*	(1) *a*	(1) *ab*
Dip 2:	*a* *ab*	*b* *ab*	*a* *b*

If Plan I of Table 14.1 is used, the blocks (dips) are confounded with the radius effect, since all zero radius readings are in Dip 1 and all maximum radius readings are in Dip 2. In Plan II, the depth effect is confounded with the dips, as low-level depth readings are both in Dip 1 and high-level depth readings are in Dip 2. In Plan III, neither main effect is confounded, but the interaction is confounded with the dips. To see that the interaction is confounded, recall the expression for the *AB* interaction in a 2^2 factorial found in Chapter 7.

$$AB = \tfrac{1}{2}[(1) - a - b + ab]$$

Note that the two treatment effects with the plus sign, (1) and *ab*, are both in Dip 1, and the two with a minus sign, *a* and *b*, are in Dip 2. Hence we cannot distinguish between a block effect (dips) and the interaction effect (*AB*). In most cases it is better to confound an interaction than to confound a main effect. The hope is, of course, that there is no interaction, and that information on the main effects can still be found from such an experiment.

14.2   Confounding Systems

In order to design an experiment in which the number of treatments which can be run in a block is less than the total number of treatment combinations, the experimenter must first decide on what effects he is willing to confound. If, as in the example above, he has only one interaction in the experiment and decides that he can confound this interaction with blocks, the problem is simply which treatment combinations to place in each block. One way to accomplish this is to place in one block those treatment combinations with a plus sign in the effect to be confounded, and those with a minus sign in the other block. A more general method is necessary when the number of blocks and the number of treatments increases.

First, a *defining contrast* is set up. This is merely an expression stating which effects are to be confounded with blocks. In the simple example above, to confound AB, write AB as the defining contrast. Once the defining contrast has been set up, several methods are available for determining which treatment combinations will be placed in each block. One method was shown above — place in one block the treatment combinations which have a plus sign in AB and those with a minus sign in the other block. Another method is to consider each treatment combination. Those which have an even number of letters in common with the effect letters in the defining contrast go in one block. Those which have an odd number of letters in common with the defining contrasts go into the other block. Here (1) has no letters in common with AB or an even number. Type a has one letter in common with AB (a and A) or an odd number. b also has one letter in common with AB. ab has two letters in common with AB. Thus the block contents are those in Fig. 14.2.

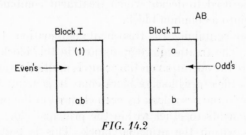

FIG. 14.2

One disadvantage of the two methods given above is that they are only good on 2^n factorials. A more general method is attributed to Kempthorne [10]. Consider the linear expression

$$A_1X_1 + A_2X_2 + \cdots + A_nX_n = L$$

Here A_i is the exponent on the ith factor appearing in each independent defining contrast, and X_i is the level of the ith factor appearing in a given treatment combination. Every treatment combination with the same L value will be placed in the same block. For the simple example above where the defining contrast is AB, $A_1 = 1$, $A_2 = 1$, and all other A_i's $= 0$. Hence

$$L = 1 \cdot X_1 + 1 \cdot X_2$$

For each treatment combination the L values are

$$(1): L = 1 \cdot 0 + 1 \cdot 0 = 0$$

$$a: L = 1 \cdot 1 + 1 \cdot 0 = 1$$

$$b: L = 1 \cdot 0 + 1 \cdot 1 = 1$$

$$ab: L = 1 \cdot 1 + 1 \cdot 1 = 2$$

Hence 0 and 2 are both 0, since a 2^n factorial is of modulus 2 (see Sec. 9.2). The assignment of treatment combinations to blocks is then

$$L = 0 \quad \text{Block 1} \quad \boxed{(1) \quad ab}$$

$$L = 1 \quad \text{Block 2} \quad \boxed{b \quad a}$$

For a more complex defining contrast such as ABC^2, the expression is

$$L = X_1 + X_2 + 2X_3$$

and this can be used to decide which treatment combinations in a 3^3 experiment go into a common block.

The block containing the treatment combination (1) is called the *principal block*. The treatment combinations in this block are elements of a group where the operation on the group is multiplication, modulus 2. The elements of the other block or blocks may be generated by multiplying one element in the new block by each element in the principal block. Multiplying elements together within the principal block will generate more elements within the principal block. This is best seen with a slightly more complex factorial, say 2^3. If the highest-order interaction is to be confounded and the eight treatment combinations are to be placed into two blocks of four treatments each, then confounding ABC gives:

$$L = X_1 + X_2 + X_3$$

Testing each of the eight treatment combinations gives

$$(1): L = 0 + 0 + 0 = 0$$

$$a: L = 1 + 0 + 0 = 1$$

$$b: L = 0 + 1 + 0 = 1$$

$$ab: L = 1 + 1 + 0 = 2 = 0$$

$$c: L = 0 + 0 + 1 = 1$$

$$ac: L = 1 + 0 + 1 = 2 = 0$$

$$bc: L = 0 + 1 + 1 = 2 = 0$$

$$abc: L = 1 + 1 + 1 = 3 = 1$$

The blocks are then

Block I $(L = 0)$ Block II $(L = 1)$

(1)	a
ab	b
ac	c
bc	abc

Group theory can simplify this procedure: Determine two elements in the principal block; e.g., ab and bc. Multiply these two to get $ab^2c = ac$, the fourth element. Generate Block II by finding one element, say a. Multiply this element by each element in the principal block, thus generating all the elements of the second block as follows:

$$a \cdot (1) = a$$

$$a \cdot ab = a^2b = b$$

$$a \cdot ac = a^2c = c$$

$$a \cdot bc = abc$$

These concepts may be extended to more complex confounding examples, as will be shown in later sections.

14.3   Block Confounding with Replication

Whenever an experiment is restricted so that all treatments cannot appear in one block, some interaction is usually confounded with blocks. If several replications of the whole experiment (all blocks) is possible, as in the case of the split-plot, the same interaction may be confounded in all replications. In this case, the design is said to be *completely confounded*. If, on the other hand, one interaction is confounded in the first replication, a different interaction is confounded in the second replication, and so on, the design is said to be *partially confounded*.

Complete Confounding

Considering a 2^3 factorial experiment in which only four treatment combinations can be finished in one day yields a 2^3 factorial run in two incomplete blocks of four treatment combinations each. We might confound the highest-order interaction ABC as follows:

$$ABC$$

As seen in Sec. 14.2, the blocks would be

Block I	Block II
(1)	a
ab	b
ac	c
bc	abc

If this whole experiment (2^3 in 2 blocks of 4 each) can be replicated, say three times, the layout might be

	Rep. I			Rep. II			Rep. III	
Block 1		Block 2	Block 1		Block 2	Block 1		Block 2
ac		a	c		(1)	ab		c
(1)		c	abc		ac	(1)		b
ab		abc	b		bc	ac		abc
bc		b	a		ab	bc		a

The confounding scheme in the above (ABC) is the same for all three replications, but the order of experimentation has been randomized within each block. Also the decision as to which block is to be run first in each replication is made at random. An analysis layout for this experiment appears in Table 14.2.

TABLE 14.2 — *Analysis Layout for Completely Confounded 2^3 Factorial*

Source	df	df
Replications	2 ⎫	
Blocks or ABC	1 ⎬	Between plots — 5
Replications × Block Interactions	2 ⎭	
A	1 ⎫	
B	1 ⎪	
AB	1 ⎪	
C	1 ⎬	Within plots — 18
AC	1 ⎪	
BC	1 ⎪	
Replications × all others	12 ⎭	
TOTALS	23	23

Here the replications' interaction with all three main effects and their interactions are usually taken as the error term for testing the important effects. The replication effect and the Block (or ABC) effect could be tested against the Replication × Block Interaction, but the degrees of freedom are low and the power of such a test is poor. Such a design is quite powerful, however, in testing the main effects A, B and C and their first-order interactions. However, it will give no clean information on the ABC interaction.

Partial Confounding

In the example just considered, we might be concerned with some test on the ABC interaction. This could be found by confounding some interactions other than ABC in some of the replications. We might use four replications and confound ABC in the first one, AB in the second, AC in the third, and BC in the fourth. Thus the four replications will yield full information on A, B and C but three-fourths information on AB, AC, BC and ABC, since we can compute an unconfounded interaction such as AB in three out of four of the replications. The layout below shows the proper block entries for each replication.

	Rep. I		Rep. II		Rep. III		Rep. IV
Confound:	ABC		AB		AC		BC

(1)	a		(1)	a		(1)	a		(1)	b
ab	b		c	b		ac	c		bc	c
ac	c		ab	ac		abc	bc		a	ab
bc	abc		abc	bc		b	ab		abc	ac

$$L = X_1 + X_2 + X_3 \quad L = X_1 + X_2 \quad L = X_1 + X_3 \quad L = X_2 + X_3$$

The analysis layout would be that shown in Table 14.3.

TABLE 14.3 — Analysis Layout for Partially Confounded 2^3 Factorial

Source	df		df
Replications	3 ⎫		Between plots — 7
Blocks within Replications	4 ⎭		
in			
Or ABC (Rep. I)	1		
AB (Rep. II)	1		
AC (Rep. III)	1		
BC (Rep. IV)	1		
A	1		
B	1		
C	1		
AB	1	only from	Within plots — 24
AC	1	replications	
BC	1	where not	
ABC	1	confounded	
Replications × all effects — 17			
Totals	31		31

The residual term with its 17 df can be explained as follows. In all four replications, the main effects A, B and C can be isolated. This gives 3×1 df for each replication by main effect interaction, or a total of 9 df. The AB, AC, BC and ABC interactions can be isolated in only three out of the four replications. Hence the replications by AC has $2 \times 1 = 2$ df, or a total of 8 df for all such interactions. This gives $9 + 8 = 17$ df for effects by replications, which is usually taken as the error estimate. The blocks and replications are separated out in the top of Table 14.3 only to reduce the experimental error. The numerical analysis of problems like this is carried out in the same manner as given in earlier chapters.

14.4   Block Confounding — No Replication

In many cases an experimenter cannot afford several replications of an experiment, and he is further restricted in that he cannot run the complete factorial in one block or at one time. Again, the experiment may be blocked and information recovered on all but some high-order interactions, which may be confounded. Designs for such experiments will be considered for the special cases of 2^n and 3^n factorials because they appear often in practice.

Confounding in 2^n Factorials

The methods given earlier in this chapter can be used to determine the block composition for a specific confounding scheme. If only one replication is possible, one is run, and some of the higher-order interaction terms must be used as experimental error unless some independent measure of error is available from previous data. This type of design is used mostly when there are several factors involved (say four or more), some high-order interactions may be confounded with blocks, and some others are yet available for an error estimate. For example, consider a 2^4 factorial where only eight treatment combinations can be run at one time. One possible confounding scheme would be

Confound: $ABCD$ and $L = X_1 + X_2 + X_3 + X_4$

Block I	(1)	ab	bc	ac	abcd	cd	ad	bd		$L = 0$

Block II	a	b	abc	c	bcd	acd	d	abd		$L = 1$

and the analysis would be as shown in Table 14.4.

The three-way interactions may be pooled here to give 4 df for error, assuming that these interactions are actually nonexistent. All main effects and first-order interactions could then be tested with 1 and 4 df.

TABLE 14.4 — 2^4 Factorial in Two Blocks

Source	df
A	1
B	1
C	1
D	1
AB	1
AC	1
AD	1
BC	1
BD	1
CD	1
ABC	1 ⎫
ABD	1 ⎪ 4 df
ACD	1 ⎬ for
BCD	1 ⎭ error
Blocks or ABCD	1
TOTALS	15 df

After examining the results, it might be possible to pool some of the two-way interactions that have small mean squares with the three-way interactions if more degrees of freedom are desired in the error term.

If only four treatment combinations can be run in a block, one may confound the 2^4 factorial in four blocks of four treatment combinations each. For four blocks, 3 df must be confounded with blocks. If two interactions are confounded, the product (modulus 2) of these two is also confounded, since the product of the signs in two effects gives the signs for the product. Thus, if AB and CD are confounded, so also will $ABCD$ be confounded. This scheme would confound two first-order interactions and one third order. It might be better to confound two second-order interactions and one first order:

$$ABC, \quad BCD, \quad AD$$

(Note here that $(ABC)(BCD) = AB^2C^2D = AD$ (modulus 2). Hence 3 df are confounded with blocks. Before proceeding to the block compositions, consider a problem where four factors (A, B, C and D) are involved, each at two levels, and only four treatment combinations can be run in one day. The measured variable is yield. The confounding scheme given above gives two independent equations

$$L_1 = X_1 + X_2 + X_3$$
$$L_2 = X_2 + X_3 + X_4$$

Each treatment combination will give one of the following four pairs when substituted into both L_1 and $L_2 = 00, 01, 10, 11$. For example

$$(1): L_1 = 0, \qquad L_2 = 0$$

$$a: L_1 = 1, \qquad L_2 = 0$$

$$b: L_1 = 1, \qquad L_2 = 1$$

$$ab: L_1 = 2 = 0, \quad L_2 = 1$$

etc.

All treatment combinations with the same pair of L values will be placed together in one block. Thus the 16 treatment combinations will be assigned to four blocks as shown in Table 14.5.

TABLE 14.5 — 2^4 Example in four Blocks of Four with Data

Block 1	Block 2	Block 3	Block 4
(1) = 82	a = 76	b = 79	ab = 85
bc = 55	abc = 74	c = 71	ac = 84
acd = 81	cd = 72	$abcd$ = 89	bcd = 84
abd = 88	bd = 73	ad = 79	d = 80
$L_1 = 0$	$L_1 = 1$	$L_1 = 1$	$L_1 = 0$
$L_2 = 0$	$L_2 = 0$	$L_2 = 1$	$L_2 = 1$

In Table 14.5, the order of experimentation within each block is randomized and the resulting responses are given for each treatment combination. The proper treatment combinations for each block can be generated from the principal block. If bc and acd are in the principal block, then their product

$$(bc)(acd) = abc^2d = abd$$

is also in the principal block. For another block, consider a and multiply a by all the combinations in the principal block, giving

$$a(1) = a, \quad a(bc) = abc, \quad a(acd) = cd, \quad a(abd) = bd$$

the entries in the second block. In the same manner, the other two blocks may be generated. This means that only a few readings in the principal block need to be determined by the L_1, L_2 values, and all the rest of the design can be generated from these few treatment combinations. Tables are also available for designs when certain effects are confounded [5].

This experiment is then a 2^4 factorial experiment. The design is a randomized incomplete block design where blocks are confounded with the interactions ABC, BCD and AD. For the analysis, we might use the Yates method of Chapter 7. (See Table 14.6.)

TABLE 14.6 — Yates Method Analysis for 2^4 Example

Treatment Combination	Response	(1)	(2)	(3)	(4)	SS
(1)	82	158	322	606	1252	—
a	76	164	284	646	+60	225.00
b	79	155	320	+32	2	0.25
ab	85	129	326	28	30	56.25
c	71	159	0	−20	−32	64.00
ac	84	161	+32	22	+32	64.00
bc	55	153	14	+18	−14	12.25
abc	74	173	14	12	−26	42.25*
d	80	−6	6	−38	40	100.00
ad	79	+6	−26	6	−4	1.00*
bd	73	+13	2	+32	42	110.25
abd	88	+19	20	0	−6	2.25
cd	72	−1	12	−32	44	121.00
acd	81	15	+6	18	−32	64.00
bcd	84	9	16	−6	50	156.25*
abcd	89	5	−4	−20	−14	12.25

*Confounded with blocks   Total   1031.00

In Table 14.6 the sums of squares in the last column correspond to the effect for the treatment combination on the left. That is

$$\text{SS}_A = 225.00, \quad \text{SS}_B = 0.25, \quad \text{etc.}$$

Note that the effects ABC, BCD and AD are confounded with blocks. Their total sum of squares is $42.25 + 156.25 + 1.00 = 199.50$. If the block totals are computed in Table 14.5, they yield

Block 1 — 306   Block 3 — 318

Block 2 — 295   Block 4 — 333

and the sum of squares between these blocks is

$$\frac{(306)^2 + (295)^2 + (318)^2 + (333)^2}{4} - \frac{(1252)^2}{16}$$

$$\text{SS}_{\text{blocks}} = 98,168.50 - 97,969.00 = 199.50$$

which is identical with the sum of the three interactions with which blocks are confounded. If all three-way and four-way interactions that are not confounded are pooled for an error term, the resulting analysis is that shown in Table 14.7.

TABLE 14.7 — ANOVA for 2^4 in four Blocks

Source	df	SS	MS
A	1	225.00	225.00
B	1	0.25	0.25
C	1	64.00	64.00
D	1	100.00	100.00
AB	1	56.25	56.25
AC	1	64.00	64.00
BC	1	12.25	12.25
BD	1	110.25	110.25
CD	1	121.00	121.00
Error (ABD, ACD, $ABCD$)	3	78.50	26.17
Blocks (ABC, BCD, AD)	3	199.50	66.50
TOTALS	15	1031.00	

With only 1 and 3 df, none of the four main effects nor the five, two-way interactions can be declared significant at the 5 percent significance level. Since the B effect and the BC interaction are not significant even at the 25 percent level, we might wish to pool these with the error to increase the error degrees of freedom. The resulting error sum of squares would then be

$$0.25 + 12.25 + 78.50 = 91.00$$

with 5 df. The error mean square then $= 91.00/5 = 18.20$. Using this error mean square, A and CD are now significant at the 5 percent level. We might conclude that the effect of Factor A is important, that B is not present, and that there may be a CD interaction. As 2^n experiments are often run to get an over-all picture of the important factors, each set at the extremes of its range, another experiment might now be planned without Factor B, since its effect is negligible over the range considered here. The next experiment might include Factors A, C and D at, perhaps, three levels each, or a 3^3 experiment. This experiment might also require blocking.

Confounding in 3^n Factorials

When a 3^n factorial experiment cannot be completely randomized, it is usually blocked in blocks which are multiples of 3. The use of the I and J components of interaction introduced in Sec. 9.2 is helpful in confounding only part of an interaction with blocks. Kempthorne's rule also applies, using such interactions as AB, AB^2, ABC^2, etc., and treatment combinations in the form 00, 10, 01, 11 instead of (1), a, b, ab as in 2^n. Here treatment combinations can be multiplied which will actually add these exponents (modulus 3).

If a 3^2 factorial is restricted so that only three of the nine treatment combinations can be run in one block, we usually confound AB or AB^2, as each carries 2 df. The defining contrast might be AB^2 which gives $L = X_1 + 2X_2$.

Each of the nine treatment combinations then yields

$$00, \ L = 0 \qquad 01, \ L = 2 \qquad 02, \ L = 4 = 1$$
$$10, \ L = 1 \qquad 11, \ L = 3 = 0 \qquad 12, \ L = 5 = 2$$
$$20, \ L = 2 \qquad 21, \ L = 4 = 1 \qquad 22, \ L = 6 = 0$$

Placing treatment combinations with the same L value in common blocks gives

Block 1	Block 2	Block 3
$L = 0$	$L = 1$	$L = 2$
00	10	20
11	21	01
22	02	12

Block 1 with 00 in it is the principal block. Block 2 is generated by *adding* one treatment combination in Block 2 to all those in Block 1, giving

$$00 + 10 = 10, \qquad 11 + 10 = 21, \qquad 22 + 10 = 32 = 02$$

Similarly for Block 3

$$00 + 20 = 20, \qquad 11 + 20 = 31 = 01, \qquad 22 + 20 = 42 = 12$$

Since there are three blocks, 2 df must be confounded. Here AB^2 is confounded with blocks. If AB with its 2 df were confounded, $L = X_1 + X_2$, and the blocking would be

Block 1	Block 2	Block 3
$L = 0$	$L = 1$	$L = 2$
00	10	20
12	22	02
21	01	11

If the data of Table 9.1 are used as an example, and AB^2 is confounded, the responses are

Block 1	Block 2	Block 3
$00 = 1$	$10 = -2$	$20 = 3$
$11 = 4$	$21 = 1$	$01 = 0$
$22 = 2$	$02 = 2$	$12 = -1$

The block sums of squares are determined from the three block totals of 7, 1, and 2.

$$SS_{blocks} = \frac{7^2 + 1^2 + 2^2}{3} - \frac{(10^2)}{9} = 6.89$$

which is identical with the $I(AB)$ interaction component computed in Sec. 9.2 (Table 9.6) as it should be. The remainder of the analysis proceeds the same as in Sec. 9.2, and the resulting ANOVA table is that exhibited in Table 14.8.

TABLE 14.8 — ANOVA for 3^2 Example

Source	df	SS	MS
A	2	4.22	2.11
B	2	1.56	0.78
AB	2	16.22	8.11
Blocks or AB^2	2	6.89	3.44
TOTALS	8	28.89	

If these were real data, the AB part of the interaction might be considered as error, but then neither main effect is significant. The purpose here is only to illustrate the blocking of a 3^2 experiment.

Consider now a 3^3 experiment in which the 27 treatment combinations (such as given in Table 9.7, Chapter 9) cannot all be completely randomized. If nine can be randomized and run on one day, nine on another day, etc., we might use a 3^3 factorial in three blocks of nine treatment combinations each. This requires 2 df to be confounded with blocks. Since the ABC interaction with 8 df can be partitioned into

ABC, ABC^2, AB^2C and AB^2C^2, each with 2 df, one of these four could be confounded with blocks. If AB^2C is confounded

$$L = X_1 + 2X_2 + X_3$$

and the three blocks are

$L = 0$	$L = 1$	$L = 2$
000	100	200
011	111	211
110	210	010
121	221	021
102	202	002
212	012	112
220	020	120
022	122	222
201	001	101

The analysis of data for this design would yield Table 14.9.

TABLE 14.9 — 3^3 Factorial in Three Blocks

Source	df
A	2
B	2
AB	4
C	2
AC	4
BC	4
Error or ABC, ABC^2, AB^2C^2	6
Blocks or AB^2C	2
TOTAL	26

This is a useful design, since we can retrieve all main effects (A, B, C) and all two-way interactions, if we are willing to pool the 6 df in ABC as error. The determination of sums of squares, etc., is the same as for a complete 3^3 given in Example 9.1. Confounding other parts of the ABC interaction would, of course, yield different blocking arrangements, although the outline of the analysis would be the same. In practice, different blocking arrangements might yield different responses.

More complex confounding schemes can be found in tables such as in Chapter 9 of Davies [5].

For practice, consider confounding a 3^3 in nine blocks of three treatment combinations each. Here 8 df must be confounded with blocks. One confounding scheme might be

$$AB^2C^2, \qquad AB, \qquad BC^2, \qquad AC$$

Note that

$$(AB^2C^2)(AB) = A^2C^2 = AC$$

and

$$(AB)(BC^2) = AB^2C^2$$

These are not all independent. In fact only two of the expressions are. For this reason, we need only two expressions for the L values

$$L_1 = X_1 + 2X_2 + 2X_3$$

$$L_2 = X_1 + X_2$$

as these two will yield nine pairs of numbers — one pair for each block. First determine the principal block, where both L_1 and L_2 are zero. One treatment combination is obviously 000. Another is 211, as

$$L_1 = 1(2) + 2(1) + 2(1) = 6 = 0$$

$$L_2 = 1(2) + 1(1) = 3 = 0$$

A third is 122, as

$$L_1 = 1(1) + 2(2) + 2(2) = 9 = 0$$

$$L_2 = 1(1) + 1(2) = 3 = 0$$

The other eight blocks can now be generated from this principal block, giving

Block	1	2	3	4	5	6	7	8	9
	000	001	002	010	020	100	200	110	101
	211	212	210	221	201	011	111	021	012
	122	120	121	102	112	222	022	202	220

An analysis layout would be that shown in Table 14.10.

TABLE 14.10 — 3^3 Factorial in Nine Blocks

Source	df	
A	2	
B	2	
C	2	
AB^2	2	
AC^2	2	
BC	2	
ABC	2 ⎫	
AB^2C	2 ⎬ use for error with 6 df	
ABC^2	2 ⎭	
Blocks or AB, BC^2, AC, AB^2C^2	8	
Total	26	

This design might be reasonable if interest centered only in the main effects A, B and C. Such a design might be necessary where three factors are involved, each at three levels, but only three treatment combinations can be run in one day. These three might involve an elaborate environmental test where at best only three sets of environmental conditions, temperature, pressure, and humidity, can be simulated in one day.

14.5 Summary

The summary of Chapter 13 may now be extended.

Experiment	*Design*	*Analysis*
II. Two or		
More		
Factors		
A. Fac-		
torial		
	1. Completely	
	Randomized	
	2. Randomized Block	2.
	a. Complete	a. Factorial
	$X_{ijk} = \mu + R_k + A_i$	ANOVA
	$+ B_j + AB_{ij} + \epsilon_{ijk}$	

b. Incomplete —   b.
   Confounding
   (1) Main Effect —   (1) Split-Plot
       Split Plot   ANOVA
$$X_{ijk} = \mu + \underbrace{R_i + A_j + RA_{ij}}_{\text{whole plot}}$$

$$+ \underbrace{B_k + RB_{ik} + AB_{jk} + RAB_{ijk}}_{\text{split plot}}$$

   (2) Interactions —   (2)
       In 2^n and 3^n
       (a) Several   (a) ANOVA
           Replications   replica-
           $X_{jkq} = \mu + \underset{\downarrow}{R_i}$ tions

                   (rep)   and
           $+ B_j + RB_{ij} + \underset{\downarrow}{A_k} + B_q$ blocks
           (block or confounded
           interaction)
           $+ AB_{kq} + \epsilon_{ikq}$
       (b) One   (b) ANOVA
           Replication Only   (blocks)
           $X_{ijk} = \mu + B_i + \underset{\downarrow}{A_j}$
           (block or con-
           founded interaction)
           $+ B_k + AB_{jk}$, etc.

PROBLEMS

14-1. Assuming that Example 7.2 could not be run all in one day, set up a confounding scheme to confound the AC interaction using two blocks of four observations each. With the results of this problem (Table 7.9) show that you have indeed confounded AC with blocks.

14-2. For the data of Prob. 7-6, consider running the 16 treatment combinations in four blocks of four (two replications per treatment). Confound ACD, BCD, and AB, and determine the block compositions.

14-3. From the results of Prob. 7-6, show that the blocks are confounded with the interactions in Prob. 14-2 above.

14-4. For Prob. 9-5, consider this experiment as run in three blocks of nine with two replications for each treatment combination.

Confound ABC (2 df) where A is surface thickness, B is base thickness, and C is sub-base thickness, and determine the design. Also use the numerical results of Prob. 9-7 to show that ABC is indeed confounded in your design.

14-5.   Set up a scheme for confounding a 2^4 factorial in two blocks of eight each, confounding ABD with blocks.

14-6.   Repeat Prob. 14-5 and confound BCD.

14-7.   Work out a confounding scheme for a 2^5 factorial, confounding in four blocks of eight each. Show the outline of an ANOVA table.

14-8.   Repeat Prob. 14-7 in four replications confounding different interactions in each replication. Show the ANOVA table outline.

14-9.   Work out the confounding of a 3^4 factorial in three blocks of 27 each.

14-10. Repeat Prob. 14-9 in nine blocks of nine each.

CHAPTER

15 | Fractional Replication

15.1 Introduction

As the number of factors to be considered in a factorial experiment increases, the number of treatment combinations increases very rapidly. This can be seen with a 2^n factorial where $n = 5$ requires 32 experiments for one replication, $n = 6$ requires 64, $n = 7$ requires 128, etc. Along with this increase in the amount of experimentation comes an increase in the number of high-order interactions. Some of these high-order interactions may be used as error, as those above second-order (three-way) would be difficult to explain if found significant. Table 15.1 gives some idea of the number of main effects, first-order, second-order, etc., interactions that can be recovered if a complete 2^n factorial can be run.

TABLE 15.1 — Buildup of 2^n Factorial Effects

n	2^n	Main Effects	Orders of Interaction						
			1st	2nd	3rd	4th	5th	6th	7th
5	32	5	10	10	5	1			
6	64	6	15	20	15	6	1		
7	128	7	21	35	35	21	7	1	
8	256	8	28	56	70	56	28	8	1

Considering $n = 7$, there will be 7 df for the seven main effects, 21 df for the 21 first-order interactions, 35 df for the 35 second-order interactions, leaving

$$35 + 21 + 7 + 1 = 64 \text{ df}$$

for an error estimate, assuming no blocking. Even if this experiment were confounded in blocks, there is still a large number of degrees of freedom for the error estimate. In such cases, it may not be economical to run a whole replicate of 128 observations. Nearly as much information can be gleaned from half as many observations. When only a fraction of a replicate is run, the design is called a *fractional replication* or a *fractional factorial*.

For running a fractional replication, the methods of Chapter 14 are used to determine a confounding scheme such that the number of treatment combinations in a block is within the economic range of the experimenter. If, for example, he can run 60 or 70 experiments and he is interested in seven factors, each at two levels, he can use a one-half replicate of a 2^7 factorial. The complete $2^7 = 128$ experiment is laid out in two blocks of 64 by confounding some high-order interaction. Then only one of these two blocks is run; the decision is made as to which one by the toss of a coin.

15.2 Aliases

To see how a fractional replication is run, consider a simple case. Three factors are of interest, each at two levels, but the experimenter cannot afford $2^3 = 8$ experiments. He will, however, settle for four. This suggests a one-half replicate of a 2^3 factorial. Suppose ABC is confounded with blocks. The two blocks are then

$$I = ABC$$

Block 1 | (1) | *ab* | *bc* | *ac*
Block 2 | *a* | *b* | *c* | *abc*

A coin is flipped and the decision is made to run only Block 2. What information can be gleaned from Block 2 and what information is lost when only half of the experiment is run?

Referring to Table 7.7, which shows the proper coefficients ($+1$ or -1) for the treatment combinations in a 2^3 factorial to give the effects desired, box only those treatment combinations in Block 2 which are to be run. (See Table 15.2.)

TABLE 15.2 — One-half Replication of a 2^3 Factorial

Treatment Combination	Effect						
	A	B	AB	C	AC	BC	ABC
(1)	−	−	+	−	+	+	−
a	+	−	−	−	−	+	+
b	−	+	−	−	+	−	+
ab	+	+	+	−	−	−	−
c	−	−	+	+	−	−	+
ac	+	−	−	+	+	−	−
bc	−	+	−	+	−	+	−
abc	+	+	+	+	+	+	+

Note, in the boxed area, that ABC has all plus signs in Block 2, which is a result of confounding blocks with ABC. Note also that the effect of A is

$$A = +a - b - c + abc$$

and

$$BC = +a - b - c + abc$$

so that we cannot distinguish between A and BC in Block 2. Two or more effects which have the same numerical value are called *aliases*. We cannot tell them apart. B and AC are likewise aliases, as are C and AB. Because of this confounding when only a fraction of the experiment is run, we must check the aliases and be reasonably sure they are not both present if such a design is to be of value. An analysis of this one half replication of a 2^3 would be as shown in Table 15.3.

TABLE 15.3 — One-half Replication of a 2^3 Factorial

Source	df
A (or BC)	1
B (or AC)	1
C (or AB)	1
TOTAL	3

This would hardly be a practical experiment unless the experimenter is sure that no first-order interactions exist and that he has some external source of error to use in testing A, B and C. The real advantage of such fractionating will be seen on designs with larger n values.

If Block 1 were run for the experiment instead of Block 2, A has the value $-(1) + ab + ac - bc$, and BC has the value $+(1) - ab - ac + bc$, which gives the same total except for sign. The sum of squares due to A and BC are therefore the same; again they are said to be aliases. Here

$$A = -BC \qquad B = -AC \qquad C = -AB$$

The definition given above still holds where one effect is the alias of another if they have the same *numerical* value, or value regardless of sign.

A quick way to find the aliases of an effect in a fractional replication of a 2^n factorial experiment is to multiply the effect by the terms in the defining contrast, modulus 2. The results will be aliases of the original effect. In the example above

$$I = ABC$$

The alias of A is

$$A(ABC) = A^2BC = BC$$

The alias of B is

$$B(ABC) = AB^2C = AC$$

The alias of C is

$$C(ABC) = ABC^2 = AB$$

This simple rule works for any fractional replication for a 2^n factorial. It works also with a slight modification for a 3^n factorial run as a fractional replication.

15.3 Fractional Replications

2^n Factorials

As an example, consider the problem suggested in the introduction. An experimenter wishes to study the effect of seven factors, each at two levels, but he cannot afford to run all 128 experiments. He will settle for 64, or a one-half replicate of a 2^7. Deciding to confound the highest-order interaction with blocks, he has

$$I = ABCDEFG$$

The two blocks are found by placing (1) and all pairs, quadruples, and sextuples of the seven letters in one block and the single letters, triples, quintuples and one septuple of the seven letters in the other block. One of the two blocks is chosen at random and run. Before carrying out this experiment, he should check on the aliases. From the defining contrast

$$I = ABCDEFG$$

the alias of A is $A(ABCDEFG) = BCDEFG$, and all main effects are likewise aliased with fifth-order interactions.

AB is aliased with $AB(ABCDEFG) = CDEFG$, a fourth-order interaction. So all first-order interactions are aliased with fourth-order interactions. A second-order interaction such as ABC is aliased with a third-order interaction as

$$ABC(ABCDEFG) = DEFG$$

If the second and third-order interactions are taken as error, the analysis would be as in Table 15.4.

TABLE 15.4 — One-half Replication of a 2^7

Source	df	
Main effects $A, B, \cdots G$ (or fifth order)	1 each for 7	
First-order interaction: AB, AC (or fourth order)	1 each for 21	
Second-order interaction: ABC, ABD (or third order)	1 each for 35 $\Big\}$	use as error
TOTAL	63	

This is a very practical design, as there are good tests on all main effects and first-order interactions, assuming all higher-order interactions are zero. The degrees of freedom for each test would be 1 and 35. If, for some reason known to the experimenter, he suspects some second-order interaction, he could leave it out of the error estimate and still have sufficient degrees of freedom for the error estimate. The analysis of such an experiment follows the methods given in Chapter 7.

If this same experimenter is further restricted and can only afford to run 32 experiments, he might try a one-fourth replication of a 2^7. Here 3 df must be confounded with blocks. If two fourth-order interactions are confounded with blocks, one third-order is automatically confounded also, as

$$I = ABCDE = CDEFG = ABFG$$

which confounds 3 df with the four blocks. In this design, if only one of the four blocks of 32 observations is run, each effect has three aliases. These are

$$A = BCDE = ACDEFG = BFG \qquad CD = ABE = EFG = ABCDFG$$

$$B = ACDE = BCDEFG = AFG \qquad CE = ABD = DFG = ABCEFG$$

$$C = ABDE = DEFG = ABCFG \qquad CF = ABDEF = DEG = ABCG$$

$$D = ABCE = CEFG = ABDFG \qquad CG = ABDEG = DEF = ABCF$$

$$E = ABCD = CDFG = ABEFG \qquad DE = ABC = CFG = ABDEFG$$

$$F = ABCDEF = CDEG = ABG \qquad DF = ABCEF = CEG = ABDG$$

$$G = ABCDEG = CDEF = ABF \qquad DG = ABCEG = CEF = ABDF$$

$$AB = CDE = ABCDEFG = FG \qquad EF = ABCDF = CDG = ABEG$$

$$AC = BDE = ADEFG = BCFG \qquad EG = ABCDG = CDF = ABEF$$

$$AD = BCE = ACEFG = BDFG \qquad ACF = BDEF = ADEG = BCG$$

$$AE = BCD = ACDFG = BEFG \qquad ACG = BDEG = ADEF = BCF$$

$$AF = BCDEF = ACDEG = BG \qquad ADF = BCEF = ACEG = BDG$$

$$AG = BCDEG = ACDEF = BF \qquad ADG = BCEG = ACEF = BDF$$

$$BC = ADE = BDEFG = ACFG \qquad AEG = BCDG = ACDF = BEF$$

$$BD = ACE = BCEFG = ADFG \qquad BEG = ACDG = BCDF = AEF$$

$$BE = ACD = BCDFG = AEFG$$

This is quite a formidable list of aliases; but when only one block of 32 is run, there are 31 df within the block. The above list accounts for these 31 df. If, in this design, all second-order (three-way) and higher interactions can be considered negligible, the main effects are all clear of first-order interactions. Three first-order interactions (AB, AF and AG) are each aliased with another first-order interaction (FG, BG and BF). If the choice of Factors A, B, F and G can be made with the assurance that the above interactions are either negligible or not of sufficient interest to be tested, these 3 df can be either pooled with error or left out of the analysis. The remaining 15 first-order interactions are all clear of other interactions except second order or higher. There are also 6 df left over for error involving only second-order interactions or higher. An analysis might be that shown in Table 15.5.

TABLE 15.5 — One-fourth Replication of a 2^7 Factorial

Source	df
Main effects: $A, B, \cdots G$	1 each for 7
1st order Interaction: AC, AD, etc.	1 each for 15
AB (or FG), AF (or BG), AG (or BF)	1 each for 3
Second-order interaction or higher (ACF, etc.)	1 each for 6
TOTAL	31

Here tests can be made with 1 and 6 df or 1 and 9 df if the last two lines can be pooled for error. This is a fairly good design when it is necessary to run only a one-fourth replication of a 2^7 factorial.

3^n Factorials

The simplest 3^n factorial is a 3^2 requiring nine experiments for a complete factorial. If only a fraction of these can be run, we might consider a one-third replication of a 3^2 factorial. First we confound either AB or AB^2 with the three blocks. Confounding AB^2 gives

$$I = AB^2$$

$$L = X_1 + 2X_2$$

and the three blocks are

$$L = 0 \qquad L = 1 \qquad L = 2$$

00	10	20
11	21	01
22	02	12

If one of these three is run, the aliases are

$$A(AB^2) = A^2B^2 = A^4B^4 = AB$$

since the exponent on the first element is never left greater than one. A^2B^2 is squared to give $A^4B^4 = AB$ (modulus 3). However, the alias of B is

$$B(AB^2) = AB^3 = A$$

Hence all three effects, A, B and AB, are aliases and mutually confounded. In order to get both aliases from one multiplication using the defining contrast, one multiplies the effect by the square of I as well as I. This gives

$$A[(AB^2)]^2 = A(A^2B^4) = A^3B = B$$

Hence, $A = AB = B$; this is a poor experiment, since, within the block that is run, both degrees of freedom confound A, B and AB. In addition, no degrees of freedom are left for error. This example is cited only to show the slight modification necessary when determining the aliases in a 3^n factorial run as a fractional replication. The value of these fractional replications is seen when more factors are involved.

Consider a 3^3 factorial in three blocks of nine treatment combinations each. The effects can be broken down into 13, 2 df effects: A, B, C, AB, AB^2, AC, AC^2, BC, BC^2, ABC, AB^2C, ABC^2, and AB^2C^2. Confounding ABC^2 with the three blocks gives

$$I = ABC^2, \qquad L = X_1 + X_2 + 2X_3$$

and the blocks are

| $L = 0$ | 000 | 011 | 022 | 101 | 112 | 120 | 210 | 221 | 202 |

| $L = 1$ | 100 | 111 | 122 | 201 | 212 | 220 | 010 | 021 | 002 |

| $L = 2$ | 200 | 211 | 222 | 001 | 012 | 020 | 110 | 121 | 102 |

If only one of these blocks is now run, the aliases are

$$A = A(ABC^2) = A^2BC^2 = AB^2C$$

and $\quad A = A(ABC^2)^2 = A^3B^2C^4 = B^2C = B^4C^2 = BC^2$

$$B = B(ABC^2) = AB^2C^2$$

and $\quad B = B(ABC^2)^2 = A^2B^3C^4 = A^4C^8 = AC^2$

$$C = C(ABC^2) = ABC^3 = AB$$

and $\quad C = C(ABC^2)^2 = A^2B^2C^5 = A^4B^4C^{10} = ABC$

$$AB^2 = AB^2(ABC^2) = A^2B^3C^2 = A^4B^6C^4 = AC$$

and $\quad AB^2 = AB^2(ABC^2)^2 = A^3B^4C^4 = BC$

The analysis would be that in Table 15.6.

TABLE 15.6 — One-third Replication of a 3^3 Factorial

Source	df
A (or BC^2 or AB^2C)	2
B (or AB^2C^2 or AC^2)	2
C (or AB or ABC)	2
AC (or AB^2 or BC)	2
Total	8

This design would be somewhat practical if we could consider all interactions negligible and be content with 2 df for error.

These methods are easily extended to higher-order 3^n experiments. Analysis proceeds as in Chapter 9.

It might be instructive to examine somewhat further this design of a 1/3rd replication of a 3^3. A layout for 3^3 as a complete factorial was given in Table 9.7. If only one-third of this were run, say block $L = 1$, suppose the other entries in Table 9.7 were crossed out, giving the results shown in Table 15.7.

TABLE 15.7 — One-third Replication of a 3^3 Factorial

Factor B	Factor C	Factor A 0	1	2
0	0	~~000~~	100	~~200~~
	1	~~001~~	~~101~~	201
	2	002	~~102~~	~~202~~
1	0	010	~~110~~	~~210~~
	1	~~011~~	111	~~211~~
	2	~~012~~	~~112~~	212
2	0	~~020~~	~~120~~	220
	1	021	~~121~~	~~221~~
	2	~~022~~	122	~~222~~

The remaining nine entries in Table 15.7 can now be summarized by levels of Factor C only to give the result shown in Table 15.8. A second glance at Table 15.8 reveals that this design is none other than a Latin Square! In a sense our designs have now come full circle, from a Latin Square as two restrictions on a single-factor experiment (Chapter

TABLE 15.8 — *One-third Replication of a 3^3 in Terms of Factor C*

	Factor A		
Factor B	0	1	2
0	2	0	1
1	0	1	2
2	1	2	0

5) to a Latin Square as a one-third replication of a 3^3 factorial. The designs come out the same, but they result from entirely different objectives. In a single-factor experiment, the general model

$$X_{ij} = \mu + T_j + \epsilon_{ij}$$

is partitioned by refining the error term due to restrictions on the randomization to give: $X_{ijk} = \mu + T_j + \beta_i + \gamma_k + \epsilon'_{ij}$ where the block and position effects are taken from the original error term, ϵ_{ij}.

In the one-third replication of a 3^3, there are three factors of interest which comprise the treatments, giving

$$X_{ijk} = \mu + A_i + B_j + C_k + \epsilon_{ijk}$$

where A, B and C are taken from the treatment effect. Both models look alike but derive from different types of experiments. In both cases, the assumption is made that there is no interaction among the factors. This is more reasonable when the factors represent only randomization restrictions such as blocks and positions, rather than when each of the three factors are of vital concern to the experimenter.

By choosing each of the other two blocks in the confounding of ABC^2 ($L = 0$ or $L = 2$), two other Latin squares are obtained. If another confounding scheme is chosen, such as AB^2C, ABC, or AB^2C^2, more and different Latin squares can be generated. In fact, with four parts of the three-way interaction and three blocks per confounding scheme, 12 distinct Latin squares may be generated. This shows how it is possible to select a Latin square at random for a particular design.

It cannot be overstressed that we must be quite sure that no interaction exists before using these designs on a 3^3 factorial. It is not enough to say that there is no interest in the interactions, because, unfortunately, the interactions are badly confounded with main effects as aliases.

15.4 Summary

Continuing the summary at the end of Chapter 14 under incomplete randomized blocks gives

Experiment	*Design*	*Analysis*

II. Two or More
Factors
  A. Factorial

      1. Completely Randomized

      2. Randomized Block
        a. Complete
        b. Incomplete —
        Confounding
        (1) Main Effect —
        Split Plot
        (2) Interactions —
        2^n and 3^n

        (*a*) Several   (*a*) ANOVA (replica-
        Replications   tions and blocks)

$$X_{ijkq} = \mu + R_i + \beta_j + R\beta_{ij} + A_k + B_q + AB_{kq} + \epsilon_{ikq}$$

        (*b*) One Rep-   (*b*) ANOVA (blocks)
        lication only

$$X_{ijk} = \mu + \beta_i + A_j + B_k + AB_{jk} + \text{, etc.}$$

        (Blocks or Con-
        founded Interaction)
        (*c*) Fractional   (*c*) ANOVA
        Replication — Aliases
        (1) In 2^n
        (2) In $3^n - n = 3$:
        Latin Square

$$X_{ijk} = \mu + A_i + B_j + AB_{ij} = \text{, etc.}$$

PROBLEMS

15-1. If not all of Prob. 14-1 can be run, determine the aliases if a one-half replication is run. Analyze the data for the principal block only.

15-2. If only a one-fourth replication can be run in Prob. 14-2, determine the aliases.

15-3. For Prob. 14-4, use a one-third replication and determine the aliases.

15-4. Run an analysis on the block in Prob. 15-3 that contains treatment combination 022.

15-5. What would be the aliases in Prob. 14-5 if a one-half replication is run?

15-6. Determine the aliases in a one-fourth replication of Prob. 14-7.

15-7. Determine the aliases in Prob. 14-9 if a one-third replication is run.

CHAPTER
16 | Miscellaneous Topics

16.1 Introduction

There are several techniques that have been developed, based on the general design principles presented in the first 15 chapters of this book and on other well-known statistical methods. Two of these are very useful in experimental work and are mentioned briefly here. No attempt will be made to discuss these in detail, as they are presented very well in the references. It is hoped that a background in experimental design as given in the first 15 chapters will make it possible for the experimenter to read and understand the references.

The two methods to be discussed are Response Surface Experimentation and Evolutionary Operation.

16.2 Response Surface Experimentation

Philosophy

The concept of a response surface involves a dependent variable (Y), called the response variable, and several independent or controlled variables $(X_1, X_2, \cdots X_k)$. If all of these variables are assumed to be measurable, the response surface can be expressed as

$$Y = f(X_1, X_2, \cdots X_k)$$

For the case of two independent variables such as temperature (X_1) and time (X_2), the yield (Y) of a chemical process can be expressed as

$$Y = f(X_1, X_2)$$

This surface can be plotted in three dimensions, with X_1 on the abscissa, X_2 on the ordinate, and Y plotted perpendicular to the X_1X_2 plane. If the values of X_1 and X_2 that yield the same Y are connected, we can picture the surface with a series of equal-yield lines, or contours. These are similar to the contours of equal height on topographic maps and the isobars on weather maps. Some response surfaces might be of the types in Fig. 16.1.

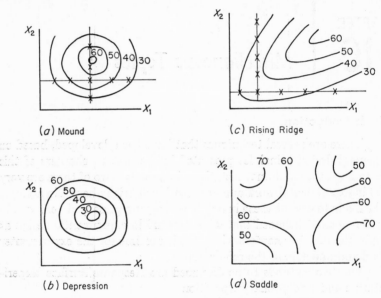

(*a*) Mound

(*c*) Rising Ridge

(*b*) Depression

(*d*) Saddle

FIG. 16.1   *Some Typical Response Surfaces in Two Dimensions*

Two excellent references for understanding response surface experimentation are given in [5] and [9].

The Twofold Problem

The problem involved in the use of response-surface experimentation is twofold: (1) to determine, on the basis of one experiment, where to move in the next experiment toward the optimal point on the underlying response surface; (2) having located the optimum, or near optimum of the surface, to determine the equation of the response surface in an area near this optimum point.

One method of experimentation that seeks the optimal point of the response surface might be the traditional one-factor-at-a-time method. As shown in Fig. 16.1(a), if X_2 is fixed and X_1 is varied, we find the X_1 optimal (or near optimal) value of response, Y, at the fixed value of X_2. Having found this X_1 value, experiments can now be run at this fixed X_1, and the X_2 for optimal response can be found. In the case of the mound in Fig. 16.1(a), this method would lead eventually to the peak of the mound or near it. However, this same method, when applied to a surface such as the rising ridge in Fig. 16.1(c), fails to lead to the maximum point on the response surface. In experimental work, the type of response surface is usually unknown, so that a better method is necessary if the optimum set of conditions is to be found for any surface.

The method developed by those who have worked in this area is called the *path of steepest ascent* method. The idea here is to run a simple experiment over a small area of the response surface, where, for all practical purposes, the surface may be regarded as a plane. We then determine the equation of this plane and from it the direction we should take from this experiment in order to move toward the optimum of the surface. Since the next experiment should be in a direction in which we hope to scale the height the fastest, this is referred to as the *path of steepest ascent*. This technique does not determine how far away from the original experiment succeeding sequential experiments should be run, but it does indicate to the experimenter the direction along which the next experiment should be performed. A simple example in the next section will illustrate this method.

In order to determine the equation of the response surface, several special experimental designs have been developed which attempt to approximate this equation using the smallest number of experiments possible. In two dimensions, the simplest surface is a plane given by

$$Y = B_0 X_0 + B_1 X_1 + B_2 X_2 + \epsilon \qquad (16.1)$$

where Y is the observed response, X_0 is taken as unity, and estimates of the B's are to be determined by the method of least squares which minimizes the sum of the squares of the errors, ϵ. Such an equation is referred to as a first-order equation, since the power on each independent variable is unity.

If there is some evidence that the surface is not planar, a second-order equation in two dimensions may be a more suitable model

$$Y = B_0 X_0 + B_1 X_1 + B_2 X_2 + B_{11} X_1^2 + B_{12} X_1 X_2 + B_{22} X_2^2 + \epsilon \qquad (16.2)$$

Here, the $X_1 X_2$ term represents an interaction between the two variables X_1 and X_2.

If there are three independent or controlled variables, the first-order equation is again a plane or hyperplane

$$Y = B_0 X_0 + B_1 X_1 + B_2 X_2 + B_3 X_3 + \epsilon \qquad (16.3)$$

and the second-order equation is

$$\begin{aligned} Y = B_0 X_0 + B_1 X_1 + B_2 X_2 + B_3 X_3 + B_{11} X_1^2 + B_{22} X_2^2 \\ + B_{33} X_3^2 + B_{12} X_1 X_2 + B_{13} X_1 X_3 + B_{23} X_2 X_3 + \epsilon \end{aligned} \qquad (16.4)$$

As the complexity of the surface increases, more coefficients must be estimated, and the number of experimental points must necessarily increase. Several very clever designs have been developed that minimize the amount of work necessary to estimate these response-surface equations.

In order to determine the coefficients for these more complex surfaces and to interpret their geometric nature, both multiple regression techniques and the methods of solid analytical geometry are used. In the example which follows, only the simplest type of surface will be explored. The references above will give many more complex examples.

EXAMPLE 16.1. Consider an example in which an experimenter is seeking the proper values for both concentration of filler to epoxy resin (X_1) and position in the mold (X_2) to minimize the abrasion on a plastic die. This abrasion or wear is measured as a decrease in thickness of the material after 10,000 cycles of abrasion. Since the maximum thickness is being sought, the first experiment should attempt to discover the direction in which succeeding experiments should be run in order to approach this maximum by the steepest path. Assuming the surface to be a plane in a small area, the first experiment will be used to determine the equation of this plane. The response surface is then

$$Y = B_0 X_0 + B_1 X_1 + B_2 X_2 + \epsilon$$

As there are three parameters to be estimated, B_0, B_1 and B_2, at least three experimental points must be taken to estimate these coefficients. Such a design might be an equilateral triangle, but, since there are two factors $(X_1$ and $X_2)$, each can be set at two levels and a 2^2 factorial may be used. Two concentrations were chosen, $1/2 : 1$, and $1 : 1$ (ratio of filler to resin), and two positions, 1 in. and 2 in. from a reference point, with responses, Y = thickness of material in 0.0001 in., as shown in Fig. 16.2.

To determine the equation of the best fitting plane for these four points, consider the error in the prediction equation

$$\epsilon = Y - B_0 X_0 - B_1 X_1 - B_2 X_2$$

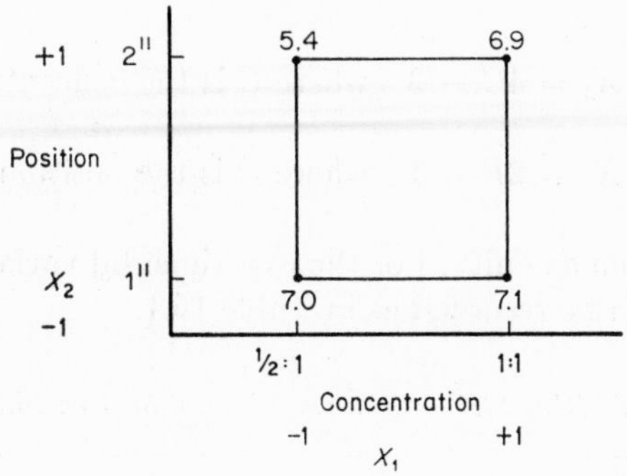

FIG. 16.2 — 2^2 Factorial Example on Response Surface

The sum of the squares for this error is

$$\sum \epsilon^2 = \sum (Y - B_0 X_0 - B_1 X_1 - B_2 X_2)^2$$

where the summation is over all points given in the design. To find the B's, we differentiate this expression with respect to each parameter and set these three expressions equal to zero. This provides three least-squares normal equations, which can be solved for the best estimates of the B's. These estimates are designated at b's.

Differentiating the expression above gives

$$\frac{\partial(\sum \epsilon^2)}{\partial B_0} = -2 \sum (Y - B_0 X_0 - B_1 X_1 - B_2 X_2) X_0 = 0$$

$$\frac{\partial(\sum \epsilon^2)}{\partial B_1} = -2 \sum (Y - B_0 X_0 - B_1 X_1 - B_2 X_2) X_1 = 0$$

$$\frac{\partial(\sum \epsilon^2)}{\partial B_2} = -2 \sum (Y - B_0 X_0 - B_1 X_1 - B_2 X_2) X_2 = 0$$

and from these results we get

$$\left. \begin{aligned} \sum X_0 Y &= b_0 \sum X_0^2 + b_1 \sum X_0 X_1 + b_2 \sum X_0 X_2 \\ \sum X_1 Y &= b_0 \sum X_0 X_1 + b_1 \sum X_1^2 + b_2 \sum X_1 X_2 \\ \sum X_2 Y &= b_0 \sum X_0 X_2 + b_1 \sum X_1 X_2 + b_2 \sum X_2^2 \end{aligned} \right\} \quad (16.5)$$

as the least-squares normal equations.

By a proper choice of experimental variables, it is possible to reduce these equations considerably for simple solution. More complex models can be solved best by the use of matrix algebra. For the 2^2 factorial, the following coding scheme simplifies the solution of Eq. (16.5).

Set: $X_1 = 4C - 3$ where C is the concentration

$X_2 = 2P - 1$ where P is the position

X_0 is always taken as unity. For the experimental variables, X_1 and X_2, the responses can be recorded as in Table 16.1.

TABLE 16.1 — Orthogonal Layout for Fig. 16.2

Y	X_0	X_1	X_2
7.0	1	−1	−1
5.4	1	−1	1
7.1	1	1	−1
6.9	1	1	1

These experimental variables are also indicated on Fig. 16.2.

An examination of the data as presented above shows that X_0, X_1 and X_2 are all orthogonal to each other as

$$\sum X_1 = \sum X_2 = 0 \quad \text{and} \quad \sum X_1 X_2 = 0$$

Hence the least-squares normal equations become

$$\left. \begin{array}{l} \sum X_0 Y = b_0 n + b_1 \cdot 0 + b_2 \cdot 0 \\[2mm] \sum X_1 Y = b_0 \cdot 0 + b_1 \cdot \sum X_1^2 + b_2 \cdot 0 \\[2mm] \sum X_2 Y = b_0 \cdot 0 + b_1 \cdot 0 + b_2 \sum X_2^2 \end{array} \right\} \qquad (16.6)$$

Solving gives

$$\left. \begin{array}{l} b_0 = \sum X_0 Y / n \\[2mm] b_1 = \sum X_1 Y / \sum X_1^2 \\[2mm] b_2 = \sum X_2 Y / \sum X_2^2 \end{array} \right\} \qquad (16.7)$$

For this problem
$$b_0 = \frac{26.4}{4} = 6.60$$

$$b_1 = \frac{1.6}{4} = 0.40$$

$$b_2 = \frac{-1.8}{4} = -0.45$$

and the response surface can be approximated as
$$\hat{Y} = 6.60 + 0.40X_1 - 0.45X_2$$

To determine the sum of squares due to each of these terms in the model, we can use the results of Sec. 3.6 where the sum of squares due to b_i is
$$SS_{b_i} = b_i \cdot \sum X_i Y$$
Here
$$SS_{b_0} = (6.60)(26.4) = 174.24$$

$$SS_{b_1} = (0.40)(1.6) = 0.64$$

$$SS_{b_2} = (-0.45)(-1.8) = 0.81$$

each carrying 1 df. The ANOVA table is shown as Table 16.2.

TABLE 16.2 — ANOVA for 2^2 Factorial Response-Surface Example

Source	SS	df
b_0	174.24	1
b_1	0.64	1
b_2	0.81	1
Residual	0.49	1
TOTALS	176.18	4

Here, all 4 df are shown, as the b_0 term represents the degree of freedom usually associated with the mean; i.e., the correction term in many examples. The total sum of squares is $\sum Y^2$ of the responses and the residual is what is left over. With this 1 df residual, no good test is available on the siginficance of each term in the model, nor is there any way to assess the adequacy of the planar model to describe the surface.

To decide on the direction for the next experiment, plot contours of equal response using the equation of the plane determined above

$$\hat{Y} = 6.60 + 0.40X_1 - 0.45X_2$$

Solve for X_2

$$X_2 = \frac{6.60 - \hat{Y} + 0.40X_1}{0.45}$$

If $\hat{Y} = 5.5$

$$X_2 = \frac{1.10 + 0.40X_1}{0.45}$$

when $X_1 = -1$ $X_2 = 1.56$

          $X_1 = 1$ $X_2 = 3.33$

If $\hat{Y} = 6.0$

$$X_2 = \frac{0.60 + 0.40X_1}{0.45}$$

when $X_1 = -1$ $X_2 = 0.44$

          $X_1 = 1$ $X_2 = 2.22$

If $\hat{Y} = 6.5$

$$X_2 = \frac{0.10 + 0.40X_1}{0.45}$$

when $X_1 = -1$ $X_2 = -0.67$

          $X_1 = 1$ $X_2 = 1.11$

If $\hat{Y} = 7.0$

$$X_2 = \frac{-0.40 + 0.40X_1}{0.45}$$

when $X_1 = -1$ $X_2 = -1.67$

          $X_1 = 1$ $X_2 = 0$

If $\hat{Y} = 7.5$

$$X_2 = \frac{-0.90 + 0.40X_1}{0.45}$$

when $X_1 = -1$ $X_2 = -2.89$

          $X_1 = 1$ $X_2 = -1.11$

Plotting these five contours on the original diagram gives the pattern shown in Fig. 16.3.

By moving in a direction normal to these contours and "up" the surface, we can anticipate larger values of response until the peak is reached. To decide on a possible set of conditions for the next experiment, consider the equation of a normal to these contours thru the point $(0, 0)$. The contours are

$$X_2 = \frac{6.60 - \hat{Y} + 0.40X_1}{0.45}$$

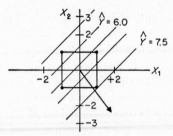

FIG. 16.3 — Contours on 2^2 Factorial Response Surface Example

and their slope is $0.40/0.45 = 8/9$. The normal will have a slope $= -9/8$, and its equation is

$$X_2 - 0 = \frac{-9}{8}(X_1 - 0)$$

$$X_2 = \frac{-9}{8}X_1 \qquad \text{(see arrow in Fig. 16.3)}$$

This technique will not tell how far to go in this direction, but we might run the next experiment with the center of the factorial at $(+1, -9/8)$. The four points would be

X_1	X_2
0	$-\frac{1}{8}$
0	$-2\frac{1}{8}$
2	$-\frac{1}{8}$
2	$-2\frac{1}{8}$

These points are expressed in terms of the experimental variables, but must be decoded to see where to set the concentration and position. Using the coding

$$X_1 = 4C - 3 \quad \text{or} \quad C = \frac{X_1 + 3}{4}$$

$$X_2 = 2P - 1 \quad \text{or} \quad P = \frac{X_2 + 1}{2}$$

the four new points would be

X_1	X_2	C	P
0	$-\frac{1}{8}$	$\frac{3}{4}:1$	$\frac{7}{16}''$
0	$-2\frac{1}{8}$	$\frac{3}{4}:1$	$-\frac{9}{16}''$
2	$-\frac{1}{8}$	$1\frac{1}{4}:1$	$\frac{7}{16}''$
2	$-2\frac{1}{8}$	$1\frac{1}{4}:1$	$-\frac{9}{16}''$

if these settings are possible. Responses may now be taken at these four points on a new 2^2 factorial, and after analysis we can again decide the direction of steepest ascent. This procedure continues until the optimum is obtained.

The above design is sufficient to indicate the direction for subsequent experiments, but it does not provide a good measure of experimental error to test the significance of b_0, b_1, and b_2, nor is there any test of how well the plane approximates the surface. One way to improve on this design is to take two or more points at the center of the square. By replication at the same point, an estimate of experimental error is obtained and the average of the center-point responses will provide an estimate of "goodness of fit" of the plane. If the experiment is near the maximum response, this center point might be somewhat above the four surrounding points, which would indicate the need of a more complex model.

To see how this design would help, consider two observations of response at the center of the example above. Using the same responses at the vertices of the square, the results might be those shown in Fig. 16.4.

Y	X_0	X_1	X_2
7.0	1	−1	−1
5.4	1	−1	1
7.1	1	1	−1
6.9	1	1	1
6.6	1	0	0
6.8	1	0	0

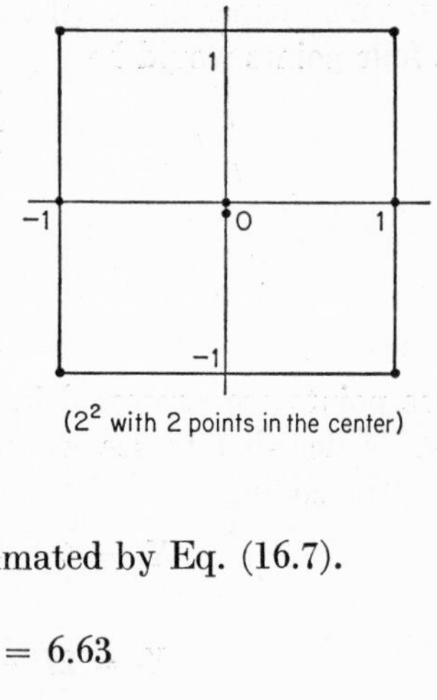

(2^2 with 2 points in the center)

FIG. 16.4

The coefficients in the model are still estimated by Eq. (16.7).

$$b_0 = \frac{\sum X_0 Y}{n} = \frac{39.8}{6} = 6.63$$

$$b_1 = \frac{\sum X_1 Y}{\sum X_1^2} = \frac{1.6}{4} = 0.40$$

$$b_2 = \frac{\sum X_2 Y}{\sum X_2^2} = \frac{-1.8}{4} = -0.45$$

and

$$SS_{b_0} = 6.63(39.8) = 263.87$$

$$SS_{b_1} = 0.40(1.6) = 0.64$$

$$SS_{b_2} = -0.45(-1.8) = 0.81$$

For the sum of squares of the error at $(0, 0)$

$$SS_e = (6.6)^2 + (6.8)^2 - \frac{(13.4)^2}{2} = 89.80 - 89.78 = 0.02$$

The analysis is shown in Table 16.3.

TABLE 16.3 — ANOVA for 2^2 + Two Center Points

Source	SS	df	MS
Total	265.98	6	
b_0	263.87	1	236.87
b_1	0.64	1	0.64
b_2	0.81	1	0.81
Residual	0.66	3	—
Error	0.02	1	0.02
Lack of Fit	0.64	2	0.32

Testing these effects against error gives

For b_0: $F_{1,1} = \dfrac{236.87}{0.02} = 11{,}843.5$

b_1: $F_{1,1} = \dfrac{0.64}{0.02} = 32$

b_2: $F_{1,1} = \dfrac{0.81}{0.02} = 40.5$

Lack of fit: $F_{2,1} = \dfrac{0.32}{0.02} = 16$

With such a small number of degrees of freedom, only b_0 shows significance at the 5 percent level. However, the tests on the b terms are larger than the test on lack of fit, which may indicate that the plane

$$\hat{Y} = 6.63 + 0.40X_1 - 0.45X_2$$

is a fair approximation to the surface where this first experiment was run.

More Complex Surfaces

For more factors — controlled variables — the model for the response variable is more complex, but several designs have been found useful in estimating the coefficients of these surfaces.

When three variables are involved, a first approximation is again a plane or hyperplane, of the form

$$Y = B_0X_0 + B_1X_1 + B_2X_2 + B_3X_3 + \epsilon$$

For this first-order surface, at least four points must be taken to estimate the four B's. Since three dimensions are involved, we might consider a

2^3 factorial. As this design has eight experimental conditions at its vertices, the design often used is a one-half replication of a 2^3 factorial with two or more points at the center of the cube. These six points (two at the center) are sufficient to estimate all four B's and to test for lack of fit of this plane to the surface in three dimensions. After this initial one-half replication of the 2^3, the other half might be run, giving more information for a better fit.

If a plane is not a good fit in two dimensions, a second-order model might be tried. Such a response surface has the form

$$Y = B_0X_0 + B_1X_1 + B_2X_2 + B_{11}X_1^2 + B_{12}X_1X_2 + B_{22}X_2^2 + \epsilon$$

Here six B's are to be estimated. The simplest design for this model would be a pentagon (five points) plus center points. This would yield six or more responses, and all six B's could be estimated.

In developing these designs, Box and others have found that the calculations can be simplified if the design can be rotated. A *rotatable design* is one which has equal predictability in all directions from the center, and the points are at a constant distance from the center. All first-order designs are rotatable, as the square and one-half replication of the cube in the cases above. The simplest second-order design that is rotatable is the pentagon with a point at the center, as given above.

In three dimensions, a second-order surface is given by

$$Y = B_0X_0 + B_1X_1 + B_2X_2 + B_3X_3 + B_{11}X_1^2 + B_{22}X_2^2$$
$$+ B_{33}X_3^2 + B_{12}X_1X_2 + B_{13}X_1X_3 + B_{23}X_2X_3 + \epsilon \quad (16.8)$$

which has 10 unknown coefficients. The cube for a three dimensional model has only eight points, so a special design has been developed, called a *central composite* design. It is a 2^3 factorial with points along each axis at a distance from the center equal to the distance to each vertex. This gives $8 + 6 = 14$ points, and a point at the center makes 15, which is adequate for estimating the B's in Eq. (16.8). This design is pictured in Fig. 16.5.

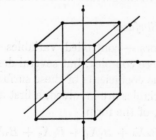

FIG. 16.5   *Central Composite Design*

In attempting to determine the equation of the response surface, some concepts in solid analytical geometry are often helpful. If a second-order model in two dimensions is

$$Y = B_0 X_0 + B_1 X_1 + B_2 X_2 + B_{11} X_1^2 + B_{12} X_1 X_2 + B_{22} X_2^2 + \epsilon$$

The shape of this surface can be determined by reducing this equation to what is called *canonical form*. This would be

$$Y = B'_{11} X_1'^2 + B'_{22} X_2'^2$$

This is accomplished by a translation of axes to remove terms in X_1 and X_2, then a rotation of axes to remove the $X_1 X_2$ term. From B'_{11} and B'_{22}, we can determine the shape of the surface — whether it is a sphere, ellipsoid, paraboloid, hyperboloid, etc. In higher dimensions this becomes more complicated, but it can still be useful in describing the response surface.

16.3   Evolutionary Operation (EVOP)

Philosophy

Evolutionary Operation is a method of process operation that has a built-in procedure to increase productivity. The technique was developed by Box, and both his original article [3] and Barnett's article [1] should be read in order to understand how the method works. Many chemical companies have reported considerable success using EVOP.

The procedure consists of running a simple experiment — usually a factorial — within the range of operability of a process as it is currently running. It is assumed that the variables to be controlled are measure-able and can be set within a short distance of the current settings without disturbing production quality. The idea is to gather data on a response variable — usually yield — at the various points of an experimental design. When one set of data has been taken at all the points, one *cycle* is said to have been completed. One cycle is usually not sufficient to detect any shift in the response, so a second cycle is taken. This continues until the effect of one or more control variables, their interactions, or a change in the mean shows up as significant when compared with a measure of experimental error. This estimate of error is obtained from the cycle data, thus making the experiment self-contained. After a significant increase in yield has been detected, one *phase* is said to have been completed, and at this point a decision is usually made to change the basic operating conditions in a direction that should improve the yield.

Several cycles may be necessary before a shift can be detected. The objective here, as with response surfaces, is to move in the direction of an optimum response. Response-surface experimentation is primarily a laboratory or research technique; evolutionary operation is a production-line method.

In order to facilitate the EVOP procedure, a simple form has been developed to be used on the production line for each cycle of a 2^2 factorial with a point at the center. In the sections that follow, an example will be run using these forms, and later the details of the form will be developed.

An EVOP Example

To illustrate the EVOP procedure, consider a chemical process in which temperature and pressure are varied over short ranges, and the resulting chemical yield is recorded. Since two controlled variables affect the yield, a 2^2 factorial should indicate the effect of each factor as well as a possible interaction between them. By taking a point at the center of a 2^2 factorial, we can also check on a change in the mean (CIM) by comparing this point at the center with the four points around the vertices of the square. If the process should be straddling a maximum, the center point should eventually (after several cycles) be significantly above the peripheral points at the vertices. The standard form for EVOP locates the five points in this design as indicated in Fig. 16.6.

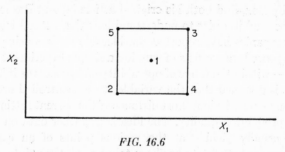

FIG. 16.6

By comparing the responses (or average responses) at points 3 and 4 with those at 2 and 5, an effect of variable X_1 may be detected. Likewise, by comparing responses at 3 and 5 with those at 2 and 4, we may assess the X_2 effect. Comparing the responses at 2 and 3 with those at 4 and 5 will indicate an interaction effect, and comparing the responses at 2, 3, 4, and 5 with those at 1 will indicate a change in the mean, if present. The forms shown in Table 16.4 are filled in with data to show their use, which is self-explanatory.

Not much can be learned from the first cycle unless some separate

TABLE 16.4 — EVOP Work Sheet — First Cycle

```
5 ┌───┐ 3
  │ .1│
2 └───┘ 4
```

CALCULATION WORK SHEET

Cycle: $n = 1$
Response: Yield

Project: 424
Phase: 1
Date: 10/12

Calculation of Averages

	(1)	(2)	(3)	(4)	(5)
Operating Conditions					
(i) Previous Cycle Sum					
(ii) Previous Cycle Average					
(iii) New Observations	94.0	94.5	96.5	94.5	94.5
(iv) Differences [(ii) less (iii)]					
(v) New Sums	94.0	94.5	96.5	94.5	94.5
(vi) New Averages ($\bar{Y}_i$)	94.0	94.5	96.5	94.5	94.5

Calculation of Effects

Temperature effect $= \frac{1}{2}(\bar{Y}_3 + \bar{Y}_4 - \bar{Y}_2 - \bar{Y}_5) = 1.00$

Pressure effect $= \frac{1}{2}(\bar{Y}_3 + \bar{Y}_5 - \bar{Y}_2 - \bar{Y}_4) = 1.00$

$T \times P$ Interaction effect $= \frac{1}{2}(\bar{Y}_2 + \bar{Y}_3 - \bar{Y}_4 - \bar{Y}_5) = 1.00$

Change in Mean effect $= \frac{1}{5}(\bar{Y}_2 + \bar{Y}_3 + \bar{Y}_4 + \bar{Y}_5 - 4\bar{Y}_1) = 0.80$

Calculation of Standard Deviation

Previous Sum $S =$

Previous Average $S =$

New $S = $ Range $\times f_{k,n} =$

Range $=$

New Sum $S =$

New Average $s = \dfrac{\text{New Sum } S}{n-1} =$

Calculations of Error Limits

For New Average $\dfrac{2}{\sqrt{n}} s =$

For New Effects $\dfrac{2}{\sqrt{n}} s =$

For Change in Mean $\dfrac{1.78}{\sqrt{n}} s =$

TABLE 16.5 — EVOP Work Sheet — Second Cycle

CALCULATION WORK SHEET

Cycle: $n = 2$
Response: Yield

Project: 424
Phase: 1
Date: 10/12

```
  5 |   | 3
    | .1 |
  2 |   | 4
```

Calculations of Averages

Operating Conditions	(1)	(2)	(3)	(4)	(5)
(i) Previous Cycle Sum	94.0	94.5	96.5	94.5	94.5
(ii) Previous Cycle Average	94.0	94.5	96.5	94.5	94.5
(iii) New Observations	96.0	95.0	95.0	96.5	94.0
(iv) Differences [(ii) less (iii)]	−2.0	−0.5	1.5	−2.0	−0.5
(v) New Sums	190.0	189.5	191.5	191.0	188.5
(vi) New Averages ($\bar{Y}_i$)	95.0	94.7	95.7	95.5	94.2

Calculation of Standard Deviation

Previous Sum $S =$

Previous Average $S =$

New $s = $ Range $\times f_{k,n} = 1.05$

Range $= 3.5$

New Sum $S = 1.05$

New Averages $= \dfrac{\text{New Sum } S}{n-1} = 1.05$

Calculation of Effects

Temperature effect $= \frac{1}{2}(\bar{Y}_3 + \bar{Y}_4 - \bar{Y}_2 - \bar{Y}_5) = 1.15$

Pressure effect $= \frac{1}{2}(\bar{Y}_3 + \bar{Y}_5 - \bar{Y}_2 - \bar{Y}_4) = -0.15$

$T \times P$ Interaction effect $= \frac{1}{2}(\bar{Y}_2 + \bar{Y}_3 - \bar{Y}_4 - \bar{Y}_5) = 0.35$

Change in Mean Effect $= \frac{1}{5}(\bar{Y}_2 + \bar{Y}_3 + \bar{Y}_4 + \bar{Y}_5 - 4\bar{Y}_1) = 0.02$

Calculation of Error Limits

For new Average $\dfrac{2s}{\sqrt{n}} = 1.48$

For new Effects $\dfrac{2}{\sqrt{n}} s = 1.48$

For Change in Mean $\dfrac{1.78}{\sqrt{n}} s = 1.32$

estimate of standard deviation is available. The second cycle (Table 16.5) will begin to show the method for testing the effects.

Since, in the second cycle, none of the effects are numerically larger than their error limits, the true effect could easily be zero. In this case another cycle must be run. The only items that might need explaining are under the calculation of standard deviation. The range referred to here is the range of the differences (iv), and $f_{k,n}$ is found in a table where $k = 5$ for these five point designs, and n is the cycle number. Part of such a table shows

$$n = \quad 2 \quad\quad 3 \quad\quad 4 \quad\quad 5 \quad\quad 6 \quad\quad 7 \quad\quad 8$$

$$f_{5,n} = 0.30 \quad 0.35 \quad 0.37 \quad 0.38 \quad 0.39 \quad 0.40 \quad 0.40$$

The third cycle is shown in Table 16.6. Here the temperature effect is seen to be significant, with an increase in temperature giving a higher yield. Once a significant effect has been found, the first *phase* of the EVOP procedure has been completed. The average results at this point are usually displayed on an EVOP bulletin board as in Fig. 16.7.

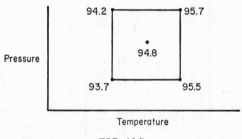

FIG. 16.7

Now an EVOP committee usually reviews these data and decides whether or not to reset the operating conditions. If they change the operating conditions [Point (1)], then EVOP is reinstated around this new point and the second phase is begun. EVOP is continued again until significant changes are detected. In fact, it goes on continually, seeking to optimize a process.

This is a very simple example with just two independent variables. The references should be consulted for more complex situations.

EVOP Form Rationale

Most of the steps in the EVOP form above are quite clear. It may be helpful to see where some of the constants come from.

TABLE 16.6 — EVOP Work Sheet — Third Cycle

$$5 \quad 3$$
$$2 \quad \boxed{.1} \quad 4$$

CALCULATION WORK SHEET

Cycle: $n = 3$
Response: Yield

Project: **424**
Phase: 1
Date: 10/12

Calculations of Averages

Operating Conditions	(1)	(2)	(3)	(4)	(5)
(i) Previous Cycle Sum	190.0	189.5	191.5	191.0	188.5
(ii) Previous Cycle Average	95.0	94.7	95.7	95.5	94.2
(iii) New Observations	94.5	91.5	96.0	97.0	94.0
(iv) Differences [(ii) less (iii)]	0.5	1.2	-0.3	-1.5	0.2
(v) New Sums	284.5	281.0	287.2	286.5	282.7
(vi) New Averages ($\bar{Y}_i$)	94.8	93.7	95.7	95.5	94.2

Calculation of Standard Deviation

Previous Sum $S = 1.05$
Previous Average $S = 1.05$
New $s = \text{Range} \times f_{k, n} = 0.95$
Range = 2.7
New Sum $S = 2.00$
New Average $s = \dfrac{\text{New Sum } S}{n - 1} = 1.00$

Calculation of Effects

Temperature effect $= \frac{1}{2}(\bar{Y}_3 + \bar{Y}_4 - \bar{Y}_2 - \bar{Y}_5) = 1.65^*$

Pressure effect $= \frac{1}{2}(\bar{Y}_3 + \bar{Y}_5 - \bar{Y}_2 - \bar{Y}_4) = 0.35$

$T \times P$ Interaction effect $= \frac{1}{2}(\bar{Y}_2 + \bar{Y}_3 - \bar{Y}_4 - \bar{Y}_5) = -0.15$

Change in Mean Effect $= \frac{1}{5}(\bar{Y}_2 + \bar{Y}_3 + \bar{Y}_4 + \bar{Y}_5 - 4\bar{Y}_1) = -0.02$

Calculation of Error Limits

For New Average $\dfrac{2}{\sqrt{n}}\, s = 1.16$

For New Effects $\dfrac{2}{\sqrt{n}}\, s = 1.16$

For Change in Mean $\dfrac{1.78}{\sqrt{n}}\, s = 1.02$

In estimating the standard deviation from the range of differences in step (iv), consider a general expression for these differences

$$D_p = \frac{X_{p1} + X_{p2} + \cdots + X_{p,n-1}}{n - 1} - X_{p,n}$$

where D_p represents the difference at any point p of the design. X_{pi} represents the observation at point p in the ith cycle. n is, of course, the number of cycles. Since the variance of a sum equals the sum of the variances for independent variables, and since the variance of a constant times a random variable equals the square of the constant times the variance of the random variable

$$\sigma_{D_p}^2 = \frac{1}{(n - 1)^2}[\sigma_{xp1}^2 + \sigma_{xp2}^2 + \cdots + \sigma_{xp,n-1}^2] + \sigma_{xp,n}^2$$

Since all these x's represent the same population, their variances are all alike, and then

$$\sigma_D^2 = \frac{1}{(n - 1)^2}[(n - 1)\sigma_x^2] + \sigma_x^2 = \frac{n}{n - 1}\sigma_x^2$$

and

$$\sigma_D = \sqrt{\frac{n}{n - 1}} \cdot \sigma_x$$

The standard deviation of the population can then be written in terms of the standard deviation of these differences

$$\sigma_x = \sqrt{\frac{n - 1}{n}} \cdot \sigma_D$$

σ_D can now be estimated from the range of these differences (R_d). From the quality control field

$$\sigma_D = \frac{R_d}{d_2}$$

where d_2 depends on the number of differences in the range, which is 5 on this form. Here $d_2 = 2.326$ for samples of 5,

$$\sigma_D = \frac{R_d}{2.326}$$

and the standard deviation of the population is estimated by

$$\sigma_x = \sqrt{\frac{n - 1}{n}} \cdot \frac{R_d}{2.326}$$

The quantity

$$\sqrt{\frac{n - 1}{n}} \cdot \frac{1}{2.326}$$

is called $f_{k,n}$ in the EVOP form where $k = 5$.

Note that

$$f_{5,2} = \sqrt{\frac{1}{2}} \cdot \frac{R_d}{2.326} = 0.30 R_d$$

$$f_{5,6} = \sqrt{\frac{5}{6}} \cdot \frac{R_d}{2.326} = 0.39 R_d$$

which tallies with the table values given.

To determine the error limits for the effects, two standard deviation limits are used, as they represent the approximate 95 percent confidence limits on the parameter being estimated.

For any effect such as

$$E = \tfrac{1}{2}(\bar{Y}_3 + \bar{Y}_4 - \bar{Y}_2 - \bar{Y}_5)$$

its variance would be

$$V_E = \frac{1}{4}(\sigma_{\bar{Y}_3}^2 + \sigma_{\bar{Y}_4}^2 + \sigma_{\bar{Y}_2}^2 + \sigma_{\bar{Y}_5}^2) = \frac{1}{4} \cdot (4\sigma_{\bar{Y}}^2) = \sigma_{\bar{Y}}^2 = \frac{\sigma_Y^2}{n}$$

and two standard deviation limits on an effect would be

$$\pm 2 \cdot \frac{\sigma_Y}{\sqrt{n}} \quad \text{estimated by} \quad \pm 2 \frac{s}{\sqrt{n}}$$

For the change in mean effect

$$\text{CIM} = \frac{1}{5}(\bar{Y}_2 + \bar{Y}_3 + \bar{Y}_4 + \bar{Y}_5 - 4\bar{Y}_1)$$

$$V_{\text{CIM}} = \frac{1}{25}(\sigma_{\bar{Y}_2}^2 + \sigma_{\bar{Y}_3}^2 + \sigma_{\bar{Y}_4}^2 + \sigma_{\bar{Y}_5}^2 + 16\sigma_{\bar{Y}_1}^2)$$

$$= \frac{20}{25}(\sigma_{\bar{Y}}^2) = \frac{20}{25} \frac{\sigma_Y^2}{n}$$

$$\sigma_{\text{CIM}} = \sqrt{\frac{4}{5}} \cdot \frac{\sigma_Y}{\sqrt{n}}$$

and two standard deviation limits would be

$$\pm 2 \cdot \sqrt{\frac{4}{5}} \frac{s}{\sqrt{n}} = \pm 1.78 \frac{s}{\sqrt{n}}$$

as given on the EVOP form.

CHAPTER

17 | Summary

Throughout this book the three phases of an experiment have been emphasized: the experiment, the design, and the analysis. At the end of most chapters an outline of the designs considered up to that point has been presented. It may prove useful to the reader to have a complete outline as a summary of the designs presented in Chapters 1–15.

This is not the only way such an outline could be constructed, but it represents an attempt to see each design as part of the over-all picture of designed experiments. A look at the outline will reveal that the same design is often used for an entirely different experiment, which simply illustrates the fact that much care must be taken to spell out the experiment and its design or method of randomization before an experiment is performed.

For each experiment, the chapter reference in this book is given.

Experiment	Design	Analysis	Chapter Reference
I. Single Factor	A. Completely Randomized $X_{ij} = \mu + T_j + \epsilon_{ij}$	A. One-way ANOVA	Chapter 3
	B. Randomized Block $X_{ij} = \mu + B_i + T_j + \epsilon_{ij}$ 1. Complete	B. 1. Two-way ANOVA	Chapter 4
	2. Incomplete — Balanced 3. Incomplete — General	2. Special ANOVA 3. General Regression Method.	
	C. Latin Square $X_{ijk} = \mu + B_i + T_j + \gamma_k + \epsilon_{ijk}$ 1. Complete	C. 1. Three-way ANOVA	Chapter 5
	2. Incomplete — Youden Square	2. Special ANOVA (like B-2 above)	
	D. Graeco-Latin Square $X_{ijkm} = \mu + B_i + T_j + \gamma_k + W_m + \epsilon_{ijkm}$	D. Four-way ANOVA	Chapter 5
II. Two or More Factors A. Factorial (crossed)	A. Completely Randomized $X_{ijk} = \mu + A_i + B_j + AB_{ij} + \epsilon_{k(ij)}$, etc., for more factors	A.	

Experiment	Design	Analysis	Chapter Reference
	1. General Case	1. ANOVA with interactions	Chapter 6
	2. 2^n Case	2. Yates Method or General ANOVA	Chapter 7
		Use: (1), a, b, ab, etc.	
	3. 3^n Case	3. General ANOVA	Chapter 9
		Use: 00, 10, 20, etc., and $AB = AB + AB^2$ etc., for interaction.	
	B. Randomized Block	*B*.	
	1. Complete	1. Factorial ANOVA with replications (R_k)	Chapter 12

$$X_{ijk} = \mu + R_k + A_i + B_j + AB_{ij} + \epsilon_{ijk}$$

| | 2. Incomplete — Confounding: | 2. | |
| | *a*. Main Effect — Split Plot | *a*. Split-Plot ANOVA | Chapter 13 |

$$X_{ijk} = \mu + \underbrace{R_i + A_j + RA_{ij}}_{\text{whole plot}}$$
$$+ \underbrace{B_k + RB_{ik} + AB_{jk} + RAB_{ijk}}_{\text{split plot}}$$

Experiment	Design	Analysis	Chapter Reference
	b. Interactions — in 2^n and 3^n	*b.* (1) Factorial ANOVA with reps (R_i) and blocks (β_i)	Chapter 14
	(1) Several Replications		
	$X_{ijkq} = \mu + R_i + \beta_j + R\beta_{ij} + A_k + B_q + AB_{kq} + \epsilon_{ikq}$ replications (blocks or confounded interaction)		
	(2) One Replication only	(2) Factorial ANOVA with blocks (β_i)	Chapter 14
	$X_{ijk} = \mu + \beta_i + A_j + B_k + AB_{jk} +$, etc. (Blocks or confounded interaction)		
	(3) Fractional Replication — Aliases	(3) Factorial ANOVA with aliases	Chapter 15
	$X_{ijk} = \mu + A_i + B_j + AB_{ij} +$, etc. (aliased interactions)		
	i. in 2^n		
	ii. in 3^n; $n = 3 - a$ Latin Square		
	C. Latin Square	*C.*	
	1. Complete	1. Factorial ANOVA with reps. and positions	Chapter 12
	$X_{ijkm} = \mu + R_k + \gamma_m + A_i + B_j + AB_{ij} + \epsilon_{ijkm}$		

Experiment	Design	Analysis	Chapter Reference
B. Nested (hierarchical)	A. Completely Randomized $$X_{ijk} = \mu + A_i + B_{j(i)} + \epsilon_{k(ij)}$$ B. Randomized Block 1. Complete $$X_{ijk} = \mu + R_k + A_i + B_{j(i)} + \epsilon_{ijk}$$ C. Latin Square 1. Complete $$X_{ijkm} = \mu + R_k + \gamma_m + A_i + B_{j(i)} + \epsilon_{ijkm}$$	A. Nested ANOVA B. 1. Nested ANOVA with blocks (R_k) C. 1. Nested ANOVA with blocks and positions	Chapter 11 Chapters 4 and 11 Chapters 5 and 11
C. Nested-Factorial	A. Completely Randomized $$X_{ijkm} = \mu + A_i + B_{j(i)} + C_k + AC_{ik} + BC_{kj(i)} + \epsilon_{m(ijk)}$$ B. Randomized Block 1. Complete $$X_{ijkm} = \mu + R_k + A_i + B_{j(i)} + C_m + AC_{im} + BC_{mj(i)} + \epsilon_{ijkm}$$ C. Latin Square 1. Complete $$X_{vjkmq} = \mu + R_k + \gamma_m + A_i + B_{j(i)} + C_q + AC_{iq} + BC_{qj(i)} + \epsilon_{ijkmq}$$	A. Nested-factorial ANOVA B. 1. Nested-factorial ANOVA with blocks (R_k) C. 1. Nested-factorial ANOVA with blocks and positions	Chapter 11 Chapters 4 and 11 Chapters 5 and 11

GLOSSARY OF TERMS

Alias. An effect in a fractionally replicated design which "looks like" or cannot be distinguished from another effect.

Alpha (α). Size of the Type-I error or probability of rejecting a hypothesis when true.

Beta (β). Size of the Type-II error or probability of accepting a hypothesis when some alternative hypothesis is true.

Canonical Form. Form of a second-degree response-surface equation which allows determination of the type of surface.

Completely Randomized Design. A design in which all treatments are assigned to the experimental units in a completely random manner.

Confidence Limits. Two values between which a parameter is said to lie with a specified degree of confidence.

Confounding. An experimental arrangement in which certain effects cannot be distinguished from others. One such effect is usually blocks.

Consistent Estimator. An estimator of a parameter whose value becomes closer to the parameter as the sample size is increased.

Contrast. A linear combination of treatment totals or averages where the sum of the coefficients is zero.

Critical Region. A set of values of a test statistic where the hypothesis under test is rejected.

Defining Contrast. An expression that indicates which effects are confounded with blocks in a factorial design that is confounded.

Effect of a Factor. The change in response produced by a change in level of the factor.

Errors. (Type I). Rejecting a hypothesis when true. (Type II). Accepting a hypothesis when false.

Evolutionary Operation. An experimental procedure for collecting information to improve a process without disturbing production.

Expected Value of a Statistic. The average value of a statistic if it were calculated from an infinite number of equal-sized samples from a given population.

Factorial Experiment. An experiment in which all levels of each factor in the experiment are combined with all levels of every other factor.

Fractional Replication. An experimental design in which only a fraction of a complete factorial is run.

Graeco-Latin Square. An experimental design in which four factors are so arranged that each level of each factor is combined only once with each level of the other three factors.

Incomplete Block Design. A randomized block design in which not all treatment combinations can be included in one block. Such a design is called a *balanced* design if each pair of treatments occurs together the same number of times.

Interaction. An interaction between two factors means that a change in response between levels of one factor is not the same for all levels of the other factor.

Latin Square. An experimental design in which each level of each factor is combined only once with each level of two other factors.

Mean. of a sample

$$\bar{X} = \sum_{i=1}^{n} X_i/n$$

of a population

$$\mu = E(X)$$

Mean Square. An unbiased estimate of a population variance. Determined by dividing a sum of squares by its degrees of freedom.

Minimum Variance Estimate. If two or more estimates, $u_1, u_2, \cdots u_k$, are made of the same parameter, θ, the estimate with the smallest variance is called the minimum variance estimate.

Mixed Model. The model of a factorial experiment in which one or more factors are at fixed levels and at least one factor is at random levels.

Nested Experiment. An experiment in which the levels of one factor are chosen within the levels of another factor.

Nested Factorial Experiment. An experiment in which some factors are factorial or crossed with others and some factors are nested within others.

Operating Characteristic Curve (OC Curve). A plot of the probability of acceptance of a hypothesis under test, versus the true parameter of the population.

Orthogonal Contrasts. Two contrasts are said to be orthogonal if the products of their corresponding coefficients add to zero.

Parameter (θ). A characteristic of a population, such as the population mean or variance.

Point Estimate. A single statistic used to estimate a parameter.

Power of a Test. A plot of the probability of rejection of a hypothesis under test versus the true parameter. It is the complement of the OC Curve.

Principal Block. The block in a confounded design that contains the treatment combination in which all factors are at their lowest level.

Random Model. A model of a factorial experiment in which the levels of the factor are chosen at random.

Random Sample. A sample in which each member of the population sampled has an equal chance of being selected in this sample.

Randomized Block Design. An experimental design in which the treatment combinations are randomized within a block and several blocks are run.

Rotatable Design. An experimental design that has equal predictive power in all directions from a center point, and in which all experimental points are equidistant from this center point.

Split-Plot Design. An experimental design in which a main effect is confounded with blocks due to the practical necessities of the order of experimentation.

Steepest Ascent Method. A method of sequential experiments that will direct the experimenter toward the optimum of a response surface.

Statistic (u). A measure computed from a sample.

Statistics. Decision-making in the light of uncertainty.

Statistical Hypothesis (H_0). An assumption about a population being sampled.

Statistical Inference. Inferring something about a population of measures from a sample of that population.

Test of a Hypothesis. A rule by which a hypothesis is accepted or rejected.

Test Statistic. A statistic used to test a hypothesis.

Treatment Combination. A given combination showing the levels of all factors to be run for that set of experimental conditions.

Unbiased Statistic. A statistic whose expected value equals the parameter it is estimating.

Variance. of a sample

$$s^2 = \frac{\sum_{i=1}^{n} (X_i - \bar{X})^2}{n - 1} = \frac{\text{SS}}{\text{df}}$$

of a population

$$\sigma^2 = E(X - \mu)^2$$

Youden Square. An incomplete Latin Square.

REFERENCES

1. BARNETT, E. H. "Introduction to Evolutionary Operation," *Industrial and Engineering Chemistry*, Vol. 52 (June 1960), 500.
2. BENNETT, C. A., and N. L. FRANKLIN. *Statistical Analysis in Chemistry and the Chemical Industry*. New York: John Wiley & Sons, Inc., 1954.
3. BOX, G. E. P. "Evolutionary Operation: A Method for Increasing Industrial Productivity," *Applied Statistics*, Vol. VI, No. 2 (1957).
4. BURR, I. W. *Engineering Statistics and Quality Control*. New York: McGraw-Hill Book Company, 1953.
5. DAVIES, O. L. *Design and Analysis of Industrial Experiments*. New York: Hafner Publishing Company, 1954.
6. DIXON, W. J., and F. J. MASSEY. *An Introduction to Statistical Analysis* (2nd Ed.). New York: McGraw-Hill Book Company, 1957.
7. DUNCAN, D. B. "Multiple Range and Multiple F Tests," *Biometrics*, No. 11 (1956).
8. FISHER, R. A., and F. YATES. *Statistical Tables for Biological, Agricultural and Medical Research* (4th Ed.). Edinburgh and London: Oliver & Boyd, Ltd., 1953.
9. HUNTER, J. S. "Determination of Optimum Operating Conditions by Experimental Methods," *Industrial Quality Control* (December–February, 1958–59).
10. KEMPTHORNE, O. *The Design and Analysis of Experiments*. New York: John Wiley & Sons, Inc., 1952.
11. McCALL, C. H. JR. "Linear Contrasts, Parts I, II and III," *Industrial Quality Control* (July–September, 1960).
12. MILLER, L. D. "An Investigation of the Machinability of Malleable Iron using Ceramic Tools." Unpublished MSIE thesis, Purdue University, 1959.
13. OWEN, D. B. *Handbook of Statistical Tables*. Boston: Addison-Wesley Publishing Company, Inc., 1962.
14. WORTHAM, A. W., and T. E. SMITH. *Practical Statistics in Experimental Design*. Dallas: Dallas Publishing House, 1960.
15. YATES, F. *Design and Analysis of Factorial Experiments*. London: Imperial Bureau of Soil Sciences, 1937.

STATISTICAL TABLES

TABLE A — Areas Under the Normal Curve*

(*Proportion of total area under the curve from* $-\infty$ *to designated Z value*)

Z	0.09	0.08	0.07	0.06	0.05	0.04	0.03	0.02	0.01	0.00
−3.5	0.00017	0.00017	0.00018	0.00019	0.00019	0.00020	0.00021	0.00022	0.00022	0.00023
−3.4	0.00024	0.00025	0.00026	0.00027	0.00028	0.00029	0.00030	0.00031	0.00033	0.00034
−3.3	0.00035	0.00036	0.00038	0.00039	0.00040	0.00042	0.00043	0.00045	0.00047	0.00048
−3.2	0.00050	0.00052	0.00054	0.00056	0.00058	0.00060	0.00062	0.00064	0.00066	0.00069
−3.1	0.00071	0.00074	0.00076	0.00079	0.00082	0.00085	0.00087	0.00090	0.00094	0.00097
−3.0	0.00100	0.00104	0.00107	0.00111	0.00114	0.00118	0.00122	0.00126	0.00131	0.00135
−2.9	0.0014	0.0014	0.0015	0.0015	0.0016	0.0016	0.0017	0.0017	0.0018	0.0019
−2.8	0.0019	0.0020	0.0021	0.0021	0.0022	0.0023	0.0023	0.0024	0.0025	0.0026
−2.7	0.0026	0.0027	0.0028	0.0029	0.0030	0.0031	0.0032	0.0033	0.0034	0.0035
−2.6	0.0036	0.0037	0.0038	0.0039	0.0040	0.0041	0.0043	0.0044	0.0045	0.0047
−2.5	0.0048	0.0049	0.0051	0.0052	0.0054	0.0055	0.0057	0.0059	0.0060	0.0062
−2.4	0.0064	0.0066	0.0068	0.0069	0.0071	0.0073	0.0075	0.0078	0.0080	0.0082
−2.3	0.0084	0.0087	0.0089	0.0091	0.0094	0.0096	0.0099	0.0102	0.0104	0.0107
−2.2	0.0110	0.0113	0.0116	0.0119	0.0122	0.0125	0.0129	0.0132	0.0136	0.0139
−2.1	0.0143	0.0146	0.0150	0.0154	0.0158	0.0162	0.0166	0.0170	0.0174	0.0179
−2.0	0.0183	0.0188	0.0192	0.0197	0.0202	0.0207	0.0212	0.0217	0.0222	0.0228
−1.9	0.0233	0.0239	0.0244	0.0250	0.0256	0.0262	0.0268	0.0274	0.0281	0.0287
−1.8	0.0294	0.0301	0.0307	0.0314	0.0322	0.0329	0.0336	0.0344	0.0351	0.0359
−1.7	0.0367	0.0375	0.0384	0.0392	0.0401	0.0409	0.0418	0.0427	0.0436	0.0446
−1.6	0.0455	0.0465	0.0475	0.0485	0.0495	0.0505	0.0516	0.0526	0.0537	0.0548
−1.5	0.0559	0.0571	0.0582	0.0594	0.0606	0.0618	0.0630	0.0643	0.0655	0.0668
−1.4	0.0681	0.0694	0.0708	0.0721	0.0735	0.0749	0.0764	0.0778	0.0793	0.0808
−1.3	0.0823	0.0838	0.0853	0.0869	0.0885	0.0901	0.0918	0.0934	0.0951	0.0968
−1.2	0.0985	0.1003	0.1020	0.1038	0.1057	0.1075	0.1093	0.1112	0.1131	0.1151
−1.1	0.1170	0.1190	0.1210	0.1230	0.1251	0.1271	0.1292	0.1314	0.1335	0.1357
−1.0	0.1379	0.1401	0.1423	0.1446	0.1469	0.1492	0.1515	0.1539	0.1562	0.1587
−0.9	0.1611	0.1635	0.1660	0.1685	0.1711	0.1736	0.1762	0.1788	0.1814	0.1841
−0.8	0.1867	0.1894	0.1922	0.1949	0.1977	0.2005	0.2033	0.2061	0.2090	0.2119
−0.7	0.2148	0.2177	0.2207	0.2236	0.2266	0.2297	0.2327	0.2358	0.2389	0.2420
−0.6	0.2451	0.2483	0.2514	0.2546	0.2578	0.2611	0.2643	0.2676	0.2709	0.2743
−0.5	0.2776	0.2810	0.2843	0.2877	0.2912	0.2946	0.2981	0.3015	0.3050	0.3085
−0.4	0.3121	0.3156	0.3192	0.3228	0.3264	0.3300	0.3336	0.3372	0.3409	0.3446
−0.3	0.3483	0.3520	0.3557	0.3594	0.3632	0.3669	0.3707	0.3745	0.3783	0.3821
−0.2	0.3859	0.3897	0.3936	0.3974	0.4013	0.4052	0.4090	0.4129	0.4168	0.4207
−0.1	0.4247	0.4286	0.4325	0.4364	0.4404	0.4443	0.4483	0.4522	0.4562	0.4602
−0.0	0.4641	0.4681	0.4721	0.4761	0.4801	0.4840	0.4880	0.4920	0.4960	0.5000

*Adapted from E.L. Grant, "Statistical Quality Control," 2d ed., Table A, pp. 510–511, McGraw-Hill Book Company, Inc., New York, 1952. By permission from the publisher.

TABLE A — *Areas Under the Normal Curve* (*Continued*)
(*Proportion of total area under the curve from* $-\infty$ *to designated Z value*)

Z	0.00	0.01	0.02	0.03	0.04	0.05	0.06	0.07	0.08	0.09
+0.0	0.5000	0.5040	0.5080	0.5120	0.5160	0.5199	0.5239	0.5279	0.5319	0.5359
+0.1	0.5398	0.5438	0.5478	0.5517	0.5557	0.5596	0.5636	0.5675	0.5714	0.5753
+0.2	0.5793	0.5832	0.5871	0.5910	0.5948	0.5987	0.6026	0.6064	0.6103	0.6141
+0.3	0.6179	0.6217	0.6255	0.6293	0.6331	0.6368	0.6406	0.6443	0.6480	0.6517
+0.4	0.6554	0.6591	0.6628	0.6664	0.6700	0.6736	0.6772	0.6808	0.6844	0.6879
+0.5	0.6915	0.6950	0.6985	0.7019	0.7054	0.7088	0.7123	0.7157	0.7190	0.7224
+0.6	0.7257	0.7291	0.7324	0.7357	0.7389	0.7422	0.7454	0.7486	0.7517	0.7549
+0.7	0.7580	0.7611	0.7642	0.7673	0.7704	0.7734	0.7764	0.7794	0.7823	0.7852
+0.8	0.7881	0.7910	0.7939	0.7967	0.7995	0.8023	0.8051	0.8079	0.8106	0.8133
+0.9	0.8159	0.8186	0.8212	0.8238	0.8264	0.8289	0.8315	0.8340	0.8365	0.8389
+1.0	0.8413	0.8438	0.8461	0.8485	0.8508	0.8531	0.8554	0.8577	0.8599	0.8621
+1.1	0.8643	0.8665	0.8686	0.8708	0.8729	0.8749	0.8770	0.8790	0.8810	0.8830
+1.2	0.8849	0.8869	0.8888	0.8907	0.8925	0.8944	0.8962	0.8980	0.8997	0.9015
+1.3	0.9032	0.9049	0.9066	0.9082	0.9099	0.9115	0.9131	0.9147	0.9162	0.9177
+1.4	0.9192	0.9207	0.9222	0.9236	0.9251	0.9265	0.9279	0.9292	0.9306	0.9319
+1.5	0.9332	0.9345	0.9357	0.9370	0.9382	0.9394	0.9406	0.9418	0.9429	0.9441
+1.6	0.9452	0.9463	0.9474	0.9484	0.9495	0.9505	0.9515	0.9525	0.9535	0.9545
+1.7	0.9554	0.9564	0.9573	0.9582	0.9591	0.9599	0.9608	0.9616	0.9625	0.9633
+1.8	0.9641	0.9649	0.9656	0.9664	0.9671	0.9678	0.9686	0.9693	0.9699	0.9706
+1.9	0.9713	0.9719	0.9726	0.9732	0.9738	0.9744	0.9750	0.9756	0.9761	0.9767
+2.0	0.9773	0.9778	0.9783	0.9788	0.9793	0.9798	0.9803	0.9808	0.9812	0.9817
+2.1	0.9821	0.9826	0.9830	0.9834	0.9838	0.9842	0.9846	0.9850	0.9854	0.9857
+2.2	0.9861	0.9864	0.9868	0.9871	0.9875	0.9878	0.9881	0.9884	0.9887	0.9890
+2.3	0.9893	0.9896	0.9898	0.9901	0.9904	0.9906	0.9909	0.9911	0.9913	0.9916
+2.4	0.9918	0.9920	0.9922	0.9925	0.9927	0.9929	0.9931	0.9932	0.9934	0.9936
+2.5	0.9938	0.9940	0.9941	0.9943	0.9945	0.9946	0.9948	0.9949	0.9951	0.9952
+2.6	0.9953	0.9955	0.9956	0.9957	0.9959	0.9960	0.9961	0.9962	0.9963	0.9964
+2.7	0.9965	0.9966	0.9967	0.9968	0.9969	0.9970	0.9971	0.9972	0.9973	0.9974
+2.8	0.9974	0.9975	0.9976	0.9977	0.9977	0.9978	0.9979	0.9979	0.9980	0.9981
+2.9	0.9981	0.9982	0.9983	0.9983	0.9984	0.9984	0.9985	0.9985	0.9986	0.9986
+3.0	0.99865	0.99869	0.99874	0.99878	0.99882	0.99886	0.99889	0.99893	0.99896	0.99900
+3.1	0.99903	0.99906	0.99910	0.99913	0.99915	0.99918	0.99921	0.99924	0.99926	0.99929
+3.2	0.99931	0.99934	0.99936	0.99938	0.99940	0.99942	0.99944	0.99946	0.99948	0.99950
+3.3	0.99952	0.99953	0.99955	0.99957	0.99958	0.99960	0.99961	0.99962	0.99964	0.99965
+3.4	0.99966	0.99967	0.99969	0.99970	0.99971	0.99972	0.99973	0.99974	0.99975	0.99976
+3.5	0.99977	0.99978	0.99978	0.99979	0.99980	0.99981	0.99981	0.99982	0.99983	0.99983

TABLE B — Student's t Distribution

df	Percentile point						
	70	80	90	95	97.5	99	99.5
1	.73	1.38	3.08	6.31	12.71	31.82	63.66
2	.62	1.06	1.89	2.92	4.30	6.96	9.92
3	.58	.98	1.64	2.35	3.18	4.54	5.84
4	.57	.94	1.53	2.13	2.78	3.75	4.60
5	.56	.92	1.48	2.01	2.57	3.36	4.03
6	.55	.91	1.44	1.94	2.45	3.14	3.71
7	.55	.90	1.42	1.90	2.36	3.00	3.50
8	.55	.89	1.40	1.86	2.31	2.90	3.36
9	.54	.88	1.38	1.83	2.26	2.82	3.25
10	.54	.88	1.37	1.81	2.23	2.76	3.17
11	.54	.88	1.36	1.80	2.20	2.72	3.11
12	.54	.87	1.36	1.78	2.18	2.68	3.06
13	.54	.87	1.35	1.77	2.16	2.65	3.01
14	.54	.87	1.34	1.76	2.14	2.62	2.98
15	.54	.87	1.34	1.75	2.13	2.60	2.95
16	.54	.86	1.34	1.75	2.12	2.58	2.92
17	.53	.86	1.33	1.74	2.11	2.57	2.90
18	.53	.86	1.33	1.73	2.10	2.55	2.88
19	.53	.86	1.33	1.73	2.09	2.54	2.86
20	.53	.86	1.32	1.72	2.09	2.53	2.84
21	.53	.86	1.32	1.72	2.08	2.52	2.83
22	.53	.86	1.32	1.72	2.07	2.51	2.82
23	.53	.86	1.32	1.71	2.07	2.50	2.81
24	.53	.86	1.32	1.71	2.06	2.49	2.80
25	.53	.86	1.32	1.71	2.06	2.48	2.79
26	.53	.86	1.32	1.71	2.06	2.48	2.78
27	.53	.86	1.31	1.70	2.05	2.47	2.77
28	.53	.86	1.31	1.70	2.05	2.47	2.76
29	.53	.85	1.31	1.70	2.04	2.46	2.76
30	.53	.85	1.31	1.70	2.04	2.46	2.75
40	.53	.85	1.30	1.68	2.02	2.42	2.70
50	.53	.85	1.30	1.67	2.01	2.40	2.68
60	.53	.85	1.30	1.67	2.00	2.39	2.66
80	.53	.85	1.29	1.66	1.99	2.37	2.64
100	.53	.84	1.29	1.66	1.98	2.36	2.63
200	.52	.84	1.29	1.65	1.97	2.34	2.60
500	.52	.84	1.28	1.65	1.96	2.33	2.59
∞	.52	.84	1.28	1.64	1.96	2.33	2.58

TABLE C — Table of Chi Square*

(For larger values of ν, the expression $\sqrt{2\chi^2} - \sqrt{2\nu - 1}$ may be used as a normal deviate with unit variance, remembering that the probability for χ^2 corresponds with that of a single tail of a normal curve.)

ν	Probability										
	0.99	0.98	0.95	0.90	0.80	0.20	0.10	0.05	0.02	0.01	0.001
1	0.0³157	0.0³628	0.00393	0.0158	0.0642	1.642	2.706	3.841	5.412	6.635	10.827
2	0.0201	0.0404	0.103	0.211	0.446	3.219	4.605	5.991	7.824	9.210	13.815
3	0.115	0.185	0.352	0.584	1.005	4.642	6.251	7.815	9.837	11.341	16.268
4	0.297	0.429	0.711	1.064	1.649	5.989	7.779	9.488	11.668	13.277	18.465
5	0.554	0.752	1.145	1.610	2.343	7.289	9.236	11.070	13.388	15.086	20.517
6	0.872	1.134	1.635	2.204	3.070	8.558	10.645	12.592	15.033	16.812	22.457
7	1.239	1.564	2.167	2.833	3.822	9.803	12.017	14.067	16.622	18.475	24.322
8	1.646	2.032	2.733	3.490	4.594	11.030	13.362	15.507	18.168	20.090	26.125
9	2.088	2.532	3.325	4.168	5.380	12.242	14.684	16.919	19.679	21.666	27.877
10	2.558	3.059	3.940	4.865	6.179	13.442	15.987	18.307	21.161	23.209	29.588
11	3.053	3.609	4.575	5.578	6.989	14.631	17.275	19.675	22.618	24.725	31.264
12	3.571	4.178	5.226	6.304	7.807	15.812	18.549	21.026	24.054	26.217	32.909
13	4.107	4.765	5.892	7.042	8.634	16.985	19.812	22.362	25.472	27.688	34.528
14	4.660	5.368	6.571	7.790	9.467	18.151	21.064	23.685	26.873	29.141	36.123
15	5.229	5.985	7.261	8.547	10.307	19.311	22.307	24.996	28.259	30.578	37.697
16	5.812	6.614	7.962	9.312	11.152	20.465	23.542	26.296	29.633	32.000	39.252
17	6.408	7.255	8.672	10.085	12.002	21.615	24.769	27.587	30.995	33.409	40.790
18	7.015	7.906	9.390	10.865	12.857	22.760	25.989	28.869	32.346	34.805	42.312
19	7.633	8.567	10.117	11.651	13.716	23.900	27.204	30.144	33.687	36.191	43.820
20	8.260	9.237	10.851	12.443	14.578	25.038	28.412	31.410	35.020	37.566	45.315
21	8.897	9.915	11.591	13.240	15.445	26.171	29.615	32.671	36.343	38.932	46.797
22	9.542	10.600	12.338	14.041	16.314	27.301	30.813	33.924	37.659	40.289	48.268
23	10.196	11.293	13.091	14.848	17.187	28.429	32.007	35.172	38.968	41.638	49.728
24	10.856	11.992	13.848	15.659	18.062	29.553	33.196	36.415	40.270	42.980	51.179
25	11.524	12.697	14.611	16.473	18.940	30.675	34.382	37.652	41.566	44.314	52.620
26	12.198	13.409	15.379	17.292	19.820	31.795	35.563	38.885	42.856	45.642	54.052
27	12.879	14.125	16.151	18.114	20.703	32.912	36.741	40.113	44.140	46.963	55.476
28	13.565	14.847	16.928	18.939	21.588	34.027	37.916	41.337	45.419	48.278	56.893
29	14.256	15.574	17.708	19.768	22.475	35.139	39.087	42.557	46.693	49.588	58.302
30	14.953	16.306	18.493	20.599	23.364	36.250	40.256	43.773	47.962	50.892	59.703

*This table is reproduced in abridged form from Table IV of Fisher and Yates, "Statistical Tables for Biological, Agricultural, and Medical Research," published by Oliver & Boyd, Ltd., Edinburgh, by permission of the authors and publishers.

TABLE D — F Distribution*

df for denom.	1 − α	\multicolumn{12}{c}{df for numerator}

df for denom.	1 − α	1	2	3	4	5	6	7	8	9	10	11	12
1	.75	5.83	7.50	8.20	8.58	8.82	8.98	9.10	9.19	9.26	9.32	9.36	9.41
	.90	39.9	49.5	53.6	55.8	57.2	58.2	58.9	59.4	59.9	60.2	60.5	60.7
	.95	161	200	216	225	230	234	237	239	241	242	243	244
2	.75	2.57	3.00	3.15	3.23	3.28	3.31	3.34	3.35	3.37	3.38	3.39	3.39
	.90	8.53	9.00	9.16	9.24	9.29	9.33	9.35	9.37	9.38	9.39	9.40	9.41
	.95	18.5	19.0	19.2	19.2	19.3	19.3	19.4	19.4	19.4	19.4	19.4	19.4
	.99	98.5	99.0	99.2	99.2	99.3	99.3	99.4	99.4	99.4	99.4	99.4	99.4
3	.75	2.02	2.28	2.36	2.39	2.41	2.42	2.43	2.44	2.44	2.44	2.45	2.45
	.90	5.54	5.46	5.39	5.34	5.31	5.28	5.27	5.25	5.24	5.23	5.22	5.22
	.95	10.1	9.55	9.28	9.12	9.10	8.94	8.89	8.85	8.81	8.79	8.76	8.74
	.99	34.1	30.8	29.5	28.7	28.2	27.9	27.7	27.5	27.3	27.2	27.1	27.1
4	.75	1.81	2.00	2.05	2.06	2.07	2.08	2.08	2.08	2.08	2.08	2.08	2.08
	.90	4.54	4.32	4.19	4.11	4.05	4.01	3.98	3.95	3.94	3.92	3.91	3.90
	.95	7.71	6.94	6.59	6.39	6.26	6.16	6.09	6.04	6.00	5.96	5.94	5.91
	.99	21.2	18.0	16.7	16.0	15.5	15.2	15.0	14.8	14.7	14.5	14.4	14.4
5	.75	1.69	1.85	1.88	1.89	1.89	1.89	1.89	1.89	1.89	1.89	1.89	1.89
	.90	4.06	3.78	3.62	3.52	3.45	3.40	3.37	3.34	3.32	3.30	3.28	3.27
	.95	6.61	5.79	5.41	5.19	5.05	4.95	4.88	4.82	4.77	4.74	4.71	4.68
	.99	16.3	13.3	12.1	11.4	11.0	10.7	10.5	10.3	10.2	10.1	9.96	9.89
6	.75	1.62	1.76	1.78	1.79	1.79	1.78	1.78	1.77	1.77	1.77	1.77	1.77
	.90	3.78	3.46	3.29	3.18	3.11	3.05	3.01	2.98	2.96	2.94	2.92	2.90
	.95	5.99	5.14	4.76	4.53	4.39	4.28	4.21	4.15	4.10	4.06	4.03	4.00
	.99	13.7	10.9	9.78	9.15	8.75	8.47	8.26	8.10	7.98	7.87	7.79	7.72
7	.75	1.57	1.70	1.72	1.72	1.71	1.71	1.70	1.70	1.69	1.69	1.69	1.68
	.90	3.59	3.26	3.07	2.96	2.88	2.83	2.78	2.75	2.72	2.70	2.68	2.67
	.95	5.59	4.74	4.35	4.12	3.97	3.87	3.79	3.73	3.68	3.64	3.60	3.57
	.99	12.2	9.55	8.45	7.85	7.46	7.19	6.99	6.84	6.72	6.62	6.54	6.47
8	.75	1.54	1.66	1.67	1.66	1.66	1.65	1.64	1.64	1.64	1.63	1.63	1.62
	.90	3.46	3.11	2.92	2.81	2.73	2.67	2.62	2.59	2.56	2.54	2.52	2.50
	95	5.32	4.46	4.07	3.84	3.69	3.58	3.50	3.44	3.39	3.35	3.31	3.28
	.99	11.3	8.65	7.59	7.01	6.63	6.37	6.18	6.03	5.91	5.81	5.73	5.67
9	.75	1.51	1.62	1.63	1.63	1.62	1.61	1.60	1.60	1.59	1.59	1.58	1.58
	.90	3.36	3.01	2.81	2.69	2.61	2.55	2.51	2.47	2.44	2.42	2.40	2.38
	.95	5.12	4.26	3.86	3.63	3.48	3.37	3.29	3.23	3.18	3.14	3.10	3.07
	.99	10.6	8.02	6.99	6.42	6.06	5.80	5.61	5.47	5.35	5.26	5.18	5.11
10	.75	1.49	1.60	1.60	1.59	1.59	1.58	1.57	1.56	1.56	1.55	1.55	1.54
	.90	3.28	2.92	2.73	2.61	2.52	2.46	2.41	2.38	2.35	2.32	2.30	2.28
	.95	4.96	4.10	3.71	3.48	3.33	3.22	3.14	3.07	3.02	2.98	2.94	2.91
	.99	10.0	7.56	6.55	5.99	5.64	5.39	5.20	5.06	4.94	4.85	4.77	4.71
11	.75	1.47	1.58	1.58	1.57	1.56	1.55	1.54	1.53	1.53	1.52	1.52	1:51
	.90	3.23	2.86	2.66	2.54	2.45	2.39	2.34	2.30	2.27	2.25	2.23	2.21
	.95	4.84	3.98	3.59	3.36	3.20	3.09	3.01	2.95	2.90	2.85	2.82	2.79
	.99	9.65	7.21	6.22	5.67	5.32	5.07	4.89	4.74	4.63	4.54	4.46	4.40
12	.75	1.46	1.56	1.56	1.55	1.54	1.53	1.52	1.51	1.51	1.50	1.50	1.49
	.90	3.18	2.81	2.61	2.48	2.39	2.33	2.28	2.24	2.21	2.19	2.17	2.15
	.95	4.75	3.89	3.49	3.26	3.11	3.00	2.91	2.85	2.80	2.75	2.72	2.69
	.99	9.33	6.93	5.95	5.41	5.06	4.82	4.64	4.50	4.39	4.30	4.22	4.16

TABLE D (Continued)

df for numerator													1 − α	df for denom.
15	20	24	30	40	50	60	100	120	200	500	∞			
9.49	9.58	9.63	9.67	9.71	9.74	9.76	9.78	9.80	9.82	9.84	9.85	.75	
61.2	61.7	62.0	62.3	62.5	62.7	62.8	63.0	63.1	63.2	63.3	63.3	.90	1
246	248	249	250	251	252	252	253	253	254	254	254	.95	
3.41	3.43	3.43	3.44	3.45	3.45	3.46	3.47	3.47	3.48	3.48	3.48	.75	
9.42	9.44	9.45	9.46	9.47	9.47	9.47	9.48	9.48	9.49	9.49	9.49	.90	2
19.4	19.4	19.5	19.5	19.5	19.5	19.5	19.5	19.5	19.5	19.5	19.5	.95	
99.4	99.4	99.5	99.5	99.5	99.5	99.5	99.5	99.5	99.5	99.5	99.5	.99	
2.46	2.46	2.46	2.47	2.47	2.47	2.47	2.47	2.47	2.47	2.47	2.47	.75	
5.20	5.18	5.18	5.17	5.16	5.15	5.15	5.14	5.14	5.14	5.14	5.13	.90	3
8.70	8.66	8.64	8.62	8.59	8.58	8.57	8.55	8.55	8.54	8.53	8.53	.95	
26.9	26.7	26.6	26.5	26.4	26.4	26.3	26.2	26.2	26.2	26.1	26.1	.99	
2.08	2.08	2.08	2.08	2.08	2.08	2.08	2.08	2.08	2.08	2.08	2.08	.75	
3.87	3.84	3.83	3.82	3.80	3.80	3.79	3.78	3.78	3.77	3.76	3.76	.90	
5.86	5.80	5.77	5.75	5.72	5.70	5.69	5.66	5.66	5.65	5.64	5.63	.95	4
14.2	14.0	13.9	13.8	13.7	13.7	13.7	13.6	13.6	13.5	13.5	13.5	.99	
1.89	1.88	1.88	1.88	1.88	1.88	1.87	1.87	1.87	1.87	1.87	1.87	.75	
3.24	3.21	3.19	3.17	3.16	3.15	3.14	3.13	3.12	3.12	3.11	3.10	.90	5
4.62	4.56	4.53	4.50	4.46	4.44	4.43	4.41	4.40	4.39	4.37	4.36	.95	
9.72	9.55	9.47	9.38	9.29	9.24	9.20	9.13	9.11	9.08	9.04	9.02	.99	
1.76	1.76	1.75	1.75	1.75	1.75	1.74	1.74	1.74	1.74	1.74	1.74	.75	
2.87	2.84	2.82	2.80	2.78	2.77	2.76	2.75	2.74	2.73	2.73	2.72	.90	6
3.94	3.87	3.84	3.81	3.77	3.75	3.74	3.71	3.70	3.69	3.68	3.67	.95	
7.56	7.40	7.31	7.23	7.14	7.09	7.06	6.99	6.97	6.93	6.90	6.88	.99	
1.68	1.67	1.67	1.66	1.66	1.66	1.65	1.65	1.65	1.65	1.65	1.65	.75	
2.63	2.59	2.58	2.56	2.54	2.52	2.51	2.50	2.49	2.48	2.48	2.47	.90	7
3.51	3.44	3.41	3.38	3.34	3.32	3.30	3.27	3.27	3.25	3.24	3.23	.95	
6.31	6.16	6.07	5.99	5.91	5.86	5.82	5.75	5.74	5.70	5.67	5.65	.99	
1.62	1.61	1.60	1.60	1.59	1.59	1.59	1.58	1.58	1.58	1.58	1.58	.75	
2.46	2.42	2.40	2.38	2.36	2.35	2.34	2.32	2.32	2.31	2.30	2.29	.90	8
3.22	3.15	3.12	3.08	3.04	3.02	3.01	2.97	2.97	2.95	2.94	2.93	.95	
5.52	5.36	5.28	5.20	5.12	5.07	5.03	4.96	4.95	4.91	4.88	4.86	.99	
1.57	1.56	1.56	1.55	1.55	1.54	1.54	1.53	1.53	1.53	1.53	1.53	.75	
2.34	2.30	2.28	2.25	2.23	2.22	2.21	2.19	2.18	2.17	2.17	2.16	.90	9
3.01	2.94	2.90	2.86	2.83	2.80	2.79	2.76	2.75	2.73	2.72	2.71	.95	
4.96	4.81	4.73	4.65	4.57	4.52	4.48	4.42	4.40	4.36	4.33	4.31	.99	
1.53	1.52	1.52	1.51	1.51	1.50	1.50	1.49	1.49	1.49	1.48	1.48	.75	
2.24	2.20	2.18	2.16	2.13	2.12	2.11	2.09	2.08	2.07	2.06	2.06	.90	10
2.85	2.77	2.74	2.70	2.66	2.64	2.62	2.59	2.58	2.56	2.55	2.54	.95	
4.56	4.41	4.33	4.25	4.17	4.12	4.08	4.01	4.00	3.96	3.93	3.91	.99	
1.50	1.49	1.49	1.48	1.47	1.47	1.47	1.46	1.46	1.46	1.45	1.45	.75	
2.17	2.12	2.10	2.08	2.05	2.04	2.03	2.00	2.00	1.99	1.98	1.97	.90	11
2.72	2.65	2.61	2.57	2.53	2.51	2.49	2.46	2.45	2.43	2.42	2.40	.95	
4.25	4.10	4.02	3.94	3.86	3.81	3.78	3.71	3.69	3.66	3.62	3.60	.99	
1.48	1.47	1.46	1.45	1.45	1.44	1.44	1.43	1.43	1.43	1.42	1.42	.75	
2.10	2.06	2.04	2.01	1.99	1.97	1.96	1.94	1.93	1.92	1.91	1.90	.90	12
2.62	2.54	2.51	2.47	2.43	2.40	2.38	2.35	2.34	2.32	2.31	2.30	.95	
4.01	3.86	3.78	3.70	3.62	3.57	3.54	3.47	3.45	3.41	3.38	3.36	.99	

TABLE D (Continued)

df for denom.	1 − α	df for numerator											
		1	2	3	4	5	6	7	8	9	10	11	12
13	.75	1.45	1.54	1.54	1.53	1.52	1.51	1.50	1.49	1.49	1.48	1.47	1.47
	.90	3.14	2.76	2.56	2.43	2.35	2.28	2.23	2.20	2.16	2.14	2.12	2.10
	.95	4.67	3.81	3.41	3.18	3.03	2.92	2.83	2.77	2.71	2.67	2.63	2.60
	.99	9.07	6.70	5.74	5.21	4.86	4.62	4.44	4.30	4.19	4.10	4.02	3.96
14	.75	1.44	1.53	1.53	1.52	1.51	1.50	1.48	1.48	1.47	1.46	1.46	1.45
	.90	3.10	2.73	2.52	2.39	2.31	2.24	2.19	2.15	2.12	2.10	2.08	2.05
	.95	4.60	3.74	3.34	3.11	2.96	2.85	2.76	2.70	2.65	2.60	2.57	2.53
	.99	8.86	6.51	5.56	5.04	4.69	4.46	4.28	4.14	4.03	3.94	3.86	3.80
15	.75	1.43	1.52	1.52	1.51	1.49	1.48	1.47	1.46	1.46	1.45	1.44	1.44
	.90	3.07	2.70	2.49	2.36	2.27	2.21	2.16	2.12	2.09	2.06	2.04	2.02
	.95	4.54	3.68	3.29	3.06	2.90	2.79	2.71	2.64	2.59	2.54	2.51	2.48
	.99	8.68	6.36	5.42	4.89	4.56	4.32	4.14	4.00	3.89	3.80	3.73	3.67
16	.75	1.42	1.51	1.51	1.50	1.48	1.48	1.47	1.46	1.45	1.45	1.44	1.44
	.90	3.05	2.67	2.46	2.33	2.24	2.18	2.13	2.09	2.06	2.03	2.01	1.99
	.95	4.49	3.63	3.24	3.01	2.85	2.74	2.66	2.59	2.54	2.49	2.46	2.42
	.99	8.53	6.23	5.29	4.77	4.44	4.20	4.03	3.89	3.78	3.69	3.62	3.55
17	.75	1.42	1.51	1.50	1.49	1.47	1.46	1.45	1.44	1.43	1.43	1.42	1.41
	.90	3.03	2.64	2.44	2.31	2.22	2.15	2.10	2.06	2.03	2.00	1.98	1.96
	.95	4.45	3.59	3.20	2.96	2.81	2.70	2.61	2.55	2.49	2.45	2.41	2.38
	.99	8.40	6.11	5.18	4.67	4.34	4.10	3.93	3.79	3.68	3.59	3.52	3.46
18	.75	1.41	1.50	1.49	1.48	1.46	1.45	1.44	1.43	1.42	1.42	1.41	1.40
	.90	3.01	2.62	2.42	2.29	2.20	2.13	2.08	2.04	2.00	1.98	1.96	1.93
	.95	4.41	3.55	3.16	2.93	2.77	2.66	2.58	2.51	2.46	2.41	2.37	2.34
	.99	8.29	6.01	5.09	4.58	4.25	4.01	3.84	3.71	3.60	3.51	3.43	3.37
19	.75	1.41	1.49	1.49	1.47	1.46	1.44	1.43	1.42	1.41	1.41	1.40	1.40
	.90	2.99	2.61	2.40	2.27	2.18	2.11	2.06	2.02	1.98	1.96	1.94	1.91
	.95	4.38	3.52	3.13	2.90	2.74	2.63	2.54	2.48	2.42	2.38	2.34	2.31
	.99	8.18	5.93	5.01	4.50	4.17	3.94	3.77	3.63	3.52	3.43	3.36	3.30
20	.75	1.40	1.49	1.48	1.46	1.45	1.44	1.42	1.42	1.41	1.40	1.39	1.39
	.90	2.97	2.59	2.38	2.25	2.16	2.09	2.04	2.00	1.96	1.94	1.92	1.89
	.95	4.35	3.49	3.10	2.87	2.71	2.60	2.51	2.45	2.39	2.35	2.31	2.28
	.99	8.10	5.85	4.94	4.43	4.10	3.87	3.70	3.56	3.46	3.37	3.29	3.23
22	.75	1.40	1.48	1.47	1.45	1.44	1.42	1.41	1.40	1.39	1.39	1.38	1.37
	.90	2.95	2.56	2.35	2.22	2.13	2.06	2.01	1.97	1.93	1.90	1.88	1.86
	.95	4.30	3.44	3.05	2.82	2.66	2.55	2.46	2.40	2.34	2.30	2.26	2.23
	.99	7.95	5.72	4.82	4.31	3.99	3.76	3.59	3.45	3.35	3.26	3.18	3.12
24	.75	1.39	1.47	1.46	1.44	1.43	1.41	1.40	1.39	1.38	1.38	1.37	1.36
	.90	2.93	2.54	2.33	2.19	2.10	2.04	1.98	1.94	1.91	1.88	1.85	1.83
	.95	4.26	3.40	3.01	2.78	2.62	2.51	2.42	2.36	2.30	2.25	2.21	2.18
	.99	7.82	5.61	4.72	4.22	3.90	3.67	3.50	3.36	3.26	3.17	3.09	3.03
26	.75	1.38	1.46	1.45	1.44	1.42	1.41	1.40	1.39	1.37	1.37	1.36	1.35
	.90	2.91	2.52	2.31	2.17	2.08	2.01	1.96	1.92	1.88	1.86	1.84	1.81
	.95	4.23	3.37	2.98	2.74	2.59	2.47	2.39	2.32	2.27	2.22	2.18	2.15
	.99	7.72	5.53	4.64	4.14	3.82	3.59	3.42	3.29	3.18	3.09	3.02	2.96
28	.75	1.38	1.46	1.45	1.43	1.41	1.40	1.39	1.38	1.37	1.36	1.35	1.34
	.90	2.89	2.50	2.29	2.16	2.06	2.00	1.94	1.90	1.87	1.84	1.81	1.79
	.95	4.20	3.34	2.95	2.71	2.56	2.45	2.36	2.29	2.24	2.19	2.15	2.12
	.99	7.64	5.45	4.57	4.07	3.75	3.53	3.36	3.23	3.12	3.03	2.96	2.90

TABLE D (Continued)

15	20	24	30	40	50	60	100	120	200	500	∞	1 − α	df for denom.
\multicolumn{12}{c	}{df for numerator}		
1.46	1.45	1.44	1.43	1.42	1.42	1.42	1.41	1.41	1.40	1.40	1.40	.75	
2.05	2.01	1.98	1.96	1.93	1.92	1.90	1.88	1.88	1.86	1.85	1.85	.90	13
2.53	2.46	2.42	2.38	2.34	2.31	2.30	2.26	2.25	2.23	2.22	2.21	.95	
3.82	3.66	3.59	3.51	3.43	3.38	3.34	3.27	3.25	3.22	3.19	3.17	.99	
1.44	1.43	1.42	1.41	1.41	1.40	1.40	1.39	1.39	1.39	1.38	1.38	.75	
2.01	1.96	1.94	1.91	1.89	1.87	1.86	1.83	1.83	1.82	1.80	1.80	.90	
2.46	2.39	2.35	2.31	2.27	2.24	2.22	2.19	2.18	2.16	2.14	2.13	.95	14
3.66	3.51	3.43	3.35	3.27	3.22	3.18	3.11	3.09	3.06	3.03	3.00	.99	
1.43	1.41	1.41	1.40	1.39	1.39	1.38	1.38	1.37	1.37	1.36	1.36	.75	
1.97	1.92	1.90	1.87	1.85	1.83	1.82	1.79	1.79	1.77	1.76	1.76	.90	15
2.40	2.33	2.29	2.25	2.20	2.18	2.16	2.12	2.11	2.10	2.08	2.07	.95	
3.52	3.37	3.29	3.21	3.13	3.08	3.05	2.98	2.96	2.92	2.89	2.87	.99	
1.41	1.40	1.39	1.38	1.37	1.37	1.36	1.36	1.35	1.35	1.34	1.34	.75	
1.94	1.89	1.87	1.84	1.81	1.79	1.78	1.76	1.75	1.74	1.73	1.72	.90	16
2.35	2.28	2.24	2.19	2.15	2.12	2.11	2.07	2.06	2.04	2.02	2.01	.95	
3.41	3.26	3.18	3.10	3.02	2.97	2.93	2.86	2.84	2.81	2.78	2.75	.99	
1.40	1.39	1.38	1.37	1.36	1.35	1.35	1.34	1.34	1.34	1.33	1.33	.75	
1.91	1.86	1.84	1.81	1.78	1.76	1.75	1.73	1.72	1.71	1.69	1.69	.90	17
2.31	2.23	2.19	2.15	2.10	2.08	2.06	2.02	2.01	1.99	1.97	1.96	.95	
3.31	3.16	3.08	3.00	2.92	2.87	2.83	2.76	2.75	2.71	2.68	2.65	.99	
1.39	1.38	1.37	1.36	1.35	1.34	1.34	1.33	1.33	1.32	1.32	1.32	.75	
1.89	1.84	1.81	1.78	1.75	1.74	1.72	1.70	1.69	1.68	1.67	1.66	.90	18
2.27	2.19	2.15	2.11	2.06	2.04	2.02	1.98	1.97	1.95	1.93	1.92	.95	
3.23	3.08	3.00	2.92	2.84	2.78	2.75	2.68	2.66	2.62	2.59	2.57	.99	
1.38	1.37	1.36	1.35	1.34	1.33	1.33	1.32	1.32	1.31	1.31	1.30	.75	
1.86	1.81	1.79	1.76	1.73	1.71	1.70	1.67	1.67	1.65	1.64	1.63	.90	19
2.23	2.16	2.11	2.07	2.03	2.00	1.98	1.94	1.93	1.91	1.89	1.88	.95	
3.15	3.00	2.92	2.84	2.76	2.71	2.67	2.60	2.58	2.55	2.51	2.49	.99	
1.37	1.36	1.35	1.34	1.33	1.33	1.32	1.31	1.31	1.30	1.30	1.29	.75	
1.84	1.79	1.77	1.74	1.71	1.69	1.68	1.65	1.64	1.63	1.62	1.61	.90	20
2.20	2.12	2.08	2.04	1.99	1.97	1.95	1.91	1.90	1.88	1.86	1.84	.95	
3.09	2.94	2.86	2.78	2.69	2.64	2.61	2.54	2.52	2.48	2.44	2.42	.99	
1.36	1.34	1.33	1.32	1.31	1.31	1.30	1.30	1.30	1.29	1.29	1.28	.75	
1.81	1.76	1.73	1.70	1.67	1.65	1.64	1.61	1.60	1.59	1.58	1.57	.90	22
2.15	2.07	2.03	1.98	1.94	1.91	1.89	1.85	1.84	1.82	1.80	1.78	.95	
2.98	2.83	2.75	2.67	2.58	2.53	2.50	2.42	2.40	2.36	2.33	2.31	.99	
1.35	1.33	1.32	1.31	1.30	1.29	1.29	1.28	1.28	1.27	1.27	1.26	.75	
1.78	1.73	1.70	1.67	1.64	1.62	1.61	1.58	1.57	1.56	1.54	1.53	.90	24
2.11	2.03	1.98	1.94	1.89	1.86	1.84	1.80	1.79	1.77	1.75	1.73	.95	
2.89	2.74	2.66	2.58	2.49	2.44	2.40	2.33	2.31	2.27	2.24	2.21	.99	
1.34	1.32	1.31	1.30	1.29	1.28	1.28	1.26	1.26	1.26	1.25	1.25	.75	
1.76	1.71	1.68	1.65	1.61	1.59	1.58	1.55	1.54	1.53	1.51	1.50	.90	26
2.07	1.99	1.95	1.90	1.85	1.82	1.80	1.76	1.75	1.73	1.71	1.69	.95	
2.81	2.66	2.58	2.50	2.42	2.36	2.33	2.25	2.23	2.19	2.16	2.13	.99	
1.33	1.31	1.30	1.29	1.28	1.27	1.27	1.26	1.25	1.25	1.24	1.24	.75	
1.74	1.69	1.66	1.63	1.59	1.57	1.56	1.53	1.52	1.50	1.49	1.48	.90	28
2.04	1.96	1.91	1.87	1.82	1.79	1.77	1.73	1.71	1.69	1.67	1.65	.95	
2.75	2.60	2.52	2.44	2.35	2.30	2.26	2.19	2.17	2.13	2.09	2.06	.99	

TABLE D (Continued)

df for denom.	1 − α	df for numerator											
		1	2	3	4	5	6	7	8	9	10	11	12
30	.75	1.38	1.45	1.44	1.42	1.41	1.39	1.38	1.37	1.36	1.35	1.35	1.34
	.90	2.88	2.49	2.28	2.14	2.05	1.98	1.93	1.88	1.85	1.82	1.79	1.77
	.95	4.17	3.32	2.92	2.69	2.53	2.42	2.33	2.27	2.21	2.16	2.13	2.09
	.99	7.56	5.39	4.51	4.02	3.70	3.47	3.30	3.17	3.07	2.98	2.91	2.84
40	.75	1.36	1.44	1.42	1.40	1.39	1.37	1.36	1.35	1.34	1.33	1.32	1.31
	.90	2.84	2.44	2.23	2.09	2.00	1.93	1.87	1.83	1.79	1.76	1.73	1.71
	.95	4.08	3.23	2.84	2.61	2.45	2.34	2.25	2.18	2.12	2.08	2.04	2.00
	.99	7.31	5.18	4.31	3.83	3.51	3.29	3.12	2.99	2.89	2.80	2.73	2.66
60	.75	1.35	1.42	1.41	1.38	1.37	1.35	1.33	1.32	1.31	1.30	1.29	1.29
	.90	2.79	2.39	2.18	2.04	1.95	1.87	1.82	1.77	1.74	1.71	1.68	1.66
	.95	4.00	3.15	2.76	2.53	2.37	2.25	2.17	2.10	2.04	1.99	1.95	1.92
	.99	7.08	4.98	4.13	3.65	3.34	3.12	2.95	2.82	2.72	2.63	2.56	2.50
120	.75	1.34	1.40	1.39	1.37	1.35	1.33	1.31	1.30	1.29	1.28	1.27	1.26
	.90	2.75	2.35	2.13	1.99	1.90	1.82	1.77	1.72	1.68	1.65	1.62	1.60
	.95	3.92	3.07	2.68	2.45	2.29	2.17	2.09	2.02	1.96	1.91	1.87	1.83
	.99	6.85	4.79	3.95	3.48	3.17	2.96	2.79	2.66	2.56	2.47	2.40	2.34
200	.75	1.33	1.39	1.38	1.36	1.34	1.32	1.31	1.29	1.28	1.27	1.26	1.25
	.90	2.73	2.33	2.11	1.97	1.88	1.80	1.75	1.70	1.66	1.63	1.60	1.57
	.95	3.89	3.04	2.65	2.42	2.26	2.14	2.06	1.98	1.93	1.88	1.84	1.80
	.99	6.76	4.71	3.88	3.41	3.11	2.89	2.73	2.60	2.50	2.41	2.34	2.27
∞	.75	1.32	1.39	1.37	1.35	1.33	1.31	1.29	1.28	1.27	1.25	1.24	1.24
	.90	2.71	2.30	2.08	1.94	1.85	1.77	1.72	1.67	1.63	1.60	1.57	1.55
	.95	3.84	3.00	2.60	2.37	2.21	2.10	2.01	1.94	1.88	1.83	1.79	1.75
	.99	6.63	4.61	3.78	3.32	3.02	2.80	2.64	2.51	2.41	2.32	2.25	2.18

TABLE D (*Continued*)

df for numerator														df for denom.
15	20	24	30	40	50	60	100	120	200	500	∞	$1 - \alpha$		
1.32	1.30	1.29	1.28	1.27	1.26	1.26	1.25	1.24	1.24	1.23	1.23	.75		
1.72	1.67	1.64	1.61	1.57	1.55	1.54	1.51	1.50	1.48	1.47	1.46	.90		30
2.01	1.93	1.89	1.84	1.79	1.76	1.74	1.70	1.68	1.66	1.64	1.62	.95		
2.70	2.55	2.47	2.39	2.30	2.25	2.21	2.13	2.11	2.07	2.03	2.01	.99		
1.30	1.28	1.26	1.25	1.24	1.23	1.22	1.21	1.21	1.20	1.19	1.19	.75		
1.66	1.61	1.57	1.54	1.51	1.48	1.47	1.43	1.42	1.41	1.39	1.38	.90		40
1.92	1.84	1.79	1.74	1.69	1.66	1.64	1.59	1.58	1.55	1.53	1.51	.95		
2.52	2.37	2.29	2.20	2.11	2.06	2.02	1.94	1.92	1.87	1.83	1.80	.99		
1.27	1.25	1.24	1.22	1.21	1.20	1.19	1.17	1.17	1.16	1.15	1.15	.75		
1.60	1.54	1.51	1.48	1.44	1.41	1.40	1.36	1.35	1.33	1.31	1.29	.90		60
1.84	1.75	1.70	1.65	1.59	1.56	1.53	1.48	1.47	1.44	1.41	1.39	.95		
2.35	2.20	2.12	2.03	1.94	1.88	1.84	1.75	1.73	1.68	1.63	1.60	.99		
1.24	1.22	1.21	1.19	1.18	1.17	1.16	1.14	1.13	1.12	1.11	1.10	.75		
1.55	1.48	1.45	1.41	1.37	1.34	1.32	1.27	1.26	1.24	1.21	1.19	.90		120
1.75	1.66	1.61	1.55	1.50	1.46	1.43	1.37	1.35	1.32	1.28	1.25	.95		
2.19	2.03	1.95	1.86	1.76	1.70	1.66	1.56	1.53	1.48	1.42	1.38	.99		
1.23	1.21	1.20	1.18	1.16	1.14	1.12	1.11	1.10	1.09	1.08	1.06	.75		
1.52	1.46	1.42	1.38	1.34	1.31	1.28	1.24	1.22	1.20	1.17	1.14	.90		200
1.72	1.62	1.57	1.52	1.46	1.41	1.39	1.32	1.29	1.26	1.22	1.19	.95		
2.13	1.97	1.89	1.79	1.69	1.63	1.58	1.48	1.44	1.39	1.33	1.28	.99		
1.22	1.19	1.18	1.16	1.14	1.13	1.12	1.09	1.08	1.07	1.04	1.00	.75		
1.49	1.42	1.38	1.34	1.30	1.26	1.24	1.18	1.17	1.13	1.08	1.00	.90		∞
1.67	1.57	1.52	1.46	1.39	1.35	1.32	1.24	1.22	1.17	1.11	1.00	.95		
2.04	1.88	1.79	1.70	1.59	1.52	1.47	1.36	1.32	1.25	1.15	1.00	.99		

TABLE E — *Significant Ranges for a 1-percent Level New[a] Multiple Range Test*

n_2/p	2	3	4	5	6	7	8	9	10	12	14	16	18	20	50	100
1	90.0	90.0	90.0	90.0	90.0	90.0	90.0	90.0	90.0	90.0	90.0	90.0	90.0	90.0	90.0	90.0
2	14.0	14.0	14.0	14.0	14.0	14.0	14.0	14.0	14.0	14.0	14.0	14.0	14.0	14.0	14.0	14.0
3	8.26	8.5	8.6	8.7	8.8	8.9	8.9	9.0	9.0	9.0	9.1	9.2	9.3	9.3	9.3	9.3
4	6.51	6.8	6.9	7.0	7.1	7.1	7.2	7.2	7.3	7.3	7.4	7.4	7.5	7.5	7.5	7.5
5	5.70	5.96	6.11	6.18	6.26	6.33	6.40	6.44	6.5	6.6	6.6	6.7	6.7	6.8	6.8	6.8
6	5.24	5.51	5.65	5.73	5.81	5.88	5.95	6.00	6.0	6.1	6.2	6.2	6.3	6.3	6.3	6.3
7	4.95	5.22	5.37	5.45	5.53	5.61	5.69	5.73	5.8	5.8	5.9	5.9	6.0	6.0	6.0	6.0
8	4.74	5.00	5.14	5.23	5.32	5.40	5.47	5.51	5.5	5.6	5.7	5.7	5.8	5.8	5.8	5.8
9	4.60	4.86	4.99	5.08	5.17	5.25	5.32	5.36	5.4	5.5	5.5	5.6	5.7	5.7	5.7	5.7
10	4.48	4.73	4.88	4.96	5.06	5.13	5.20	5.24	5.28	5.36	5.42	5.48	5.54	5.55	5.55	5.55
11	4.39	4.63	4.77	4.86	4.94	5.01	5.06	5.12	5.15	5.24	5.28	5.34	5.38	5.39	5.39	5.39
12	4.32	4.55	4.68	4.76	4.84	4.92	4.96	5.02	5.07	5.13	5.17	5.22	5.24	5.26	5.26	5.26
13	4.26	4.48	4.62	4.69	4.74	4.84	4.88	4.94	4.98	5.04	5.08	5.13	5.14	5.15	5.15	5.15
14	4.21	4.42	4.55′	4.63	4.70	4.78	4.83	4.87	4.91	4.96	5.00	5.04	5.06	5.07	5.07	5.07
15	4.17	4.37	4.50	4.58	4.64	4.72	4.77	4.81	4.84	4.90	4.94	4.97	4.99	5.00	5.00	5.00
16	4.13	4.34	4.45	4.54	4.60	4.67	4.72	4.76	4.79	4.84	4.88	4.91	4.93	4.94	4.94	4.94
17	4.10	4.30	4.41	4.50	4.56	4.63	4.68	4.73	4.75	4.80	4.83	4.86	4.88	4.89	4.89	4.89
18	4.07	4.27	4.38	4.46	4.53	4.59	4.64	4.68	4.71	4.76	4.79	4.82	4.84	4.85	4.85	4.85
19	4.05	4.24	4.35	4.43	4.50	4.56	4.61	4.64	4.67	4.72	4.76	4.79	4.81	4.82	4.82	4.82
20	4.02	4.22	4.33	4.40	4.47	4.53	4.58	4.61	4.65	4.69	4.73	4.76	4.78	4.79	4.79	4.79
22	3.99	4.17	4.28	4.36	4.42	4.48	4.53	4.57	4.60	4.65	4.68	4.71	4.74	4.75	4.75	4.75
24	3.96	4.14	4.24	4.33	4.39	4.44	4.49	4.53	4.57	4.62	4.64	4.67	4.70	4.72	4.74	4.74
26	3.93	4.11	4.21	4.30	4.36	4.41	4.46	4.50	4.53	4.58	4.62	4.65	4.67	4.69	4.73	4.73
28	3.91	4.08	4.18	4.28	4.34	4.39	4.43	4.47	4.51	4.56	4.60	4.62	4.65	4.67	4.72	4.72
30	3.89	4.06	4.16	4.22	4.32	4.36	4.41	4.45	4.48	4.54	4.58	4.61	4.63	4.65	4.71	4.71
40	3.82	3.99	4.10	4.17	4.24	4.30	4.34	4.37	4.41	4.46	4.51	4.54	4.57	4.59	4.69	4.69
60	3.76	3.92	4.03	4.12	4.17	4.23	4.27	4.31	4.34	4.39	4.44	4.47	4.50	4.53	4.66	4.66
100	3.71	3.86	3.98	4.06	4.11	4.17	4.21	4.25	4.29	4.35	4.38	4.42	4.45	4.48	4.64	4.65
∞	3.64	3.80	3.90	3.98	4.04	4.09	4.14	4.17	4.20	4.26	4.31	4.34	4.38	4.41	4.60	4.68

From Duncan, D. B., "Multiple Range and Multiple F Tests," *Biometrics*, 11, 1956.
[a]Using special protection levels based on degrees of freedom.

TABLE E — *Significant Studentized Ranges for a 5-percent Level New[a] Multiple Range Test*

n_2/p	2	3	4	5	6	7	8	9	10	12	14	16	18	20	50·	100
1	18.0	18.0	18.0	18.0	18.0	18.0	18.0	18.0	18.0	18.0	18.0	18.0	18.0	18.0	18.0	18.0
2	6.09	6.09	6.09	6.09	6.09	6.09	6.09	6.09	6.09	6.09	6.09	6.09	6.09	6.09	6.09	6.09
3	4.50	4.50	4.50	4.50	4.50	4.50	4.50	4.50	4.50	4.50	4.50	4.50	4.50	4.50	4.50	4.50
4	3.93	4.01	4.02	4.02	4.02	4.02	4.02	4.02	4.02	4.02	4.02	4.02	4.02	4.02	4.02	4.02
5	3.64	3.74	3.79	3.83	3.83	3.83	3.83	3.83	3.83	3.83	3.83	3.83	3.83	3.83	3.83	3.83
6	3.46	3.58	3.64	3.68	3.68	3.68	3.68	3.68	3.68	3.68	3.68	3.68	3.68	3.68	3.68	3.68
7	3.35	3.47	3.54	3.58	3.60	3.61	3.61	3.61	3.61	3.61	3.61	3.61	3.61	3.61	3.61	3.61
8	3.26	3.39	3.47	3.52	3.55	3.56	3.56	3.56	3.56	3.56	3.56	3.56	3.56	3.56	3.56	3.56
9	3.20	3.34	3.41	3.47	3.50	3.52	3.52	3.52	3.52	3.52	3.52	3.52	3.52	3.52	3.52	3.52
10	3.15	3.30	3.37	3.43	3.46	3.47	3.47	3.47	3.47	3.47	3.47	3.47	3.47	3.48	3.48	3.48
11	3.11	3.27	3.35	3.39·	3.43	3.44	3.45	3.46	3.46	3.46	3.46	3.46	3.47	3.48	3.48	3.48
12	3.08	3.23	3.33	3.36	3.40	3.42	3.44	3.44	3.46	3.46	3.46	3.46	3.47	3.48	3.48	3.48
13	3.06	3.21	3.30	3.35	3.38	3.41	3.42	3.44	3.45	3.45	3.46	3.46	3.47	3.47	3.47	3.47
14	3.03	3.18	3.27	3.33	3.37	3.39	3.41	3.42	3.44	3.45	3.46	3.46	3.47	3.47	3.47	3.47
15	3.01	3.16	3.25	3.31	3.36	3.38	3.40	3.42	3.43	3.44	3.45	3.46	3.47	3.47	3.47	3.47
16·	3.00	3.15	3.23	3.30	3.34	3.37	3.39	3.41	3.43	3.44	3.45	3.46	3.47	3.47	3.47	3.47
17	2.98	3.13	3.22	3.28	3.33	3.36	3.38	3.40	3.42	3.44	3.45	3.46	3.47	3.47	3.47	3.47
18	2.97	3.12	3.21	3.27	3.32	3.35	3.37	3.39	3.41	3.43	3.45	3.46	3.47	3.47	3.47	3.47
19	2.96	3.11	3.19	3.26	3.31	3.35	3.37	3.39	3.41	3.43	3.44	3.46	3.47	3.47	3.47	3.47
20	2.95	3.10	3.18	3.25	3.30	3.34	3.36	3.38	3.40	3.43	3.44	3.46	3.47	3.47	3.47	3.47
22	2.93	3.08	3.17	3.24	3.29	3.32	3.35	3.37	3.39	3.42	3.44	3.45	3.46	3.47	3.47	3.47
24	2.92	3.07	3.15	3.22	3.28	3.31	3.34	3.37	3.38	3.41	3.44	3.45	3.46	3.47	3.47	3.47
26	2.91	3.06	3.14	3.21	3.27	3.30	3.34	3.36	3.38	3.41	3.43	3.45	3.46	3.47	3.47	3.47
28	2.90	3.04	.3.13	3.20	3.26	3.30	3.33	3.35	3.37	3.40	3.43	3.45	3.46	3.47	3.47	3.47
30	2.89	3.04	3.12	3.20	3.25	3.29	3.32	3.35	3.37	3.40	3.43	3.44	3.46	3.47	3.47	3.47
40	2.86	3.01	3.10	3.17	3.22	3.27	3.30	3.33	3.35	3.39	3.42	3.44	3.46	3.47	3.47	3.47
60	2.83	2.98	3.08	3.14	3.20	3.24	3.28	3.31	3.33	3.37	3.40	3.43	3.45	3.47	3.48	3.48
100	2.80	2.95	3.05	3.12	3.18	3.22	3.26	3.29	3.32	3.36	3.40	3.42	3.45	3.47	3.53	3.53
∞	2.77	2.92	3.02	3.09	3.15	3.19	3.23	3.26	3.29	3.34	3.38	3.41	3.44	3.47	3.61	3.67

From Duncan, D. B., "Multiple Range and Multiple F Tests," *Biometrics*, 11, 1956.

[a]Using special protection levels based on degrees of freedom.

TABLE F — *Coefficients of Orthogonal Polynomials*

k	Polynomial	X = 1	2	3	4	5	6	7	8	9	10	F	K
3	Linear	−1	0	1								2	1
	Quadratic	1	−2	1								6	3
4	Linear	−3	−1	1	3							20	2
	Quadratic	1	−1	−1	1							4	1
	Cubic	−1	3	−3	1							20	$10/3$
5	Linear	−2	−1	0	1	2						10	1
	Quadratic	2	−1	−2	−1	2						14	1
	Cubic	−1	2	0	−2	1						10	$5/6$
	Quartic	1	−4	6	−4	1						70	$35/12$
6	Linear	−5	−3	−1	1	3	5					70	2
	Quadratic	5	−1	−4	−4	−1	5					84	$3/2$
	Cubic	−5	7	4	−4	−7	5					180	$5/3$
	Quartic	1	−3	2	2	−3	1					28	$7/12$
7	Linear	−3	−2	−1	0	1	2	3				28	1
	Quadratic	5	0	−3	−4	−3	0	5				84	1
	Cubic	−1	1	1	0	−1	−1	1				6	$1/6$
	Quartic	3	−7	1	6	1	−7	3				154	$7/12$
8	Linear	−7	−5	−3	−1	1	3	5	7			168	2
	Quadratic	7	1	−3	−5	−5	−3	1	7			168	1
	Cubic	−7	5	7	3	−3	−7	−5	7			264	$2/3$
	Quartic	7	−13	−3	9	9	−3	−13	7			616	$7/12$
	Quintic	−7	23	−17	−15	15	17	−23	7			2184	$7/10$
9	Linear	−4	−3	−2	−1	0	1	2	3	4		60	1
	Quadratic	28	7	−8	−17	−20	−17	−8	7	28		2772	3
	Cubic	−14	7	13	9	0	−9	−13	−7	14		990	$5/6$
	Quartic	14	−21	−11	9	18	9	−11	−21	14		2002	$7/12$
	Quintic	−4	11	−4	−9	0	9	4	−11	4		468	$3/20$
10	Linear	−9	−7	−5	−3	−1	1	3	5	7	9	330	2
	Quadratic	6	2	−1	−3	−4	−4	−3	−1	2	6	132	$1/2$
	Cubic	−42	14	35	31	12	−12	−31	−35	−14	42	8580	$5/3$
	Quartic	18	−22	−17	3	18	18	3	−17	−22	18	2860	$5/12$
	Quintic	−6	14	−1	−11	−6	6	11	1	−14	6	780	$1/10$

ANSWERS TO ODD-NUMBERED PROBLEMS

CHAPTER 2

2-1. $\bar{X} = 18{,}472.9$, $s^2 = 41.7$.

2-3. For a two-sided alternative, some points are
$\mu = 18{,}473; 18{,}472; 18{,}471; 18{,}470; 18{,}469; 18{,}468; 18{,}467$
$P_a = \beta = 0.08, 0.39, 0.80, 0.95, 0.80, 0.39, 0.08$

2-5. $n = 7$.

2-7. Do not reject hypothesis as $\chi^2 = 17.05$ with 11 df.

2-9. Do not reject hypothesis as $F = 1.8$.

2-11. Reject hypothesis at 1 percent level as $|t| = 13.4$.

CHAPTER 3

3-1.

Source	df	SS	MS	
Between A levels	4	253.04	63.26	Significant at the
Error	20	76.80	3.84	1 percent level
Total	24	329.84		

3-3. Two such contrasts might be

	SS	
$C_1 = T_A - T_C = 31$	60.06	Neither is significant
$C_2 = T_A - 2T_B + T_C = -79$	130.02	at the 5 percent
	190.08	level

3-5.

$$\begin{array}{ccc} & B & A & C \\ \bar{X}_{.j}: & \underline{25.4} & \underline{22.4} & 18.5 \end{array}$$

B and *C* are significantly different at the 5 percent level.

3-7. Two sets and their sum of squares might be

$$
\begin{array}{lrr}
 & & \text{SS} \\
\hline
\text{Set 1: } C_1 = 2T_1 - 2T_5 = -28 & 49.0 \\
C_2 = \phantom{11T_1 + {}}4T_2 - 6T_4 = -108 & 48.6 \\
C_3 = 11T_1 + 11T_2 - 14T_3 + 11T_4 + 11T_5 = 71 & 1.3 \\
C_4 = 10T_1 - 4T_2 - 4T_4 + 10T_5 = 8 & 0.1 \\
\hline
& & 99.0
\end{array}
$$

$$
\begin{array}{lrr}
 & & \text{SS} \\
\hline
\text{Set 2: } C_1 = 6T_1 - 2T_2 = -18 & 3.4 \\
C_2 = 11T_1 + 11T_2 - 8T_3 = -237 & 33.6 \\
C_3 = 4T_1 + 4T_2 + 4T_3 - 19T_4 = -252 & 36.3 \\
C_4 = 2T_1 + 2T_2 + 2T_3 + 2T_4 - 23T_5 = -172 & 25.7 \\
\hline
& & 99.0
\end{array}
$$

3-9. Proofs.

CHAPTER 4

4-1.

Source	df	SS	MS	
Bet. Coater Types	3	1.53	0.51*	Significant at 5 percent level
Bet. Days	2	0.21	0.10	
Error	6	0.54	0.09	
Total	11	2.28		

4-3.

$$\begin{array}{cccc} & K & A & L & M \\ \bar{X}_{.j}: & 5.27 & 4.87 & 4.73 & 4.27 \end{array}$$

K and *M* are significantly different at the 5 percent level.

4-5. (5.57)

Source	df	SS	MS	
Coater Types	3	1.93	0.64*	Significant at the 5 percent level
Days	2	0.32	0.16	
Error	5	0.46	0.09	
Total	10	2.71		

4-7.   Three possible contrasts are

			SS	
$C_1 = Q_1 - Q_2$	$= 4$	0.33		
$C_2 = Q_1 + Q_2 - 2Q_3$	$= 6$	0.25		none significant
$C_3 = Q_1 + Q_2 + Q_3 - 3Q_4$	$= 36$	4.50		
		5.08		

4-9. $SS_{error} = 50.25$ (as before)

CHAPTER 5

5-1.

Source	df	SS	MS	
Electrodes	4	1.04	0.26	
Strips	4	3.44	0.86	none significant
Positions	4	1.84	0.46	
Error	12	9.92	0.83	
Total	24	16.24		

5-3.

	B	C	E	D	A
$\bar{X}_{.j}$:	2.26	2.54	2.76	3.14	3.42

B is thus better (less time) than E, D, or A. It is not significantly better than C.

5-5.

Source	df	SS	MS	
Electrodes	4	3.82	0.96**	Significant at 1 percent level
Positions	3	0.55	0.18	
Strips (unadjusted)	4	0.26	——	
Error	8	0.42	0.05	
Total	19	5.05		

CHAPTER 6

6-1.

Source	df	SS	MS	
Exhaust Index	2	4608.17	2304.08***	highly significant
Pump Heater Voltage	1	96.34	96.34	
$P \times E$ interaction	2	283.16	141.58*	significant
Error	6	139.00	23.17	
Total	11	5126.67		

(Readings were first multiplied by 1,000)

6-3.   On Exhaust Index Means only

$$\bar{X}_{.j}: \quad \underline{9.25} \quad \underline{21.25} \quad \underline{55.50} \quad \text{(all} \times 10^{-3})$$

All are significantly different from one another.
By cell means (because of interaction)

$$\bar{X}_{ij}: \underline{7.5} \quad 11 \quad 12 \quad \underline{30.5} \quad 53 \quad 58$$

6-5.

Source	df	SS	MS
Humidity	2	9.07	4.42
Temperature	2	8.66	4.33
$T \times H$ interaction	4	6.07	1.52
Error	27	28.50	1.06
Total	35	52.30	

6-7.   At the 5 percent significance level, reject H_2 and H_3 but not H_1.

6-9.   Plot of cell totals versus feed for the two materials lines are not parallel (interaction), and both material and feed effect are obvious.

CHAPTER 7

7-1.

Source	df	SS	MS	
Factor A	1	0.08	0.08	
Factor B	1	70.08	70.08**	Significant at the
$A \times B$ interaction	1	24.08	24.08	1 percent level
Error	8	36.68	4.58	
Total	11	130.92		

7-3.

Source	df	SS	MS	
A	1	2,704.00	2,704.00	
B	1	26,732.25	26,732.25	
AB	1	7,744.00	7,744.00	
C	1	24,025.00	24,025.00	Nothing significant
AC	1	16,256.25	16,256.25	at the 5 percent level
BC	1	64,516.00	64,516.00	
ABC	1	420.25	420.25	
Error	8	246,284.00	30,785.50	
Total	15	388,681.75		

7-5.   No plots, as there are no significant effects at the 5 percent levels.

7-7.

Source	df	SS	MS	
A	1	13,736.5		
B	1	6,188.3	Same	
AB	1	22,102.5		
C	1	22.7	as	
AC	1	22,525.0		
BC	1	12,051.3	SS	
ABC	1	20,757.0		
D	1	81,103.8		
AD	1	145,665.0*		Significant at 5 percent level
BD	1	9,214.3		
ABD	1	126,630.3*		Significant at 5 percent level
CD	1	148.8		
ACD	1	6,757.0		
BCD	1	294.0		
ABCD	1	19,453.8		
Error	16	431,599.4	26,975.0	
Total	31	918,249.7		

CHAPTER 8

8-1.

Source	df	SS	MS	
Linear A	1	16.82	16.82*	Significant at 5 percent
Quadratic A	1	202.30	202.30**	Significant at 1 percent
Cubic A	1	28.88	28.88*	Significant at 5 percent
Quartic A	1	5.04	5.04	
Error	20	76.80	3.84	
Total	24	329.84		

8-3.

Source	df	SS	MS	
Lacquer	3	63.79	21.26**	Significant at 1 percent
Times	2	126.59	63.29**	Significant at 1 percent
$L \times T$ interaction	6	38.07	6.35	
Error	12	34.51	2.88	
Total	23	262.96		

8-5. As no interactions are significant, plot averages for lacquer concentrations and note an obvious cubic effect. Also, after averages for the three standing times are plotted, both a linear and quadratic effect can be seen. However, points in between those set should be taken before concluding that these higher-order effects are as high as we need to go.

9-1.

Source	df	SS	MS	
Temperature	2	348.44	174.22	
Humidity	2	333.77	166.88	None significant at
$T \times H$ interaction	4	358.23	89.56	5 percent level
Error	9	680.00	75.66	
Total	17	1720.44		

9-3. $\left.\begin{array}{l} AB = 320.11 \\ AB^2 = 38.11 \end{array}\right\} 358.22$

9-5.   After coding data by subtracting 2.6 and multiplying by 10, we have

Source	df	SS	MS	
Surface Th(A)	2	2,544.71	1,272.35	All except $B \times C$ are
Base Th(B)	2	4,787.37	2,393.68	significant at 5 per-
$A \times B$ interaction	4	185.18	46.29	cent level, but the
Sub-base Th(C)	2	4,165.15	2,082.57	main effects pre-
$A \times C$ interaction	4	189.72	47.48	dominate
$B \times C$ interaction	4	27.74	6.93	
$A \times B \times C$ interaction	8	100.06	12.51	
Error	27	71.50	2.65	

9-7.

Source	df	SS	
AB	2	66.93	$\left.\right\}$ 185.19
AB^2	2	118.26	
AC	2	58.93	$\left.\right\}$ 189.75
AC^2	2	130.82	
BC	2	5.82	$\left.\right\}$ 27.75
BC^2	2	21.93	
ABC	2	17.60	
ABC^2	2	8.26	$\left.\right\}$ 100.05
AB^2C	2	53.48	
AB^2C^2	2	20.71	

9-9.   Plots show strong linear effects of A, B and C. They show AB and AC interaction — but it is slight compared to the main effects. A slight quadratic trend in A is also noted.

CHAPTER 10

10-1.

Source	EMS
O_i	$\sigma_e^2 + 10\sigma_O^2$
A_j	$\sigma_e^2 + 2\sigma_{OA}^2 + 6\sigma_A^2$
OA_{ij}	$\sigma_e^2 + 2\sigma_{OA}^2$
$\epsilon_{k(ij)}$	σ_e^2

Tests are indicated by arrows.
None significant at 5 percent

10-3.

Source	EMS
A_i	$\sigma_e^2 + nc\sigma_{AB}^2 + nbc\sigma_A^2$
B_j	$\sigma_e^2 + nc\sigma_{AB}^2 + nac\sigma_B^2$
AB_{ij}	$\sigma_e^2 + nc\sigma_{AB}^2$
C_k	$\sigma_e^2 + n\sigma_{ABC}^2 + na\sigma_{BC}^2 + nb\sigma_{AC}^2 + nab\sigma_C^2$
AC_{ik}	$\sigma_e^2 + n\sigma_{ABC}^2 + nb\sigma_{AC}^2$
BC_{jk}	$\sigma_e^2 + n\sigma_{ABC}^2 + na\sigma_{BC}^2$
ABC_{ijk}	$\sigma_e^2 + n\sigma_{ABC}^2$
$\epsilon_{m(ijk)}$	σ_e^2

Tests are obvious

No direct test on C.

10-5.

Source	EMS
A_i	$\sigma_e^2 + nb\sigma_{ACD}^2 + nbc\sigma_{AD}^2 + nbd\sigma_{AC}^2 + nbcd\sigma_A^2$
B_j	$\sigma_e^2 + na\sigma_{BCD}^2 + nac\sigma_{BD}^2 + nad\sigma_{BC}^2 + nacd\sigma_B^2$
AB_{ij}	$\sigma_e^2 + n\sigma_{ABCD}^2 + nc\sigma_{ABD}^2 + nd\sigma_{ABC}^2 + ncd\sigma_{AB}^2$
C_k	$\sigma_e^2 + nab\sigma_{CD}^2 + nabd\sigma_C^2$
AC_{ik}	$\sigma_e^2 + nb\sigma_{ACD}^2 + nbd\sigma_{AC}^2$
BC_{jk}	$\sigma_e^2 + na\sigma_{BCD}^2 + nad\sigma_{BC}^2$
ABC_{ijk}	$\sigma_e^2 + n\sigma_{ABCD}^2 + nd\sigma_{ABC}^2$
D_m	$\sigma_e^2 + nab\sigma_{CD}^2 + nabc\sigma_D^2$
AD_{im}	$\sigma_e^2 + nb\sigma_{ACD}^2 + nbc\sigma_{AD}^2$
BD_{jm}	$\sigma_e^2 + na\sigma_{BCD}^2 + nac\sigma_{BD}^2$
ABD_{ijm}	$\sigma_e^2 + n\sigma_{ABCD}^2 + nc\sigma_{ABD}^2$
CD_{km}	$\sigma_e^2 + nab\sigma_{CD}^2$
ACD_{ikm}	$\sigma_e^2 + nb\sigma_{ACD}^2$
BCD_{jkm}	$\sigma_e^2 + na\sigma_{BCD}^2$
$ABCD_{ijkm}$	$\sigma_e^2 + n\sigma_{ABCD}^2$
$\epsilon_{q(ijkm)}$	σ_e^2

No direct test on A, B, or AB

10-7. $N_0 = 4.44$ $s_e^2 = 1.16$ $s_A^2 = 5.32$

CHAPTER 11

11-1.

Source	df	SS	MS	EMS
L_i	2	27.42	13.71	$\sigma_e^2 + 3\sigma_R^2 + 12\sigma_L^2$
$R_{j(i)}$	9	36.38	4.04	$\sigma_e^2 + 3\sigma_R^2$
$\epsilon_{k(ij)}$	24	21.80	0.91	σ_e^2
Total	35	85.60		

Difference between rolls within lots is significant at the 1 percent level.

11-3.

Source	EMS
A_i	$\sigma_e^2 + 2\sigma_C^2 + 6\sigma_B^2 + 24\sigma_A^2$
$B_{j(i)}$	$\sigma_e^2 + 2\sigma_C^2 + 6\sigma_B^2$
$C_{k(ij)}$	$\sigma_e^2 + 2\sigma_C^2$
$\epsilon_{m(ijk)}$	σ_e^2

Tests are obvious

11-5.

Source	df	SS	MS	EMS
T_i	1	5,489,354	5,489,354	$\sigma_e^2 + 6\sigma_M^2 + 12\sigma_T^2$
$M_{j(i)}$	2	408,250	204,125	$\sigma_e^2 + 6\sigma_M^2$
S_k	1	8,971	8,971	$\sigma_e^2 + 3\sigma_{MS}^2 + 12\sigma_S^2$
TS_{ik}	1	37,445	37,445	$\sigma_e^2 + 3\sigma_{MS}^2 + 6\sigma_{TS}^2$
$MS_{kj(i)}$	2	31,520	15,760	$\sigma_e^2 + 3\sigma_{MS}^2$
$\epsilon_{m(ijk)}$	16	316,930	19,808	σ_e^2

11-7.

Source	EMS
T_i	$\sigma_e^2 + 18\sigma_m^2 + 36\sigma_t^2$
$M_{j(i)}$	$\sigma_e^2 + 18\sigma_m^2$
S_k	$\sigma_e^2 + 9\sigma_{ms}^2 + 36\sigma_s^2$
TS_{ik}	$\sigma_e^2 + 9\sigma_{ms}^2 + 18\sigma_{ts}^2$
$MS_{kj(i)}$	$\sigma_e^2 + 9\sigma_{ms}^2$
P_m	$\sigma_e^2 + 6\sigma_{mp}^2 + 24\sigma_p^2$
TP_{im}	$\sigma_e^2 + 6\sigma_{mp}^2 + 12\sigma_{tp}^2$
$MP_{mj(i)}$	$\sigma_e^2 + 6\sigma_{mp}^2$
SP_{km}	$\sigma_e^2 + 3\sigma_{msp}^2 + 12\sigma_{sp}^2$
TSP_{ikm}	$\sigma_e^2 + 3\sigma_{msp}^2 + 6\sigma_{tsp}^2$
$MSP_{mkj(i)}$	$\sigma_e^2 + 3\sigma_{msp}^2$
$\epsilon_{q(ijkm)}$	σ_e^2

11-9.

Source	df	SS	MS	EMS
F_i	4	3,886	971**	$\sigma_e^2 + 9\sigma_s^2 + 54\sigma_f^2$
C_j	1	109	109**	$\sigma_e^2 + 9\sigma_s^2 + 135\sigma_c^2$
FC_{ij}	4	721	180**	$\sigma_e^2 + 9\sigma_s^2 + 27\sigma_{fc}^2$
$S_{k(ij)}$	20	39	1.95**	$\sigma_e^2 + 9\sigma_s^2$
P_m	2	161	80.5**	$\sigma_e^2 + 3\sigma_{sp}^2 + 90\sigma_p^2$
FP_{im}	8	114	14.3**	$\sigma_e^2 + 3\sigma_{sp}^2 + 18\sigma_{fp}^2$
CP_{jm}	2	3	1.5	$\sigma_e^2 + 3\sigma_{sp}^2 + 45\sigma_{cp}^2$
FCP_{ijm}	8	15	1.9	$\sigma_e^2 + 3\sigma_{sp}^2 + 9\sigma_{fcp}^2$
$SP_{mk(ij)}$	40	66	1.65	$\sigma_e^2 + 3\sigma_{sp}^2$
$\epsilon_{q(ijkm)}$	180	30	0.17	σ_e^2
Total	269	5,144		**Significant at 1 percent

CHAPTER 12

12-1.

Source	df	SS	MS	EMS
R_i	2	337.15	168.58	$\sigma_e^2 + 18\sigma_R^2$
S_j	1	16.66	16.66	$\sigma_e^2 + 9\sigma_{RS}^2 + 27\sigma_S^2$
RS_{ij}	2	126.78	63.39	$\sigma_e^2 + 9\sigma_{RS}^2$
H_k	2	15.59	7.80	$\sigma_e^2 + 6\sigma_{RH}^2 + 18\sigma_H^2$
HS_{jk}	2	80.12	40.06	$\sigma_e^2 + 3\sigma_{SRH}^2 + 9\sigma_{HS}^2$
RH_{ik}	4	62.85	15.71	$\sigma_e^2 + 6\sigma_{RH}^2$
SRH_{ijk}	4	229.44	57.36	$\sigma_e^2 + 3\sigma_{SRH}^2$
$\epsilon_{m(ijk)}$	36	200.00	5.56	σ_e^2
Total	53	1068.59		

Replications (blocks) and replications by all other factors are significant at the 5 percent level; however, these are not the factors of chief interest.

12-3.

Source	df	SS	EMS
R_i	1		$\sigma_e^2 + 3\sigma_{RM}^2 + 12\sigma_R^2$
T_j	1		$\sigma_e^2 + 3\sigma_{RM}^2 + 6\sigma_M^2 + 6\sigma_{RT}^2 + 12\sigma_T^2$
RT_{ij}	1	As before with R in place of S	$\sigma_e^2 + 3\sigma_{RM}^2 + 6\sigma_{RT}^2$
$M_{k(j)}$	2		$\sigma_e^2 + 3\sigma_{RM}^2 + 6\sigma_M^2$
$RM_{ik(j)}$	2		$\sigma_e^2 + 3\sigma_{RM}^2$
$\epsilon_{m(ijk)}$	16		σ_e^2
Total	23		

No direct test on types, but results look highly significant. No other significant effects.

12-5.   Compare models.

13-1.

	Source	df	EMS
Whole	R_i	1	$\sigma_e^2 + 6\sigma_{RS}^2 + 18\sigma_R^2$
Plot	H_j	2	$\sigma_e^2 + 2\sigma_{RHS}^2 + 4\sigma_{HS}^2 + 6\sigma_{RH}^2 + 12\sigma_H^2$
	RH_{ij}	2	$\sigma_e^2 + 2\sigma_{RHS}^2 + 6\sigma_{RH}^2$
	S_k	2	$\sigma_e^2 + 6\sigma_{RS}^2 + 12\sigma_S^2$
Split	RS_{ik}	2	$\sigma_e^2 + 6\sigma_{RS}^2$
Plot	HS_{jk}	4	$\sigma_e^2 + 2\sigma_{RHS}^2 + 4\sigma_{HS}^2$
	RHS_{ijk}	4	$\sigma_e^2 + 2\sigma_{RHS}^2$
	$\epsilon_{m(ijk)}$	18	σ_e^2
	Total	35	

13-3. $F_{1,v}' = 24.3$ and $v = 1530$; significant at 1 percent.

13-5.

	Source	df	EMS
	R_i	3	$\sigma_e^2 + 8\sigma_{RA}^2 + 40\sigma_R^2$
	S_j	1	$\sigma_e^2 + 4\sigma_{RSA}^2 + 16\sigma_{SA}^2 + 20\sigma_{RS}^2 + 80\sigma_S^2$
Whole	RS_{ij}	3	$\sigma_e^2 + 4\sigma_{RSA}^2 + 20\sigma_{RS}^2$
Plot	J_k	1	$\sigma_e^2 + 4\sigma_{RJA}^2 + 16\sigma_{JA}^2 + 20\sigma_{RJ}^2 + 80\sigma_J^2$
	RJ_{ik}	3	$\sigma_e^2 + 4\sigma_{RJA}^2 + 20\sigma_{RJ}^2$
	SJ_{jk}	1	$\sigma_e^2 + 2\sigma_{RSJA}^2 + 10\sigma_{RSJ}^2 + 8\sigma_{SJA}^2 + 40\sigma_{SJ}^2$
	RSJ_{ijk}	3	$\sigma_e^2 + 2\sigma_{RSJA}^2 + 10\sigma_{RSJ}^2$
	A_m	4	$\sigma_e^2 + 8\sigma_{RA}^2 + 32\sigma_A^2$
	RA_{im}	12	$\sigma_e^2 + 8\sigma_{RA}^2$
	SA_{jm}	4	$\sigma_e^2 + 4\sigma_{RSA}^2 + 16\sigma_{SA}^2$
Split	RSA_{ijm}	12	$\sigma_e^2 + 4\sigma_{RSA}^2$
Plot	JA_{km}	4	$\sigma_e^2 + 4\sigma_{RJA}^2 + 16\sigma_{JA}^2$
	RJA_{ikm}	12	$\sigma_e^2 + 4\sigma_{RJA}^2$
	SJA_{jkm}	4	$\sigma_e^2 + 2\sigma_{RSJA}^2 + 8\sigma_{SJA}^2$
	$RSJA_{ijkm}$	12	$\sigma_e^2 + 2\sigma_{RSJA}^2$
	$\epsilon_{q(ijkm)}$	80	σ_e^2

13-7.

	Source	df	MS	EMS
	R_i	2	75.46	$\sigma_e^2 + 5\sigma_{RO}^2 + 20\sigma_R^2$
Whole	D_j	4	272.10	$\sigma_e^2 + \sigma_{RDO}^2 + 3\sigma_{DO}^2 + 4\sigma_{RD}^2 + 12\sigma_D^2$
Plot	RD_{ij}	8	42.30	$\sigma_e^2 + \sigma_{RDO}^2 + 4\sigma_{RD}^2$
	O_k	3	1.72	$\sigma_e^2 + 5\sigma_{RO}^2 + 15\sigma_O^2$
Split	RO_{ik}	6	56.62	$\sigma_e^2 + 5\sigma_{RO}^2$
Plot	DO_{jk}	12	18.34	$\sigma_e^2 + 3\sigma_{DO}^2$
	RDO_{ijk}	24	43.01	$\sigma_e^2 + \sigma_{RDO}^2$
	Total	59		Days are significant by an F' test.

13-9. In a nested experiment the levels of B, say, are different within each level of A. In a split-plot, the same levels of B (in the split) are used at each level of A.

CHAPTER 14

14-1. Confounding AC (each value is sum of four readings) gives

Block I	Block II
$(1) = 2$	$a = -5$
$b = 15$	$ab = 13$
$ac = -17$	$c = -12$
$abc = -7$	$ac = -2$
-7	-6

and $SS_{block} = SS_{AC} = 0.13$

14-3. $SS_{blocks} = 29{,}153.5 = SS_{AB} + SS_{ACD} + SS_{BCD}$

14-5. The principal block contains: (1), ab, ad, bd, c, abc, acd, bcd.

14-7. One scheme is to confound ABC, CDE, and $ABDE$. The principal block contains (1), ab, de, $abde$, ace, bce, acd, bcd.

Source	df
Main effects	5
2-way interaction	10
3-way interaction	8
4-way interaction	4
5-way interaction	1
Blocks (or ABC, CDE, $ABDE$)	3
Total	31

14-9. One scheme is to confound $ABCD^2$. The principal block contains
0000, 1110, 1102, 1012, 2111, 2122, 0221, 0210, 0120, 0101, 1211,
1200, 2220, 0022, 0011, 0202, 0112, 1121, 1020, 1001, 1222, 2010,
2201, 2100, 2002, 2021, 2212.

CHAPTER 15

15-1. Aliases are $A = C$, $B = ABC$, $AB = BC$. $SS_{effects}$ for A (or C) =
105.06, for B (or ABC) = 33.06, for AB (or BC) = 0.56.

15-3. Aliases are
$$A = BC = AB^2C^2$$
$$B = AB^2C = AC$$
$$C = ABC^2 = AB$$
$$AB^2 = AC^2 = BC^2$$

15-5. $A = BD$, $B = AD$, $C = ABCD$, $D = AB$, $AC = BCD$, $BC =$
ACD, $CD = ABC$.

15-7.
$$A = AB^2C^2D = BCD^2$$
$$B = AB^2CD^2 = ACD^2$$
$$C = ABC^2D^2 = ABD^2$$
$$D = ABC = ABCD$$
$$AB = ABC^2D = CD^2$$
$$AB^2 = AC^2D = BC^2D$$
$$AC = AB^2CD = BD^2$$
$$AC^2 = AB^2D = BC^2D^2$$
$$AD = AB^2C^2 = BCD$$
$$BC = AB^2C^2D^2 = AD^2$$
$$BC^2 = AB^2D^2 = AC^2D^2$$
$$BD = AB^2C = ACD$$
$$CD = ABC^2 = ABD$$

INDEX

α, probability of a type-I error, 13, 259
Alias, 222–224, 259
Analysis, general, 3, 4
Analysis of variance
  fundamental equations, 25, 49
  one-way, 22
  rationale, 23, 48, 85, 169
  three-way, 67
  two-way, 46

β, probability of a type-II error, 13–14, 259
Barnett, E.H., 245, 263
Bennett, C.A., 149, 197, 263
Block, 46
  randomized (see Randomized block design)
Box, G.E.P., 245, 263
Burr, I.W., 11, 138, 263

Canonical form, 245, 259
Central composite design, 244
Change in mean effect, 246, 252

Chi-Square, table of, 269
Completely randomized design, 5, 21, 45, 259
Components of variance, 33–34, 52
Confidence
  interval, 11
  limits, 12, 33, 51, 259
Confounding, 259
  complete, 206–220
  in blocks, 201
  in 2^n, 209
  in 3^n, 213
  partial, 206
  systems, 203
Consistent statistic, 11, 259
Contrast, 29, 31, 107, 259
Critical region, 12, 259

Davies, O.L., 18, 217, 263
Defining contrast, 203, 259
Design
  completely randomized, 5, 21, 45, 259

Design (*Cont'd*)
  general, 2–4
  Graeco-Latin square, 68, 260
  incomplete block, 57–64, 260
  Latin square, 66–72, 229, 260
  randomized block, 44–65, 261
  split-plot, 190–200, 261
  Youden square, 69, 261
Dixon, W.J., 14, 263
Duncan, D.B., 263
  multiple range test, 31, 49, 84, 276, 277

Effect of a factor, 97, 107, 259
Error
  split-plot, 193
  type-I, 13, 259
  type-II, 13, 259
  whole-plot, 193
Estimates
  intervals, 10
  point, 10–11
Estimation, 10–12
Evolutionary operation, 245–252, 259
Expected mean squares, 28, 150–163
Expected value, 10, 156–157, 260
Experiment
  factorial, 75–92, 260
  general, 1–4
  nested, 165–170, 260
  nested-factorial, 171–175, 260
  single factor, 21, 44, 66

F distribution, 18, 26
  table, 270–275
F' (psuedo F), 197
Factorial experiment
  general, 75–93, 260
  2^n, 95–109
  3^n, 130–147

in randomized blocks, 179–185
in Latin squares, 185–187
Fisher, R.A., 57, 67, 111, 263
Fractional factorial, 222
Fractional replication, 221–231, 260
  in 2^n, 224–227
  in 3^n, 227–230
Franklin, N.L., 149, 197, 263

General regression significance test, 35–41, 52–54, 61-64
Graeco-Latin square, 68–69, 260

Hierarchical, 166
Hypothesis
  statistical, 12, 261
  test of, 12–14, 18

I and J interaction, 135
Incomplete block design, 57–64, 260
Inference, statistical, 9, 261
Interaction, 77–78, 89, 98, 260

J and I interaction, 135

Kempthorne, O., 203, 263

Latin square, 66–72, 229, 260
Levels of factor
  fixed, 22–24, 148–163
  qualitative, 2–4, 110–129
  quantitative, 2–4, 110-129
  random, 22–24, 148–163

Massey, F.J., 14, 263
McCall, C.H. Jr., 263
Mean of population, 9, 260
  of sample, 10, 260
Mean square, 27, 260

Miller, L.D., 263
Minimum variance estimate, 11, 260
Missing values, 54–55
Model
    fixed, 149–163
    mathematical, 3–6
    mixed, 149–163, 260
    random, 34, 149–163, 260
    summary of, 254–257
Modulus, 135

Nested experiment, 165–170, 260
Nested-factorial experiment, 171–175, 260
Normal distribution, table of, 266–267

Operating characteristic curve, 15, 16, 260
Orthogonal contrasts, 29–31, 61, 260
Orthogonal polynomials, 111–113
    table of, 278
Owen, D.B., 18, 263

Parameter, 9, 260
Path of steepest ascent, 235, 261
Point estimate, 10, 260
Power of a test, 14–16, 260
Principal block, 204, 260
Psuedo-F (F'), 197

Randomization, 2–3
Randomized block design
    balanced, 57
    complete, 44–65
    incomplete, 57–64, 260
    symmetric, 60
Random model, 34, 149, 261
Random sample, 10, 261
Response surface, 233–245
Rotatable design, 244, 261

Sample, random, 10, 261
Sample size, 16–18
Sample statistic, 10
Satterthwaite, 197
Smith, T.E., 263
Split-plot design, 191–200, 261
Standard deviation
    of population, 9
    of sample, 11
Statistical hypothesis, 12, 261
Statistical inference, 9, 261
Statistic, 10, 261
Statistics, 9–10, 261
Steepest ascent, path of, 235, 261
Studentized ranges, table of, 276 277
Student's t distribution, 12–14, 33, 268

Test of a hypothesis, 12–14, 261
Test statistic, 12, 261
Treatment combination, 80, 96, 130, 261

Unbiased statistic, 10, 261

Variance
    of population, 9, 157, 261
    of sample, 10, 261

W, X, Y, Z interactions, 138
Whole plots, 193
Wortham, A.W., 263

X, W, Y, Z interactions, 138

Y, W, X, Z interactions, 138
Yates, F., 102, 263
Yates method, 102, 106, 212
Youden square, 69, 261

Z, W, X, Y interactions, 138